STATESMAN OF THE
ENLIGHTENMENT

Turgot at his desk

STATESMAN OF THE ENLIGHTENMENT

The Life of
Anne-Robert Turgot

Malcolm Hill

OTHILA PRESS
1999

ISBN 1 901647 07 2

*To those who can see that justice,
democracy and prosperity are required to
introduce a new order of society*

Contents

List of Illustrations

Glossary of French Terms

Abbé an ordained priest

Ancien Régime the way of life and the institutions in France which were destroyed by the revolution

Contrôleur-genéral the minister in charge of finance, home affairs, commerce, agriculture and transport

Corvées the unpaid servitudes claimed from unprivileged in respect of building and repair of roads or the transport of the army in France

Dévots those who supported the Catholic Church politique in home and foreign affairs

Don grâtuit donation to government by the Catholic Church, the first Estate, in lieu of taxation

Économistes a name given to a group which formed around Dr Quesnay because they always seemed to be urging economies in government expenditure

States-General ancient assembly of the first estate, the Church, the second estate, the nobility, and the third, the common people or roturiers. Last met before 1789 in 1614

Encyclopédist someone who wrote articles for Encylopédies

Farmers-general a company of about 40-60 financiers who purchased every six years from the state the right to collect, or farm, indirect taxes

Generalities the provinces of France

Intendants the agents of the King's Council in the generalities, answerable to the Contrôleur-général.

King's Council of Ministers the body through which the king governed

Laissez-faire the cry of French merchants of the seventeenth century when they begged government to leave commerce and trade to them

Lettres de cachet order signed by the king and a secretary of state relating to an individual, who might be imprisoned or disappeared

Lit de justice exercise of royal prerogative to bring an edict into effect, despite the refusal of a parlement to register it

Métayage in return for advancing tools and seeds the landowner received a share of the tenant's crop

Milice the compulsory recruitment of soldiers and sailors who received no pay or rights

Noblesse the second estate see page for fuller description.

Nouvellistes journalists

Parlements Thirteen regional bodies possessing powers over conscience, censorship, justice, and vetoes over laws which they declined to register

Pays d' état in general there were provinces, such as Brittany, Burgundy at a relatively late date and enjoyed a degree of autonomy in taxation

Philosophes secular intellectuals who saw all branches of knowledge as their province

The Physiocrats a name from Greek ['those who follow nature'] which the followers of Dr Quesnay adopted to describe themselves

Ponts et Chaussés body responsible for bridges and main routes

Privilege any money or power obtained by a group without effort

Produit net the natural surplus accruing after earnings and expenses to landowners

Protection interference of the state in commerce and trade

Roturiers common people or members of the Third Estate, who were not members of the Church or Noblesse

Syndic elected spokesman of a village

Taille direct tax levied on the unprivileged roturiers

Taille tarifée tax levied on land and not on possessions of roturiers. It was used in part throughout the Limousin but discouraged by authority

Venality system of buying position or rank

Vingtième a direct tax introduced in 1749 to ignore privilege. Any attempt to impose it failed

Introduction

Turgot occupies an important place in European political history. He not only extended the political thought of John Locke by adapting his basic principles to the conditions of the eighteenth century, but also played a prominent part in the formulation of economic science, introduced to the Western world by François Quesnay in about 1750. This new science emerged to provide an economic foundation for the industrial revolution. Turgot began to remove the economic causes of the French Revolution.

His political thinking was inspired by justice. He stood aside from groups of every description and never confused mass opinion with individual conviction. Turgot appeared in France at a critical period in Western history. France was heading towards revolution, America was on the brink of declaring independence from Britain and the industrial revolution was about to begin. He can be ranked with Quesnay as a founder of economic science, which arose at the moment mankind had need of it. Whereas the inspiration was provided by Quesnay, the formulation was made by Turgot. Alone in France, he might have averted the revolution by reforming its economic causes, his ideas might have saved America from economic vice and would have sown the seeds of enrichment of whole societies from the invention of technology of the nineteenth and twentieth centuries.

He had played a pivotal role in the Enlightenment. Although it was destroyed by the French Revolution before it had taken root, it stands with the Gothic and Italian Renaissances, as highlights of Western culture. Everywhere the economic thought, born in Paris around 1750, has since been ignored and arrested and poverty has been allowed to afflict the mass of society, while the privileged have maintained economic injustice.

During the 1780s Du Pont and Condorcet, both close friends of Turgot, wrote the first biographies of him. Du Pont had worked as Turgot's private secretary and before that had corresponded regularly with him. His enthusiasm for revolutionary ideas tended to make him exaggerate Turgot's ideas and to lead him to assume that Turgot was at one with his own thinking. To Du Pont's work was appended an invaluable collection of Turgot's writings.

Condorcet presented him more as a philosopher than an active statesman. He did not understand Turgot's economic ideas clearly. Neither French author was free from the censors, who did not encourage the publication of certain aspects of Turgot's life. The English translation of Condorcet's biography was commissioned by Lord Shelbourne, the maligned British Prime Minister.

During the nineteenth century a number of biographies were published in France. They were more substantial works than the earlier studies. Turgot was presented by these authors as a liberal thinker and founder of economics. At the beginning of the twentieth century Gustav Schelle produced the collected writings of Turgot and little has come to light since.

In the1960s three studies of Turgot were published in France. They have attempted to portray Turgot as incompetent, blinkered, overrated and uninteresting. They were Edgar Faure's *Le Disgrëce de Turgot* [1962], Laugier's *Turgot ou le mythe des reformes* [1979] and Kleiner & Peyronnet's *Quand Turgot régnait en Limousin* [1979] They are each severe in their criticisms and reckless in their misconceptions. They reveal themselves as socialists and the gravamen of their complaint was that Turgot was not one.

Two works have appeared in English. W.W. Stephens wrote *The Life and Writings of Turgot* [1885] and D. Dakin wrote Turgot and the *Ancien Régime* [1939]. The former is incomplete biography, the latter uninteresting.

My reasons for writing his biography are to revive interest in such an eminent figure in European political thought and to explain his thinking on questions which confront society today.

My gratitude is due to Duncan McAra for his editorial assistance, which was invaluable; to Catherine Feighan for her determination and patience in ensuring clarity of expression and comprehension; to Liz Marsh, who reworded many of the translations of the quotations drawn from Schelle and Véri to bring out the the essence of the quotation; to Paul Turner for giving the final proof read.

NOTE

The livre was gauged by the English traveller to be equal to 10 and a half pence and these conversions are taken from his table:

Livres	£
100	4.75p
1,000	43.7
10.000	437.50[1]

---

[1] J. Lough, *An Introduction to Eigthteenth Century France* p. vi.

1

Turgot's Youth

There have been periods of seminal creativity throughout history when thinking has been radically challenged and new directions revealed. One such cultural leap occurred during the Enlightenment of the eighteenth century, during which the science of economics was introduced to the Western world by a group of thinkers in Paris, who were later styled the *économistes*, after their habit of continually advising economy in government.

In 1750 the greater part of the population of Europe was engaged in agriculture and apart from a few foundries, tanneries and paperworks there was little factory production. Mining was confined to a few holes in the ground. Some writers had thrown some light on isolated economic matters such as trade and money, but none had examined the subject of economics as a whole.

Economic science was a timely introduction to Western thought. It occurred on the eve of the industrial revolution, the independence of the colonies in North America and in the decades before the French Revolution, which brought the Enlightenment to a premature and abrupt end.

The founder of economics was a surgeon, Dr François Quesnay, who had been impressed by the concept of the natural order in ancient China. The central point of the science of economics which he introduced was human conformity to the natural order of the universe. Yet the simplest and most profound formulation of his ideas was expressed by Turgot. His prodigious scholarship, nobility of character and unquestioned integrity brought to political thought a new order. Yet Turgot's contribution has been ignored and misrepresented.

Turgot was born in Paris on 10 May 1727. He was christened Anne-Robert. His ancestors stretched back over centuries with branches in Denmark and in Scotland.[1] Many had become prominent in public life. Louis XV claimed complete genealogical knowledge of the French nobility and described the Turgot family as 'good stock'.

His father, Michel Etienne, was a noted lawyer who become *prévôt des marchands*, or executive mayor, of Paris between 1729–40. During these eleven

---

[1] See *National Dictionary Biography* for Turgot, Bishop of St Andrews.

years he was responsible for the construction of a large sewer on the north bank of the Seine and the enlargement of the Quai d'Horloge, which was linked by a bridge to the opposite bank. He commissioned an elegant architectural map of Paris, which is still in print, in order to preserve the overall shape and design of the growing capital. He was known for his genuine concern for the welfare of the poor in the city. Later he became president of the Grand Council, which acted as one of the superior courts of law. He died in 1751 of hereditary gout, which had run through the male line of the Turgot family. Turgot's mother, Magdalène-Françoise, was a strict and competent mother. Supervising her children's early education, she instilled in them the virtues of kindness and piety. She was disappointed by Anne-Robert, her youngest son, because during his childhood he was so withdrawn that he would hide behind curtains, whenever her friends visited the house.

Anne-Robert had two older brothers and a younger sister. The eldest brother followed his father into law, the second brother became successful in the army. His sister married the duc de Saint-Aigan, who was some forty-five years her senior. Being the third son, Anne-Robert was destined, by tradition, to the priesthood The family was noble but poor and the priesthood offered the youngest son the sinecure of a rich provincial bishopric. Although the church had become spiritually corrupt, the education offered at its seminaries was generally the best education available.

At the age of ten, in 1737, Turgot attended the Collège Duplessis, later known as the Collège Louis-le-Grand, which was a preparatory school for the priesthood. During his early schooling, Turgot's parents became worried by their son's continual need of pocket money. His headmaster later discovered that the boy's unusual expenditure was devoted to purchasing textbooks for fellow students poorer than himself.

He moved on to the seminary Saint-Supplice when he reached the age of sixteen. Within a year he wrote to his father about his wish to abandon his religious education. But he was persuaded to persevere longer, in order to allow time for his mother to accept his abandonment of the career which had been determined for him.

At the seminary he had good teachers and, under their influence, he began to show his intellectual prowess. There was abbé Sigorne, who was an authority on Isaac Newton, abbé Guérin, a liberal teacher of the humanities, and abbé Bon, an authority on English literature. Under these three teachers Turgot became acquainted with Voltaire, who widened his thinking and interested him in English thinkers.

Voltaire had spent three years in England in the late 1720s and was exposed to the ideas of Newton and John Locke. He admitted that this experience had liberalised his thinking. 'For your Cartesians [followers of Descartes]', wrote Voltaire, 'everything is moved by a force which you do not understand completely, for Newton it is moved by gravitation, the source of which is scarcely better known. For a Cartesian light exists in the air, for a Newtonian it comes from the sun in six and a half minutes ... Locke', continued Voltaire, 'expounded human understanding as an excellent anatomist explains the mechanism of the human body. At all points he seeks the light of physics, he sometimes speaks affirmatively, but he also dares to doubt.'[1]

At the seminary Turgot's studies included the classics, ancient and modern history, philosophy, natural history, anatomy, physics, literature and languages; he could read and translate Latin, Greek, German, Italian, Spanish, Hebrew and English. According to Morellet, a fellow student, Turgot knew most of the 'occasional pieces' of Voltaire and most of his poems and tragedies. Turgot regretted that he had no mind for mathematics and no stomach for surgery.

While reluctantly continuing his religious education, he became less interested in theological conformity and more absorbed in the cause of religious toleration. In 1746, at the age of nineteen, he wrote: 'Fundamentally intolerance can only be upheld by those who regard religion as a political invention whereby everyone is obliged to follow the predominant religion, whether it be true or false.'[2] Though Britain had enjoyed a measure of religious tolerance since the late seventeenth century, intolerance was the policy of the state in France and was interwoven in the fabric of government. Thus there was a real risk of expulsion for a theological student who dared to oppose intolerance. In 1747, when he was twenty, Turgot received a special dispensation on account of his youth and entered his examination for his licence, or degree. This was procured by a recommendation of Louis XV. His father described to his elder son Turgot's oral examination with pride.

> 'Your brother, the abbé, has delivered his thesis with every possible distinction; he has gone way beyond my expectations, for he did not show the slightest timidity and he received the approbation of all those present. The examination took place in the outer schools of the Sorbonne in an immense hall. The decoration and lighting were perfect and, extensive though it was, it was full throughout the five hours of the examinations. The Lord archbishop of Tours presided. The assembly of the clergy, which is now sitting in Paris, came as a body to hear this thesis ... The archbishop stepped down from his rostrum and embraced the abbé [Turgot], telling him that he had delivered his thesis in the most splendid style. Next day the archbishop went to Versailles. The king asked him whether he had been at the assembly of the clergy the previous day because he wanted to know why he had not been at Versailles. The archbishop replied that he had been presiding over a thesis. 'Whose was

---

[1] Voltaire, *Letters on England* trans by L. Tancock [Penguin] 1980 edn. pp. 68 & 63.
[2] G. Schelle, *Les Oeuvres de Turgot* vol i pp. 96-7.

it?' enquired the king. 'The abbé Turgot.' Thereupon the king asked him whether the discourse had been a good one and the archbishop was gracious enough to say that he had never heard a thesis delivered with such distinction.'[1]

Morellet recalled that Turgot 'had a prodigious memory. I have heard him repeat pieces of 120 verses, after having heard them repeated twice, or even once ...'[2] Once this talent caused great danger to Turgot and his friends. In 1748 the seizure of Prince Charles Edward Stewart of Scotland, better known as Bonnie Prince Charlie, in Paris became the subject of several lampoons about the humiliating terms of the Treaty of Aix-la-Chapelle, under which he had been returned to Britain and about the debauchery of the king and his mistress, Mme de Pompadour. Some of these verses were recited to abbé Bon, one of Turgot's tutors, by his students. The abbé was unimpressed and agreed, when challenged, to compose something himself within two hours. He wrote a sonnet which made fun of Mme de Pompadour. The sonnet began:

> I have seen the sceptre fall
>   at the feet of Pompadour.
> But it was raised up once more
>   by the hand of l'amour ...

Bon repeated the whole sonnet to Turgot, who in turn, repeated it to Sigorne, who wrote it on a blackboard. Several students learnt it. It found its way into the streets of the capital, where it enjoyed immediate popularity. Soon the sonnet reached the ears of Mme de Pompadour. She exploded with indignation and commanded Maurepas, the minister responsible for the police, to investigate the source of this scandalous sonnet. He advised her that the matter would soon be forgotten, if nothing were done about it. She was not satisfied with this passive response, and, remembering that Maurepas had once deployed his ready wit by singing some uncomplimentary verses about her after a dinner, assuaged her anger by obtaining his exile to his country chëteau near Paris for twenty-five years. His successor, Argenson, instructed the police spies to investigate. They traced the sonnet back as far as Sigorne and he was removed to the Bastille, where he remained for four months until Turgot's name was prised out of him. The police decided not to proceed against Turgot, on account, it was said, of the reputation of his father.

Sigorne was released, but exiled to Lorraine and barred from public appointments. Many years later Turgot was in a position to have the abbé

---

[1] Ibid., pp. 98–9.
[2] Morellet, *Mémoirs*, vol. i p. 12.

returned to Paris and given a position in the Church. The sonnet's author, abbé Bon, was so frightened that he left Paris, and remained in voluntary exile thereafter. Years later he was walking with several people including Maurepas and abbé Véri, who had been a fellow student of Turgot. Maurepas jokingly recalled the incident. Whereupon one of the party remarked that its author had left France. 'What a loss!' retorted Maurepas. Véri, who knew the truth of the matter, noticed Bon's face blanch with fear at the mention of the expensive sonnet.

In 1748 the Acadèmie de Soisson organised a literary competition on the causes of the progression and the decline of the arts and sciences. Turgot, at the age of twenty-one, had planned to compete but when he learnt that abbé Bon had entered, he withdrew in order to avoid public competition with his tutor. Nevertheless, he did write notes for an essay which give evidence of the range and depth of Turgot's learning.

> The progress of the arts and sciences was dependent, he asserted, 'on the state of a language, the constitution of government and the chance appearance of a genius . . . Before a language had attained a fixed state it was liable to deterioration through blending with others and by resort to metaphors. But when it had acquired a certain richness and its analogies had become fixed, poets could raise taste and eloquence; the works of great writers became extensive reservoirs of language.[1]

The progress of science depended on freedom of thought. Turgot reflected how limited progress would have been in Greece had the legislators been disciples of Pythagoras; for a sectarian spirit descended on his school, closing minds to new and different possibilities. Fortunately in Greece there were numerous independent republics, as there were in Italy during the fourteenth century, and new knowledge was allowed the freedom to grow.

> Genius is spread among mankind like gold in a mine; the more mining, the more gold. [He distinguished genius from] those who are destined to bring together the discoveries of others in order to clarify and even perfect them, if they are not like torches shining with their own light, they are like diamonds which brilliantly reflect a borrowed light, which in total darkness remain undistinguishable from the basest stones.[2]

When these lesser lights have explored all the possibilities opened by a genius, knowledge springs again with the advent of another. Among these he cited Columbus, Bacon, Descartes, Newton and a small number of others.

---

[1] Schelle, op. cit. voi i p. 117.
[2] Ibid pp. 118–41.

Nevertheless Turgot wrote, 'The designs of men are more limited than those of nature. It would be better to be guided by nature than by bad laws.'

He likened the development of colonies to the ripening of fruit on a tree, for when they had received sufficient nourishment to sustain their independent existence, they fell from the parent branch. In time they would germinate and produce new trees. He predicted that the American colonies would shortly declare their independence from Britain.

In these notes he shows enthusiasm for new ideas and discoveries and, by contrast, his contempt for anything which hindered or suppressed their emergence:

> It is definitely not human error and it is not wars or revolutions which slow the progress of governments; it is lethargy, stubbornness, a bent for routine and everything which leads to inaction. In directing all the strength of your mind to discover new truths one is afraid of straying and one prefers to follow the accepted opinions, or, in other words, you do not want to walk for fear of breaking your limbs. But thereby one puts oneself in the place of the person with broken limbs, since your own are quite useless.[1]

These notes reveal a young thinker of profound scholarship, even though they were not entered as an essay for the competition. After spending a great deal of time collecting his thoughts, Turgot formulated his ideas swiftly and succinctly. This was a pattern which he adopted throughout his life.

In the same year Buffon, a French scholar, published his work on natural history in forty-three volumes. Turgot read each of the volumes as it appeared. He was surprised that Buffon had ignored many of Newton's discoveries and had attempted to describe the creation of the earth in fanciful language, savouring more of fiction than of science. Turgot wrote an anonymous criticism of the work. It was anonymous only because he thought the review of a theological student would not be taken seriously. In any event, it did not command widespread interest.

Around 1748 Turgot compiled an index of his writings. There appeared 'a treatise on currency interest and banking, the system of Law, credit, exchange and commerce'. Though no such treatise on money survived, he did write to a fellow student on the subject of paper money. Turgot distinguished paper money issued by governments from gold and silver and he could not imagine that any people would allow paper money to oust those precious metals. He condemned the system of John Law, a Scottish financier, who had propounded the wild notion that the power of the state to create money out of thin air was unlimited. The

---

[1] Ibid. p. 133.

implementation of his scheme caused a financial collapse in France during the 1720s.

In July 1749, at the age of twenty-two, Turgot, under one of his family titles of baron of Aulne, entered the House of the Sorbonne, the theological faculty of the University of Paris. It was likened by Morellet to a fellowship at Oxford or Cambridge. The House had its own library, study rooms, chapel, gardens and dining room. Turgot studied a range of subjects there including what would be described today as economics and sociology. Theology interested him less and less. 'I remember', recalled Morellet, 'admitting to each other our embarrassment, our doubts, or rather our disgust, at the follies by which our youth had been deceived and at the sophisms given by theologians to the reasoning by which the Socianist Crellus proved that one and one make three, and being convulsed with laughter.'[1]

While at the House of the Sorbonne Turgot's learning was drawn from a wide number of sources. He completed a large number of translations: parts of the *Odes* of *Horace*, the Fourth book of Aeneid, the beginning of of the Fourth book of the *Georgics*, all the *Eclogues* and pieces from British authors, including Johnson, Shakespeare, Hume, Tucker and Pope.

Six months after entering the House, Turgot was elected its prior. During his year of office he was obliged to deliver two discourses in Latin, at the conclusion of academic exercises, called the *sorbonniques*. The first discourse, in July 1750, concerned the advantages which Christianity had bestowed on the human race.

Man, he stated, was endowed by nature with the needs, passions, desires and reason as the means to attain happiness. Yet men showed themselves too limited in their ideas, too petty minded and too selfish to direct society to the happiness of everyone. In several places of the discourse he reiterated the need of people to raise their political thinking in order to embrace justice. In the ancient republics, for example, love of country had become hatred and mistrust of the rest of mankind; selfishness manifested in the enslavement of peoples and barbarous inequality of the sexes, which existed particularly in the Orient. Despite all the horrors, the darkness and relapses in human development, Turgot traced a progression in knowledge and understanding. He was searching for new growth in comprehension, which, though it might lie unrealised and undeveloped for centuries, at length would burst upon the human consciousness.

He concluded his first discourse with the assertion that the Christian religion had been the standard which had lifted the sights of men beyond their narrow perceptions of personal interests to consider the welfare of their fellow beings. It was a safe conclusion which suited the occasion more than it followed the course of the argument. But it was too vague and speculative for him to have employed as a conclusion; he was seeking something more dynamic than religion with its

---

[1] Morellet, *Mémoires*, vol i p. 131.

rigid traditions and time-worn ceremonies. He had been feeling listless for three months before delivering the discourse and, though it had been well received, he was not happy with it. He wrote across the front page of the speech that its tone was too didactic.

The keynote of the second discourse, delivered in December 1750, was the idea of the perfectibility of man; the idea that man could perfect his being by transcending limitations and by cultivating the qualities implanted in him. It was at once a powerful and dynamic idea; it made spiritual development dependent on the individual himself, rather than on priest and pulpits. The French word *perfectibilté* was accepted into the official language in 1835 by the Acadèmie française. The perfectibility was inevitable, because man will attain eventually his highest end. Yet he was talking of an inevitability over several centuries, for men fell continually to the same weaknesses, the same temptations, the same errors. For much of this time progress might be indiscernible. 'No-one', wrote Flint, 'had perceived with anything like the same clearness how the mental and spiritual movement in history underlies, pervades and originates the outwardly visible movement.'[1]

The discourse contained ideas which were to preoccupy Turgot throughout his life.

> We see societies and nations establishing and forming themselves and dominating others or becoming subject to them; empires raise themselves up and crash; laws and forms of government succeed each other; the arts and sciences are perfected in a progression which passes from clime to clime, sometimes accelerating, at other times checked ... The whole human race, through periods of calm and agitation, of good times and bad times marches on, though slowly, to greater perfection ... Doubtless the mind contains the potential for the same progress, but nature, unequal in her gifts, has given to certain individuals an abundance of talents or left them buried in others and from the infinite variety of these circumstances is born the inequality in the development of nations. Barbarism makes all men equal.[2]

Lord Acton, the British historian, assessed the importance of this second discourse thus:

> While Montesquieu, at the height of his fame as the foremost of living writers, was to contemplate the past, there was a student in a Paris seminary who taught men to fix hope and endeavour on the future, and led the world at twenty-three. Turgot, when he proclaimed that upward

[1] R. Flint, *Philosophy of History in Modern Europe*, 1874, p. 111.
[2] Schelle, op. cit., vol 1 pp. 214–34.

growth and progress is the law of human life was studying to become a priest ... Under the burden of sin, men accustomed themselves to the consciousness of degeneracy; each generation confessed that they were the unworthy children of their parents, and awaited with impatience the approaching end ... Turgot at once made the idea (of human perfectibility) habitual and familiar, and it became a pervading force in thoughtful minds, whilst the new sciences arose to confirm it. He imparted a deeper significance to history, giving it unity of tendency and direction, constancy where there had been motion and development instead of change.[1]

Morellet, a fellow student remembered Turgot at this period:

His modesty and reserve would have reflected honour on a maiden. It was impossible to risk the slightest *'equivoque'* on certain subjects without making him blush to the roots of his hair and making him extremely embarrassed. This did not prevent him having an open and naive sense of fun and from falling into fits of laughter at a joke, a point or an absurdity ... His mind was engaged in continual activity, but, when he set himself to work and there was need of writing or acting, he was slow and dawdling ... He would spend a lot of time arranging his desk and trimming his pens.[2]

Turgot's scholarship was drawn to the history of thought and science and the development of language and the arts. In the second discourse he described that, beneath the corruption of ancient Rome and the darkness in Europe after feudalism, there was a gradual formation of a constellation of light, burst upon Europe as the Italian Rennaisance. For centuries darkness seemed to obscure the way forward but Turgot saw the sowing of seeds which would break out of darkness to provide the next move forward.

By the age of twenty-four Turgot had received the best education available in Paris, but he did not consider that either his mind or his spirit was trained for the cloistered life of the Church or for the agreeable life, which might be enjoyed in the capital from the fruits of a provincial bishopric.

---

[1] Lord Acton, *Background to the French Revolution.* p?.
[2] W.W. Stephens, *The Life and Writings of Turgot* p. 6.

2

The *Parlements* and the *Salons*

Turgot's father died of gout in February 1751. At this point Turgot abandoned his ecclesiastical career, to which he was bound by neither inclination nor vows. Condorcet explained how Turgot could not bring himself to always hold the same opinion in public or teach as truths what appeared to him to be errors.[1]

Turgot could have pursued an academic career in classics, history, or literature. He could also have become a scientist. However, he decided to make a career in the public administration of the state. His studies had shown him that government was moved by vested interests, habit, public opinions and that principles of justice had no role in the affairs of state. He was attracted more to political thought, rather than the daily business of public administration. He did not believe that common sense or pragmatism were sufficient for the government of society.

Turgot had studied law at the House of the Sorbonne and yet at the age of twenty-four he found most openings into the law barred, on account of his youth. However, through family connections, and his reputation as a scholar, he secured a position as an under-procurator général, a legal subordinate. Two years later, in 1753, he was appointed a Master of Requests, a junior judge, even though he was still five years under the required age. This appointment entitled him to a seat along with magistrates in the *parlement* of Paris.

The *parlements* throughout France had been established since the early fourteenth century as repositories of law. Up to that date the *curia regis*, or King's Council, had handled the legislative, legal and administrative affairs of state without division. Pressure of responsibilities in these spheres had eventually dictated that the work of the Council was delegated by the crown to thirteen regional *parlements*. In time the *parlements* had added to their original function, as repositories of laws and of registrars of laws, by assuming the role of legislators in matters affecting censorship, religion, agriculture and commerce. Admission as a magistrate to a *parlement* was reserved for those anchored in nobility and money; accomplishment in law was neither necessary nor even desirable.

---

[1] A. Neymarck, *Turgot et Ses Doctrines* p. 19.

They used their additional powers invariably to suppress individual liberties and to interfere in the life of the region. They also claimed the right to register, or veto, new laws enacted by the King's Council. These rights gave them power over the King's Council. It could be exercised effectively whenever the King's Council was weak.

Soon after Turgot had taken his seat in the *parlement* of Paris, the king dissolved it and exiled the magistrates. The quarrel which had led to this extreme measure was over the duty of the Catholic Church in regard to the provision of the last rites to Protestants. In France the established Church was Roman Catholic and it was bitterly opposed to other religions.

During the eighteenth century intolerance was common and flagrant: congregations of Protestants had been broken up by troops, men had been condemned to the galleys, women had been whipped and priests had been hanged. The Catholic Church often refused to register marriages between Protestants and barred them from public employment. In 1780 the Assembly of the clergy had declared, 'that the altar and the throne would be in equal danger if heretics [protestant and non-conformist groups] was allowed to throw off its shackles'.[1] Politics and religion have always proved a combustible mixture and it is little wonder that many intelligent minds in France chose to avoid this unseemly conflict and became atheists.

In 1746, in accordance with the papal bull, entitled *Ugenitus*, the French Catholic Church had instructed their clergy not to administer last rights to persons suspected of being Jansenists, if they failed to submit to a confession, recanting their alleged heresy against the Catholic Church. The followers of Jansen, the leader of a Protestant sect, had questioned the Church's teaching on grace, free will and predestination. *Parlement*, quarrelled with the Church, as was their custom, and, in their turn, the King's Council supported the Church. In 1752 a *parlement* had fined a priest for refusing to administer the last rites to a Jansenist priest. The King's Council overruled the fine and in April 1753 Louis XV issued letters patent transferring matters concerning the sacraments from the *parlement* to the Council. When the *parlement* refused to register the letters patent and published their remonstrances against the measure, it was disbanded by the crown. It is difficult to unravel the political desire for this measure from the religious quarrel.

To continue the work of the courts, while the *parlements* were exiled, the Council formed the *Chambre Royale* as a special tribunal composed of councillors of state and forty masters of requests. Turgot thought *parlement* should not involve itself in matters of religious controversy, in order to be free to perform its judicial role impartially. He hated intolerance under any guise and thought both parties to this dispute were equally guilty of showing their intolerance of each other. Thus, he joined the tribunal.

---

[1] H. Taine, *The Ancien Regime*, 1873, p. 63.

A correspondent asked Turgot what right the Catholic Church, as the principal religion had to state protection. 'No religion', replied Turgot,' has the right to demand any other protection [from the state] than that of its own liberty and yet it loses even that right when its dogma or cult are contrary to the interests of state.'[1] However, he believed that the state did have an interest in protecting the principal religion, since its priests provided a basic education for children in villages and country districts. Its protection should extend to providing each priest with independent resources, such as land specially set aside by a community. This land should be managed by the local congregation. He did not believe that the livelihood of the cleric should be left to the free donations of congregations. In certain remote and poor districts, where a priest was most essential, he could not be expected to live from a modest collection box. His correspondent then suggested that preaching against the principal religion should be banned and that the state should not force individuals to follow that religion. Turgot agreed that no temporal ruler has any right or ability to judge any matter of truth or divinity. If the state made provision for the priests of a particular religion, it did so only to confirm its utility and not its truth.

In his reply Turgot expressed a principle of wider application.

> Every man is born free and it is never permissible to obstruct this freedom ... Liberties, like properties, are limited by each other ... One is too accustomed in government to sacrificing the happiness of the individual to the alleged rights of society. It is forgotten that society is created for individuals and that it is instituted only in order to protect the rights of everyone by assuring the performance of mutual duties.[2]

Turgot was no more at home in the *parlements* than he had been in the church; both institutions were corrupt and neither had the least desire to reform society. He felt more at home in the Parisian salons, in which the leading hostesses in the capital invited thinkers or the *philosophes* to discuss topics of government, science, education and literature. During the 1760s the Parisian salons became famous centres of intellectual life.

Turgot was introduced to this world of ideas by Mme Graffigny, one of the leading salon hostesses, who had befriended him at the House of the Sorbonne. She introduced him to other leading hostesses such as Mme Deffand, Mme Geoffrin and Mme Boufflers.

Mme Graffigny was a close friend of Voltaire and had begun writing plays and novels late in life. Her most popular novel, *Lettres d'une Peruvienne*, was due to be republished and, before she revised the work, she asked Turgot to review it. Like

---

[1] Schelle, op. cit., vol i p. 387.
[2] Ibid, p. 424.

many novels at that time, it was a philosophical commentary. One of her principal themes was the quest for equality. In primitive society equality was plainly evident but it had been so romanticised in novels that hopes for it existing in current life were quite unrealistic. What particularly dismayed Turgot was that she, in looking back into an imagined past, ignored hope in the future and in the development of society. In a review of her novel, Turgot challenged her view about the ideal of equality:

> All men are not born equal; their strength, their mind, their passions between them would break the equilibrium which laws could set; [it is] because men are born so weak that they need their parents and form an indissoluble tie with them ... Families with unequal capacities and strength compound the causes of inequality ... What would society be without this inequality of conditions? Everyone would be reduced to a life concerned merely with necessities and there were many to whom these were not assured ... Thus inequality will increase, even among the most civilised and moral peoples ... It is not an evil: it is a blessing for mankind. Where would society be if every man laboured only at his own backyard? ... The diversity of employment necessarily leads to inequality of conditions. Without it who would attract the useful arts? Who would look after the infirm? Who would spread the light of the mind? Who would bring the special and general education to men and nations which forms their customs? Who would determine peacefully the quarrels between individuals? Who would resist the brute strength of some and protect the weakness of others? Liberty! I say with a sigh that perhaps men are not worthy of you. Equality! They desire you but cannot attain you.[1]

Equality was becoming a fashionable concept; in 1754 Jean-Jacques Rousseau published his essay entitled *Discourse on Equality*. While Turgot may not have been replying directly to that book, he was opposed to the prevailing idea that man's freedom depended on his remaining a simple soul in a primitive, unpopulated world; in other words, upon his remaining a savage. Turgot believed man's freedom was greatly enhanced by the emergence of society. Indeed, he positively believed that such freedom was realisable only in a civilised society, governed by laws, enlightened by science and refined by fine taste in the arts. In order to attain freedom of the individual in such a developed society it was necessary to discover the principles which secured individual civil freedom and the nature of private property.

Another theme of Mme Graffigny's novel was the education of children. They

---

[1] W. W. Stephens, *Life and Writings of Turgot*, pp. 194–5.

were being brought up to conform to a certain meaningless etiquette of the social world and little thought was given to developing their latent qualities and talents. Turgot wrote later in the review of the novel:

> Our teaching is applied against the grain of nature. . . . We begin by wanting to cram into the heads of children a mass of the most abstract ideas. We deluge them with words which can offer no meaning to them, because the meaning of words can only be presented along with ideas and these ideas come gradually by linking them with tangible objects. We also suppress their imagination . . . We make a point of telling a child that he must be virtuous, temperate and just. But has he the least idea of virtue? Do not say to a child, 'Be virtuous', but make him find pleasure in being so. Develop in his heart the germ of the sentiments nature has placed there. We often need more defences against our education than against nature . . . It is supposed that this quiet impartiality is the gift of nature, the result of an equable temperament, and that education is powerless to effect this constant attention to oneself. We know little the power of education. I will mention one of the reasons of its failure; it is that we are content to prescribe rules when it is necessary to create natural habits . . . I believe that nature has sown in every heart the seeds of virtues, that they require only to be developed and that education (but only skillful education) can render the majority of men virtuous. I know that progress cannot be rapid; man trails along step by step. We must begin by teaching parents to feel the necessity of this real education and to know how to impart it . . . The great point in home education is to teach by example.[1]

Shortly after his introductions to the salons, Turgot was introduced to Mme Graffigny's niece, Minette de Ligniville. Often they played badminton, which was an unusual pastime for Turgot, as he had shown no inclination for sport. It was even said that he proposed marriage to her. But he had no money and no position. Minette's sister had married a rich *fermier-général*, or tax collector, and the contrast between her situation and that proposed for Minette was too stark. In any case Turgot had more of a passion for the reform of society than love of domesticity. Within a short time Minette also married a rich *fermier-général* called Helvêtius. Turgot remained a good friend of Minette, even though he came to loathe the ideas of her husband. When she was later to become a widow, Turgot persuaded her not to marry Benjamin Franklin, the American statesman, on account of their large difference in age – he being over 70 and she around 40.

At the salons Turgot met all the *philosophes*, including Diderot, Alembert,

---

[1] Ibid., pp. 196–202.

Holbach, Helvêtius, Grimm and Galiana. He was especially fond of Condorcet and Julie Lespinasse. She had been hired by Mme Deffand as a reader when her own eyesight was failing, and Julie became so popular that she was able to open her own salon to which she attracted the best minds. He also befriended the duchesse d'Enville and Mme Blondel. The latter was described as 'endowed with a superior mind and worldliness. She occupied a leading position in society on account of her relations [her husband was a diplomat] and in addition she had a vivid and brilliant imagination, quick comprehension and a perfect sense of tact.'[1]

The *philosophes* were a group of thinkers who believed in the authority of reason and materialism. Some such as Holbach, known as 'the personal enemy of the Almighty', professed atheism and others challenged only the authority of theological dogma, rather than the existence of God. Holbach wrote, 'If we go back to the beginning we shall always find that fear and ignorance always created gods, fantasy, enthusiasm or that deceit has adorned and disfigured them; credulity preserves them in life; tyranny supports it in order to make the blindness in man serve its own ends'.[2]

Turgot definitely believed in God and in nature. His theory of the perfectibility of man would have been empty without such a fundamental belief. But he accepted that atheism was a reaction against a Church that fabricated mysteries and fearful predictions and who censored literature that offended dogma and participated in temporal government only in order to preserve its own monopolies, privileges and wealth.

In 1758 Helvêtius's book *De l'Esprit* was published. It presented one stream of the *philosophes'* thought and attracted attention at home and abroad. Beccaria, the Italian juristic writer, hailed it as the great inspiration of his own writings and Jeremy Bentham confessed that he 'owed to Helvêtius's book a great part of my ideas', including the celebrated utilitarian idea of the greatest good for the greatest number. In his book Helvêtius formulated three principal ideas.

First, that man is born equal and ignorant; inequality arises from unequal education and unequal circumstances; talents and virtues are acquired by education.

Second, man is motivated by self-interest; it prevails over feelings such as sympathy and conscience; it becomes love of power in society and the so-called love of justice is also really a love of power.

Third, the concepts of good and evil are ever changing. Thus there can be no absolute good and no absolute evil.

Turgot tolerated the arguments of atheists and ideas which were opposed to his own and those which appeared to him misconceived. He could accept lies when they were attributable to ignorance rather than conscious intent. But the ideas of

---

[1] Schelle, op. cit., vol i p. 45.
[2] P Holbach, *Le Systme de la Nature* 1770 edn., vol ii p. 200.

Helvêtius attracted Turgot's condemnation of a severity which he rarely displayed on any subject. He detested the way Helvêtius scorned virtue, honesty, morality and justice and called those who upheld them them bigots and hypocrites. He despised the assertion that there was no morality between nations and the idea that international relations must invariably be dictated by narrow nationalistic interest; for the interests of nations were those of individual subjects and those were always bound up with the universal interests of peace, freedom and prosperity. He abhorred the idea that self-interest should be divorced from profound sentiments of the heart. For, when so advanced, it amounted to stating that man desired what he craved and excluded any consideration of whether a desire was in conflict with deeper reflections. He thought the severity of Helvêtius's declamation against religious intolerance would be counterproductive by persuading the Church to be more intolerant. This was a subject requiring illumination rather than condemnation. Finally, Turgot was dismayed to hear Helvêtius praised with the special fervour which to him always denoted the sectarian spirit.

There was desire in Paris in the mid-eighteenth century to summarise the whole body of human knowledge in an encyclopedia. Such a work could bring together the new sciences and older branches of knowledge. In 1751 two *philosophes*, Alembert and Diderot, combined to produce the first volume of the *Encyclopédie*, designed, according to Condorcet, to contain 'accurate and simple sketches of the different subjects of human knowledge and to demonstrate the most definite, useful and important truths in the different branches of science'.[1]

While Turgot approved of the aims of the enterprise, he was disappointed by the 'sad doctrines and the banal claims of Helvêtius, the incongruities in the ideas of Diderot and Raynal, the gross materialism of Holbach, and the dryness of heart in Grimm and Galiana'.[2] However, he was prepared to write articles for the *Encyclopédie*. Despite disagreeing with the motives of the group which promoted them, Turgot saw the value of bringing together human knowledge. His five articles appeared in 1756 and 1757.

The first was on etymology, the second on existence, the third on expansibility and the final two on charitable foundations and medieval fairs. These last two were of special interest because they provided evidence of his growing interest in economic questions. In France there were charitable foundations in every parish for saying masses for the dead, for launching Christian missions, education, relief of poverty and many for the relief of fallen women. Many charities were governed by rigid constitutions which had become obsolete. In addition, the funds of charities had been reduced by inflation so that, even though the purposes be worthy, the relief was slight. Turgot disliked individual relief of a general problem

---

[1] M-J. Condorcet, *La vie de Turgot*, ch 2.
[2] A. Neymarck, op. cit., vol i, p. 31.

such as poverty, because such measures did not affect the cause of the problem. Rather, they deflected attention from the cause to the relief. Furthermore, relief often made idleness and inertia too attractive. He argued passionately for relief of the general conditions by government. He also believed that the state should have the power to vary the constitutions of old and ineffective foundations to prevent the will of the founders controlling the living long after their deaths. In time the resources of charities might become so small and their objectives so outdated, that the foundations might no longer serve real public needs.

The last essay was on fairs. These were adopted during the Middle Ages throughout Europe to create regional markets, which had the advantage of protection from highwaymen and wars. He noted that the fairs began to attract the interest of governments and soon became objects of copious regulations, interference and permits.

After the publication of the first two volumes of the *Encyclopédies* in 1752, the clergy denounced the *encyclopédistes* as heretics, along with Bacon, Newton and Locke, who had cast doubt on theological mysteries and chronology. The Council forbade reprinting of these two volumes but said nothing about future volumes. This mild move was merely a sop to the clergy and *dévots*, or church party. For the censor, Malesherbes, a noted lawyer, adopted a characteristically tolerant attitude and encouraged the editors to continue. In 1758 the Church revived their hostilities against the *encyclopédistes* and the *parlement* appointed a commission to look into the publication. Malesherbes, however, won the patronage of Mme de Pompadour, who was too strong for the combined forces of Church and *parlements*, and work continued on the later volumes.

In 1759 Diderot begged Turgot to contribute a further eight articles. But Turgot declined because he did not like the spirit of sect which was engulfing the editors and contributors; this spirit appeared to him both a muzzle to free thought and began to threaten a militant assault on public opinion.

3

Les Économistes

Turgot's legal duties as a magistrate did not prevent him from pursuing his interest in government. At the end of 1753 Turgot translated an essay on trade by Sir Josiah Child, an English writer and Member of Parliament. His views on trade were robust and sometimes unpopular. He once described the laws of England as 'a heap of nonsense, compiled by a few ignorant country gentlemen, who hardly knew how to make laws for the good government of their own families, much less for the regulating of companies and foreign commerce'.[1] Turgot's notes to the translation revealed that he was in favour of free trade; that is trade free of government intervention and regulation. Prices, Turgot acknowledged, are settled between seller and buyer and the balance between them should not be disturbed by the state. Free competition would keep these interests in balance. There might be government control on trade in illegal articles such as poisons and armaments. but not detailed controls on trade and money. In 1753 he also translated a pamphlet on the naturalisation of foreign Protestants by Dean Tucker, an English cleric, who wrote on economic matters.

The concept of free trade was directly opposed to the prevailing spirit of protectionism, which had gripped France since the days of Jean Colbert, the finance minister of Louis XIV. Protectionism has proved a perennial weed of politics in Europe and it is as strong at the close of the twentieth century as it has ever been. Colbert has been the grand marshal of protectionism. He controlled industry by a host of regulations, price controls, subsidies, monopolies, import controls. He employed any measure, provided it altered the natural course of commerce. It should always be remembered that governments deploy neither the skill nor the experience of businessmen, nor does it risk private ruin. Colbert 'believed that international trade was a form of warfare; that the triumph of one country must be at the expense of another; that wealth was measured by bullion; that tariffs, aggression and conquest are the best means of accumulating and monopolising bullion and are therefore the weapons by which national greatness

---

[1] A. Hamilton, *Account of the East Indies*, ch. XIX.

is achieved'.[1] This state control came in time to be known as colbertism. It became as outdated in the eighteenth century as the concept that the earth was flat, for the oceans had been traversed and peoples of different continents had been joined by trade across the globe.

The idea that an import is a national loss and an export is a national gain is based on the belief of Colbert that international trade is a game in which nations succeed by accumulating gold and treasure through trade. It is impossible to reduce imports by state controls, without also restricting exports to the same extent. For the traders from whom imports are obtained, will earn less currency after controls have been imposed. Consequently a trader will be able to sell less of that currency to someone who wishes to use it to buy the exports of the importing country. Imports and exports are linked like the inward and outward breath. It is impossible to breathe out without ever breathing in; so it is impossible to restrict imports while attempting to boost exports.

There are two fundamental errors in protectionism. First, the notion that the national interest in trade during peacetime could be advanced at the expense of the economic interests of individual members of society. Second, that imports destroy domestic trade and are distinguished from exports, which are prized as a nation's pure gains. Trade is conducted between individuals situated across a street or an ocean and not between nations or their governments. The supreme national interest in peace should be to uphold the liberty of individuals to buy as they wish and producers to sell as they wish.

Turgot was to show that it is facile to promote a supposed national benefit from trade above the liberties of individuals. To pretend that a national interest is enhanced by protectionism is disingenuous; for the actual reason for benefiting producers is purchasing their political support. He believed that a free national or international market represented a perfect balance between the interests of producer and consumer. There is a world free market price, set by competition, in every agricultural produce. It is sophistry to pretend otherwise.

Turgot's keen interest in economic matters taken together with his unusual intellectual abilities, might have developed his economic thinking unaided. However, around 1753 he met Dr François Quesnay and Vincent Gournay, who were the founders of a group who became as the *économistes* because they seemed to be ever urging economies in government expenditure.

These two men had a profound influence on Turgot's thinking. He adopted his main principles from them. But he formed his own conclusions and later he wrote a succinct and reasonable formulation of his thoughts on economics.

Quesnay was born in 1694 into a poor family of peasants. He received no formal education and he learnt to read by the age of ten, with the help, it was said, of a gardener. Thereafter, his appetite for learning became insatiable. He taught

---

[1] D Ogg, *Louis XIV* ch. 3.

himself Greek and Latin and learnt from a village doctor the rudiments of surgery, which soon became his chosen profession. He practised at first in the provinces before he came to Paris in 1730 as the private surgeon of the duc de Villeroi. One evening during a party the Countess d'Estrades was stricken with an epileptic fit and Quesnay, who happened to be present, ordered everyone from the room. He handled the situation with such competence that the countess recommended him to a friend, Mme de Pompadour. She was the mistress of Louis XV. She proved herself a stronger character than her debauched master and soon became the power on the throne. At her insistence Quesnay became surgeon-in-ordinary to the king and was installed in Versailles. In 1737 he became secretary to the Royal Academy of Surgeons and wrote several articles on surgery. In recognition he was elected a Fellow of the Royal Society in London in May 1752. Later he suffered from gout and had to abandon surgery and concentrate on medicine.

Louis appointed him his consulting physician and conferred on him letters of nobility with a coat of arms of three pansies. The French word for pansies – *pensées* – is also the word for thoughts and the king referred to the doctor as his thinker.

Quesnay's thoughts turned to economic questions during the early 1750s and he contributed articles to the *Encyclopédie* on the grain trade and agriculture. He began to attract like minds to his ideas and in 1756 he met at Versailles the Marquis de Mirabeau, the author of *The Friend of Mankind*. They became the two leaders of the *économistes*. Turgot referred to them as the 'patriarchs' of the subject. Mirabeau said before then he himself was no more an economist than his cat. They set up public lectures. Mirabeau, who continued to hold meetings on Tuesday evenings for about twenty years, was the father of Honor, the revolutionary figure. Quesnay and Mirabeau reduced economic questions to mathematical and scientific principles. In 1760 they produced a book, entitled *The Theory of Taxation*, in which they had the temerity to state that the royal treasury was empty and the management of the revenue was poor. The court found this too bold and indelicate and Mirabeau was removed to prison for a short time to cool off. The doctor was shaken by the reaction to their book and confessed to the chambermaid of Mme de Pompadour that 'it is forty years since I left my native village and I have very little experience of the world and I find it difficult to get accustomed to it. When I am in a room with the King, I think to myself, "There is a man who can remove my head" and the thought makes me uneasy.'[1]

Quesnay believed fundamentally that 'God has endowed the universe with a physical constitution by which everything is ordered in nature . . . [It is God] who gives us the power to study and to discover the link between cause and effect that establish the natural laws. We must submit to these laws under pain of losing, in proportion to our errors and deviations, the faculty of doing what is more advantageous to us . . . Considered in general, natural laws are the essential

---

[1] R. Meek, *The Economics of Physiocracy* p. 29.

conditions according to which everything operates in the order prescribed by the author of nature. These are the natural laws which provide for the meeting of men in society and which fix the regulation of this meeting according to rights, duties and the manifest interest of each.'[1] His view of government was succinct: 'Ex nature, jus, ordo et leges; ex homine, arbitrium, regimen et coercito.' [From nature, right, order and laws; from men caprice, regulation and coercion.]

Once the dauphin, who was not to survive Louis XV, sighed over the complexities of government. 'I do not see that it is so troublesome,' ventured Quesnay 'What would you do then if you were the King?' countered the dauphin. 'Nothing,' replied Quesnay. 'Then who would govern?' enquired the dauphin. 'The law,' stated Quesnay. He was referring to the laws of nature which he believed governed the world whether men heeded them or not.

Quesnay's view of the relationship between the individual and society was simple and positive: the individual gains immeasurable opportunities, rights and advantages by living in a developed society, providing the laws of that society preserve his individual birthrights in both the civil and economic spheres. Quesnay derided the idea of Thomas Hobbes that from birth the individual has only rights against the world as kings might allow, for being 'as illusory as the rights of sparrows and gnats',[2] because human activity is conditioned by surrounding forces and by the acts of fellow human beings.

Quesnay was the first man to have sought to reduce what is now called economics to a basic scientific system. Several writers in early times had written about isolated matters to do with money or trade. But it was Quesnay who first embraced the elements of economics. His leading concepts were the *tableau économique* and the *produit net*. The *tableau* was produced first in 1758. It attempted to show the circulation of wealth between the agricultural producers and the rest of society in a diagrammatic form. To many the *tableau* was totally incomprehensible and earned the label, on account of its geometric form, 'le zigzag', but Mirabeau was struck with admiration and claimed that 'since the beginning of the world there have been three great inventions which have given stability to political societies: the invention of writing, for transmitting laws, contracts and discoveries; the invention of money, which bound together the relations between civilised societies and the *tableau économique*, which completed them both.'[3]

Turgot regarded the *tableau* as unnecessarily complicated, though he found some of the underlying principles useful, in particular, the concept of the *produit net* which Quesnay had defined as the surplus remaining after the wages, costs and the current rate of profit of an activity had been deducted. This surplus arose principally in agriculture which was the main economic activity in eighteenth-century France. This surplus or *produit net* did not arise from labour, for an

---

[1] G Schelle, *Du Pont et l'École Physiocrats*, 1888, p. 51.
[2] Ibid. p. 50.
[3] Schelle, op. cit., vol i, p. 642.

equivalent amount of labour could yield a lesser surplus in a less fertile place; it was created by nature, rather than men. It was the quality of land rather than human labour and expense which determined this surplus. Quesnay argued that this surplus represented a unique fund for taxation.

Under the patronage of Mme. de Pompadour, Quesnay basked in the sunshine of royal favour at Versailles. Bertin, the *contrôleur-général*, or Minister of the Interior, was willing to listen to and, even, implement Quesnay's ideas. Quesnay and Mirabeau soon attracted several younger followers. When Mme de Pompadour died in April 1764, Bertin immediately fell from favour, along with Quesnay.

A number of younger men, like Merciérè de la Rivière and Pierre Du Pont, attempted to secure a scientific basis for Quesnay's teaching. From 1767 they called themselves *Physiocrats* – those who follow the rule of nature. They became the guardians of his thinking and in their enthusiasm and blind devotion they enlarged minor and erroneous points of his teachings. They formed themselves into a sect and had a diminishing effect on public thinking. Turgot never subscribed to any sect; he believed in justice, reasonableness and an open mind. 'Unhappily', wrote Turgot, 'the two patriarchs of the *économistes* [Quesnay and Mirabeau] do not stand up to a fine analysis of language and grammar and the reverential respect of the disciples ensures that they always connect what they say to what the masters have formulated. For this reason I conclude that the latter will talk nonsense all their lives, for in order to reason well, it is necessary to begin with an open mind, which is repugnant to the whole spirit of sect.'[1]

Quesnay abandoned the study of economics by the end of the 1760s and like Hobbes, a seventeenth-century English thinker, he became in his last years preoccupied by geometry; he was trying to square the circle and trisect the angle.

The *Physiocrats* began to dissolve in the mid-1770s. Mirabeau lost his reputation as a writer and became engulfed in a family quarrel; Morellet became a friend of Necker, Turgot had to distance himself from them because of his office. Their journal, *Ephémérides du Citoyen*, was suppressed in 1772. Du Pont left for Poland in 1772 and Le Trosne and Merciérè de la Rivière continued writing but their works drifted from favour.

Gournay, the other man to whom Turgot owed a considerable debt, was a more practical thinker than Quesnay. He was engaged for seventeen years as a merchant in Cadiz and other European trading centres and in his spare time he read books about trade and banking, principally by John de Witt and Sir Josiah Child. His studies and his practical experience convinced him of the need for freedom from government interference in trade and commerce; and that trade is an individual activity, directed by the force of individual preferences and the myriad of impulses whose subtlety and intelligence will ever elude the comprehension of governments and their bureaucrats.

---

[1] Schelle, op. cit., vol iii, p. 474.

After the death of his business partner in 1746, Gournay, then in his mid-thirties, retired from business and offered his services to Maurepas, who had not then yet incurred the displeasure of Mme de Pompadour. Maurepas was minister of the Marine. In 1749 Gournay, in accordance with French custom, purchased a seat on the Grand Council, which was a court of law in Paris. Two years later he was appointed an intendant of commerce. There were six intendants of commerce who became responsible for geographic areas and particular industries. They operated as junior ministers and reported to a Board of Commerce. Gournay became responsible for the silk industry and for the region lying between Lyons and Bordeaux. According to Turgot:

> He [Gournay] could not understand why a government had deigned to regulate by express laws the length and breadth of each piece of cloth, the number of its threads, to dedicate by the seal of the legislative power volumes in quarto filled with these important details and innumerable statutes inspired first, by the spirit of monopoly, the whole purpose of which was to discourage industry and to concentrate trade in as few hands as possible by the multiplication of formalities and expenses; secondly, by guild apprenticeships of ten years for certain jobs which could be mastered in ten days, thirdly, by the exclusion of those who were not masters of the guilds or who were born outside certain districts, and, finally, by the exclusion of women in the textile trades . . . It is delusive to believe that there are products which the state must encourage rather than others; to prohibit as a result certain products by approving others and to ban certain types of industry from fear of harming other types; to support manufacture at the expense of agriculture by forcing food prices down below their natural level; to set up certain manufacture at public expense and then shower them with subsidies and privileges. This is to misconceive the real advantages of trade and to forget that a nation cannot monopolise the entire trade of the world, or sell everything to foreigners and buy nothing back from them.[1]

Gournay advised the Board of Commerce to remove the technical regulations and monopolies imposed on trade but his advice fell on deaf ears. Nevertheless with patient and persistent argument, he did persuade Trudaine, the head of the Board, to believe in the concept of free trade. The first *contrôleur-général* under whom Gournay served as an intendant was Machault, who was a staunch protectionist. Thus Gournay made no impression with argument for freer trade. But in 1754 Machault was succeeded by Moreau de Schelle, who did share

---

[1] Schelle, op. cit., vol i, pp. 600–5.

Gournay's ideas and enacted many of them. After the outbreak of the Seven Years War in 1756, military adventure took more of the government's attention and commercial matters slipped from the agenda.

Turgot travelled with Gournay in 1755 to La Rochelle, Bordeaux, Guyenne and Bayonne. Turgot came to share his ideas on commerce and became his close friend. Unfortunately in 1758 Gournay lost money on his business and was forced to resign in order to recoup his losses. He died in the following year. He had won many converts from Colbertism throughout Europe. His memory might well have died with them. But fortunately within a few weeks of his death Turgot wrote notes for his obituary:

> Thinkers of recent times have opposed the spirit of system with as much vehemence as reason and they understand by this word – system – those arbitrary assumptions, by which others endeavour to explain phenomena alike, for they explain none of them . . . They wish to confine the Infinite in order to embrace it . . . Accustomed to receive every opinion one after the other, and find them plausible without ever being convinced, like a pane of glass reflects every image without retaining any, to ignore the intimate connection of effects to their causes; to contradict themselves, but never doubt themselves; such men can only be astonished when they meet a man inwardly convinced of a truth and who deduces from it consequences with a precise logic. They allow themselves to listen to him and the next day they listen to completely contrary opinions and will be surprised not to see the same flexibility in him. Then they do not hesitate to call him a fanatic and man of systems . . .
>
> Many have wrongly accused him of being over-cautious about the reform of abuses. He knew how the ground of reform had to be prepared and how too sudden changes were dangerous. But he believed the restraint should only be present in action, and not in thought. He did not want to abolish the whole edifice without having provided the new foundations. But he wanted to have a fully reasoned plan before putting a hand to the task, so that while destroying, conserving or building he was not acting in the dark . . .[1]

Turgot owed much to each of these men and some years after Gournay's death he wrote to a friend, 'I will hold myself honoured throughout my life to have been the follower of these two men and the memory of M. Gournay will always be dear to me as a close friend and as a citizen inflamed with zeal for the public welfare.'[2]

Quesnay gave Turgot the idea of distinguishing taxes on the *produit net* of

---

[1] Ibid. pp. 600–21.
[2] Schelle, op. cit., vol ii, p. 508.

agricultural land, rather than taxes on people and goods. This idea became a fundamental element in his thinking on economic and political matters; it provided a just basis for the distribution of wealth and, consequently, for the relations also between the individual and the state. As will be shown later, Quesnay's idea provided the means for raising revenue without reducing the value of the currency or of the real value of earnings, or discouraging economic activity, or causing unemployment in the poor regions of France and without giving reason for committing fraud against the state.

Turgot valued the ideas of Quesnay, but he did not adopt them without thorough examination. He was not convinced by the usefulness of the *tableau économique*, or much of the theoretical ideas which overlay his concept of the *produit net*; he referred to this as 'the Doctor's algebra'. He rejected Quesnay's idea of a legal despotism after the example of the Chinese, under which men were ruled by mandarins and by the immutable laws of nature. He regarded that it was less offensive to intelligent opinion to base the rights of man on self-evident principles which everyone could comprehend, without the need of accepting a rigid system of laws, which Turgot felt savoured too much of the spirit of sect. He did not accept Quesnay's view that trades and occupations was of lesser importance than agriculture, or indeed of little economic influence, merely because these produced no raw materials, as did agriculture. He refuted Quesnay's view that the rate of interest should be fixed by the state, rather than by the free play of commerce.

Turgot detested the spirit of sect, which the followers of Quesnay fostered by their blind acceptance of his pronouncements and by their arrogance in thinking that they were the chosen apostles of a new political enlightenment.

> 'This spirit of sect', wrote Turgot, 'makes enemies to useful truths. If an independently minded man states modestly what he believes to be true and if it is reasonable, one listens to him, and if one finds him to be wrong, one forgets him. But as soon as savants give themselves up with pride to constitute themselves into a body and use the term "we" and imagine themselves competent to give laws for the public, thoughtful opinion deserts them, preferring to receive laws from truth rather than from authority.[1]

At the end of his life Turgot wrote to Du Pont that, though he detested sects whether they be *économiste* or *encyclopédiste*, he had nevertheless earned the reproach of being a member of both.[2]

Gournay was a fine exponent of the idea of *laissez-faire*, which phrase had been

---

[1] S. P. Du Pont, *Les Oeuvres de Turgot*, p. 47.
[2] Schelle, op. cit., vol v, p. 628.

coined by seventeenth century French merchants. They were imploring government to leave the economy alone. He believed that individuals were competent to produce what other individuals wanted to consume and that interference by government was unnecessary and clumsy. Such interests appeared as illusory as it did dangerous to Gournay; dangerous to the maintenance of individual freedom. The spirit of Colbertism infected French government. Gournay showed a simple way out of the confusion with a few self-evident principles. He showed clearly that truth and simplicity in political thought go hand in hand and that complexity is the mark of superficiality and falsity.

Turgot opposed central control of the economy because it replaced the freedom enjoyed by millions of intelligent individuals with the less intelligent judgement of one minister, who introduced political arbitrariness and uncertainty. The minister could favour the powerful at the expense of the weak and justify his actions with disingenuous reasoning.

Neither Quesnay nor Gournay presented a complete framework for the working of a free society, which was at once just and prosperous. They produced the sketches and it fell to Turgot to furnish that framework. In the words of Foncin, the French nineteenth-century historian, 'Vauban and Boisguillbert had predicted political economy; Quesnay sketched its outline; Turgot put it together.'[1]

---

[1] P. Foncin, *Essai sur le Ministre de Turgot*, p. 17.

4

Intendant of the Limousin

After Gournay's death in 1759, Turgot travelled to south-eastern France and Switzerland, making notes on the geological features of the mountains, soils and rocks and the economic activities of communities. While in Geneva he met Voltaire, who had been such an influence in his youth. Voltaire wrote to Alembert afterwards, 'I am still taken with meeting M. Turgot. I have scarcely met a more likable and learned man, and, which is quite rare among metaphysicians, he has fine and reliable taste.'[1]

While staying in Lausanne, Turgot experienced his first attack of gout. It caused swelling of the joints, particularly the big toe, on account of an excess of uric acid in the blood. The pain varied with the severity of the attack. It damages the kidneys and can shorten the sufferer's life. Having seen his father struck down by hereditary gout, Turgot must have sensed that he could not hope for a normal life span.

When Turgot returned to Paris, he applied for several judicial and administrative positions. In August 1761 he was appointed the Intendant, or administrative head, of the province of the Limousin. At that time Bertin was the *contrôleur-général*, who was inclined to listen to Quesnay. Probably Turgot was encouraged to take the intendancy of the Limousin with the hope that he could introduce and test ideas formulated by Dr Quesnay.

The Limousin was a poor, land-locked province to the east of Bordeaux. Turgot was familiar with this region, as he had travelled there with Gournay. The position of intendant in the Limousin was not widely sought; the region was isolated and poor. Turgot saw the Limousin as an opportunity to put his principles of justice into practice, for there the urgent need of reform was patent; for if his measures succeeded there, they would be applicable elsewhere.

Turgot wrote to Voltaire to say, 'I have the misfortune to be an intendant. I say misfortune, for in this century of quarrels and remonstrances, there is no happiness apart from living a philosophic life with study and friends, but still one allows oneself to get caught up in the torrent of events.'[2] Voltaire replied, 'M.

---

[1] Letter dated 18/10/1760.
[2] Schelle, op. cit., vol ii, p. 86.

Omer [an intendant] advised me that an intendant was only good at doing harm; with respect I suggest he is lying ... you will perhaps become the *contrôleur-général*, but I will be dead by then.'[1]

Perhaps Voltaire numbered the appointment of Turgot among the promising signs which enabled him to write in 1764, 'Everything I see scatters the seeds of a revolution which will indubitably arise, and which I shall not have the happiness to witness ... The young ones are indeed happy, for they will see great things.'[2]

An intendant was a subordinate of central government. Louis XV governed either directly himself or through his Council of Ministers. There was hardly any local government and nor was there any democratic participation by the people. During the seventeenth century the key positions had been allowed to fall into the hands of local potentates. There were no complaints when the offices of mayors, aldermen and lesser officials were sold in perpetuity in 1692. Yet during the eighteenth century these transactions were often overturned and these perpetual rights had to be repurchased from the crown on no less than seven occasions.

The ministers and their departments in Paris controlled central and local administration, even down to the most parochial business. Government in the provinces was entrusted to thirty-four intendants, responsible to the *contrôleur-général*, the most powerful minister in the Council. In theory, the authority delegated by the *contrôleur-général* to the intendant was minimal, allowing the intendants only to plead and to advise for changes of policy and legislation, but in practice an intelligent intendant could usurp a limited amount of authority. An intendant, wrote Condorcet, 'is the officer of the government and possesses its confidence. Government sees but with his eyes and acts with his hands.'[3]

The villages, however, retained the right to appoint an individual, called a *syndic*, to represent its interest, principally in taxation. As the responsibilities were heavy, no-one put themselves forward as a candidate and the position was often filled by an official appointee.

In order to appreciate the role of the intendant and his relationships with the Council and the people, it is necessary to consider briefly the historical development of government during the previous reign. Louis XV did not want to share power with anyone, not even the Pope, and he detested the mere mention of the States-General, which had been an assembly composed of nobles, the clergy and representatives of the people. It had not been convened since 1614 as his predecessor, Louis XIV, whose reign (1648–1715) spanned the larger part of this interval, had likewise hated the body. The nobles and the Church, who between them represented the great part of the wealth in France, had been denied a

---

[1] Ibid., p. 88.
[2] Rocquain, *Esprit Révolutionaire avant la Revolution*, p. 245.
[3] Condorcet, *La Vie de Turgot*, Ch. 3.

constitutional role in the governance of France. Instead they were placated with substantial privileges, immunities from taxation and commercial rights. The court in Versailles attracted and mollified the nobility by caressing its vanities.

During the *ancien régime* France was marked principally by the division of society into three orders comprising the nobility, the Church and the remainder of society, called the *Tiers États* or *roturiers*. For practical purposes there were two orders in the Church; higher clergy were included among the nobles and the lesser among the plebeians. The church held immense tracts of rural and urban land, allowing the cardinal and bishop to feel themselves in a different social and economic class from the country *curé* or simple monk. The nobility were not from the same paddock. At the apex of nobility were the *noblesse d'épée*, dating from feudal times; the *noblesse de robe*, who had purchased official positions in the law or higher grades of the civil service; *noblesse de cloche*, who purchased positions on towns councils and finally there were *lettres de noblesse* who had bought themselves out of the middle classes. However, so simple a ranking discounts pretension and money, either from land, commerce, or state pension. The former divided nobility into court and provincial, new and old, *haute* and *petite*, whilst the latter acted like a cement between disparate ranks. Unlike the English practice, the children of noblemen were classed as nobles. The numbers of the nobility were estimated between 140,000, according to Taine, the French historian, and 80,000, according to a contemporary writer.[1] In addition Taine estimated the number of clergy at 120,000.

It was the privileges of the nobility, rather than their airs or number, which caused much hatred during the *ancien régime*. Apart from seignorial rights, such as wine pressing, grinding and baking flour there was the more serious and unpopular was their exclusive right to hunting wild game. There were three other privileges that seemed especially unjust. First, they were above the general law. They were tried in special courts and, if found guilty, could not be subject to the plebeian penalties of hanging or whipping. Second, they were exempt from the *taille* and other taxes. Taxes to overcome their privileges generally failed. Third, many openings in government, civil service, law, army and Church were closed to people of the *Tiers État.*

At the beginning of the sixteenth century the crown had appointed governors, who were responsible for providing guards in the border provinces on the eastern frontiers of France, which the state was unable to defend. Naturally the governors needed, and indeed demanded, a degree of autonomy. Their power depended on the weakness of the state at the time of the grant of powers. But by the beginning of the following century the crown found itself sufficiently powerful to take back this function itself. Richelieu, the chief minister, decided to suppress the

---

[1] Considered a gross underestimate by M. Marion, *Dictionnaire des Institutions de La France aux XV11 et XV111* Siècles, p. 302.

governors. He removed all but four by exile, disgrace and execution. Louis XIV wanted to suppress the authority of the governors and do away with their office altogether. But he listened to moderate advice and, consequently, cancelled only their powers to raise taxation and employ their own troops. He demanded the presence of the surviving governors at Versailles, where they could be seduced into docility with comforts and titles. Throughout the eighteenth century the position of provincial border governors continued to be merely ornamental.

The *parlements* provided the only effective opposition to the crown during the eighteenth century. But they did not represent anybody but themselves. When it suited them, they pretended to support the people, but when things changed, they forgot them. The *parlements* at first attracted lawyers, who, in keeping with their customary instincts, drew themselves into a well-knit body. They handled concepts of the dusty and antique past, to argue a point of law with ingenuity, which the precision and the imprecision of words allowed, and to separate themselves from ordinary folk. The *parlements* provided the legal administration.

During the minority of Louis XV in the 1720s and the early 1730s, when the crown was weak, the *parlements* had their chance to usurp power. In 1732 they advanced a claim that *parlements* were 'as ancient as the crown and had been born with the state' and that their authority derived from the fundamental laws of the state, rather than from the crown. But once the young Louis took over the government himself in 1743, after the expiry of the regency, which had governed during his minority, he wanted to share the stage with no one else. The *parlements* had to wait for an opportunity to augment their powers. That occurred as the lasciviousness of the king began to sap the strength of his government. Then they demanded the right to veto legislation, if it offended their interests and privileges. The weakened king replied to the strange pretensions of his *parlements*: 'It is in my person alone the sovereign power resides. It is from me that my courts derive their existence and their authority; it is to me alone that legislative power belongs without dependence and without division.'

'The king of France', wrote the English historian W. Lecky of Louis XV, 'claimed a power that was essentially that of an oriental despot. And the sovereign who used this language was not a Caesar, or a Frederick or a Napoleon. He was contemptible in his abilities, sunk in sloth and in degrading vice, and he spoke not in a moment of victory or of prosperity, but at a time when his country was reduced by bad government to the verge of bankruptcy and still lay under the shadow of a disastrous war and of an ignominious peace.'[1]

The *parlements* presided over the suppression of heresy against Catholicism, the suppression of thought and of literature and they enforced many of the regulations, which Colbertism had attached to trade and industry.

---

[1] W. Lecky, *England in the Eighteenth Century*, vol v, p. 339.

In 1762, for example, the *parlement* of Toulouse condemned a Protestant priest to death on the gallows. They also condemned Jean Calas to death for the murder of his son, who had become a Catholic in order to be admitted to the legal bar in Toulouse. In despair after his apostasy the son committed suicide in his father's house. The father was ordered to be broken on the wheel and then burnt. Voltaire campaigned and after three years later obtained a new trial in 1765. Turgot was one of the fifty judges who found him innocent, his family were compensated and received by the king. While France celebrated the inhabitants of Toulouse refused to accept his innocence.

The evidence for this latter offence amounted to no more than conjecture. The *parlement* of Paris was always a leading persecutor of Huguenots, or Protestants. They instituted the annual procession to commemorate the massacre of the Protestants on St Bartholomew's Day in 1572. In proceedings dominated by traditional stupidity, the *parlements* suppressed books which cast light on science, philosophy and history or books which spread doubt on tradition and dogmas. The offensive books were often burnt ceremoniously on the steps of the *parlement* by the common hangman. The arrest of the author often followed. The notions of property and liberty may have been suspended, thinkers bludgeoned and racked, but the aspiration for freedom could never be banished from the human spirit. The *parlements* also condemned commercial money-lending as usurious, in the light of medieval dogma. Yet opportunities in trade and industry during the seventeenth and eighteenth centuries depended to a great extent on money-lending. The *parlements* even attempted to control the price of grain, provoked riots and famine instead of their declared object of securing plentiful and cheap supplies for the people. Once they banned inoculation against disease at a time when infant mortality was high and epidemics were frequent.

The reactionary behaviour of the magistrates and other institutions was attributable to the systems of venality and privilege. Venality had been introduced in France on a large scale by Francis I as a device to raise money for wars against Italy and Austria. It was a financial expedient which gave rise to generals, who purchased a rank beyond their capability, and to magistrates, who had little sense of law, buying themselves into *parlement*. Indeed, as Mercier observed, a magistrate who had purchased his seat in *parlement*, 'feared nothing so much as being taken for a magistrate. His conversation consisted of horses, social events, women and races. He was ashamed of knowing his profession and not once did a word of jurisprudence escape his mouth.'[1]

The practice of venality was generally supposed to be an efficient and a profitable means of bringing public-spirited figures into government. It was defended by Sénac de Meilhan, who was regarded as a liberal thinker. 'The most enlightened policy', he argued,' will dictate nothing better for centuries to come

---

[1] Marion, *Dictionnaire des Inst. de la France*, 1979, p. 431.

than this practice [venality] . . . the price of positions is only a pledge which guarantees that the wealth of a judge [for example] places him above want and corruption and that he is sufficiently rich to be able to support himself in a dignified way . . . the king has been able to reduce judicial fees to almost nothing and one finds oneself paid sufficiently by honour and prerogatives.'[1]

By entry into the *parlements* a magistrate gained ennoblement; a valuable right to certain privileges; he could pass his nobility to one generation only, he gained exemption from taxes such as the *gabelle* and the *vingtième* and the *corvée*, he was protected from legal action concerning debt; and he won the right to be tried by his peers, instead of by an inferior tribunal.

When the consequences of venality are taken into account, it is facile to pretend that it is a better system than that of merit, labour and remuneration. There were two negative consequences of venality. First, every privilege and position thus obtained created a vested interest, which was held as fiercely as a ferret holds its prey; any notion of progress or improvement was suppressed, as if it had emanated from a destructive revolutionary. Second, the natural development of talent and potential is arrested, causing loss to the state and frustration among the unprivileged.

Taking into account the injustices mentioned above, the preposterous boast of Louis XIV that 'L'Etat, c'est moi' was in fact true. Indeed, France was a nation without a constitution or a democratic order. Law, the Scottish speculative theorist, remarked that France had 'neither *parlements*, assemblies nor governors, but simply thirty masters [the intendants] of requests, on whom depended the happiness or misery, the fruitfulness or sterility of these provinces.'

As an intendant, Turgot found himself the regional representative of an absolute monarch, whose despotism was subject only to the intervention of the *parlements* of Paris in the north region of his intendancy and to that of Bordeaux over the rest and also to the Cours des Aides, a court of the *parlements*, which held jurisdiction in fiscal matters over the whole country. The *parlements* were competent to quash any measures executed by an intendant. Their authority over the police in a number of capacities could often override the intendant's plans.

According to De Tocqville, for example, 'Under the old order . . . there was in France no township, borough, village or hamlet, however small, no hospital, factory, convent, or college which had the right to manage its own affairs as it thought to administer its possessions without interference . . . the central power held all Frenchmen in its tutelage.'[2]

The province of the Limousin lay to the west of the mountainous region of the Auvergne and to the east of La Rochelle. Limoges, its principal town, was situated about 100 miles north-east of Bordeaux and about 180 miles east of Lyons. The

---

[1] Sénac de Meilhan, *De Government* . . ., 1795, pp. 100–1.
[2] Tocqueville, *The Ancien Regime and the French Revolution*, 1969 edn., pp. 79–80.

province was divided into the Marche in the north around Limoges, the Limousin in the south and an adjunct of territory to the east called the Angoumois with its centre in Angoulême.

The population of the province was about 600,000 of whom about 10 per cent lived in the towns, the largest being Limoges and Angoulême with 16,000 and 12,000 respectively. The predominant activity was agriculture the operation of which varied according to the fertility and climate. The land in the Angoumois was rich but elsewhere in the intendancy it was generally of poor quality. In the mountainous region of the east the soil was shallow and porous. In the rest of the Limousin and the Marche hills, dales, streams and marshes cut the land into small holdings of land. The general climate was constantly wet and the air was moist. In the summer it was stormy and ripening crops were often destroyed by hail and cloudbursts.

The conditions, however, were favourable for pasture and cattle fattening. Arthur Young, an English traveller, travelled the Limousin by horse in 1780 and was delighted by the countryside: 'I prefer [it] to every other province in France. Hill, dale, wood, enclosure, streams, lakes and scattered farms are mingled into a thousand delicious landscapes . . .'[1]

The land in the province was divided among peasant proprietors, who held about 56 per cent; the urban bourgeoisie, who held about 26 per cent, the nobility and the Church who held the remaining 15 per cent and 3 per cent respectively. The peasants, regardless of whether they owned or rented land, were subject to a number of obligations and claims owed to a seignorial lord. The peasants' position was more like that of tenant than freehold proprietor; they were obliged to pay rent, duties on sales of wines, rent charges and sums for the deemed use of the seignor's wine press, mill or oven. The resort to common land allowed the peasant to live free of these duties. But, as in England but to a lesser extent, the common land was gradually enclosed by landowners. The right of hunting game was reserved for the nobles. Lesser folk were expressly forbidden by edict to engage in hunting. The holdings of the Church, the nobles and urban bourgeoisie were let out usually to *métayer* farmers, each of whom divided half his profits with the landowner, in lieu of rent. This *métayage* system reduced farming to a subsistence level with nothing left for investment; Arthur Young described the system as 'a miserable system that perpetuates poverty'. The *métayer* farmer often cultivated the land with a pointed stick fastened to a crude contraption drawn by oxen, which tended to sow seeds too deep without burying surface weeds at all. The resulting crops were so poor and the risk of natural hazards so great that the peasants sowed cheap and hardy crops such as buckwheat, maize and root vegetables rather than wheat. The animals were mainly domestic. Turgot introduced the cultivation of lucerne, clover and pasture grass and encouraged the

---

[1] A. Young, *Travels in France*, 1929, p. 275.

growing of potatoes. This type of farming was reckoned by Turgot to account for four-sevenths of French agriculture.[1] The only large-scale farming in the Limousin during earlier centuries had been animal fattening, but this trade had moved to Normandy.

Small industries, such as paper-making, textiles, silk works and leather tanning, were located along the river Vienne, which passed through Limoges, and the Charente. The river connected the market town of Angoulême with the Atlantic port of Rochefort. In this port iron foundries produced canons for naval vessels harboured there. The paper mills in the Angoumois had once produced some of the finest papers in Europe, but the industry was crippled under taxes levied on papers. There were about seventy paper mills in the Limousin in 1750, each employing about twenty workers and about forty foundries provided employment for about 100. Young estimated that there were seventy textile looms on which up to five workers could work at once. Cotton and drugget spinning was produced on an outwork basis operated by villagers.

A further handicap for the Limousin was the lack of communication with the world outside. The Paris-Toulouse road ran through Limoges and Brive and the Paris-Bordeaux road, which was only completed as far south as Angoulême. The journey from Paris to Limoges was uncomfortable, expensive and took about five days. There was no east-west road and the journey from Limoges to Angoulême, a distance of some sixty miles, took two days for an expert muleteer. He had to pick the most direct route around marshes and though innumerable fords.

Navigation by river and by sea offered no better alternative; the Vienne was too shallow for sizeable vessels and the Charente was navigable only as far as Angoulême. Together with the intendant of the Auvergne, Turgot improved navigability by dredging river beds and strengthening river banks. He encouraged log floating on the Dordogne and the Vezire and the Corrze. The naval port of Rochefort was reserved for military purposes and closed to commerce.

News spread through provincial France through rumour and gossip more fully and speedily than through either of the two official journals. The *Gazette de France, the Journal de Savants* and the *Mercure de France* had been established during the previous century as monopolies; a monopoly of general news for the former and one covering literary and artistic matter for the latter. In the *Gazette* one might read that 'such and such a nobleman had left his home in the country, or that Mme Deuxime had acted as godmother to the granddaughter of the Duchesse de Cregny at her baptism'.[2]

In August 1789 Young was travelling through Bourbonnais about 160 miles south of Paris. He despaired of news of the revolution, one of the foremost events in modern history. 'Here is a feature', he wrote, 'of national backwardness,

---

[1] Schelle, op. cit., vol ii, pp. 449–50.
[2] F. Funck-Bretano, *The Old Regime in France*, 1929, p. 340.

ignorance and poverty. In the capital of this great province, the seat of the Intendant, at a moment like the present, with an assembly voting a revolution, and not a newspaper to inform the people whether Fayette, Mirabeau or Louis XIV is on the throne.[1]

The court at Versailles had no need of news because the universe that mattered was spread before them and those at court were its constellations. But the more sophisticated folk in the capital and elsewhere demanded news. Consequently several private, unofficial, broadsheets and journals were put out by the *nouvellistes*, or newsmen.

News was digested and dispensed at the salons, like that of of Mme Doublet de Persan. The salon was run by a *valet de chambre*, who operated strict rules and codes of conduct. The leading *nouvellistes* such as Beauchomont, Piron, Falconet and Argental had their appointed seats in the salon. Here news was gathered, verified and released to news brokers such as Métra, who specialised in political news. He broadcast his news at daily meetings under a large chestnut tree on the terrace of the Tuileries, now overlooking La Rue de Rivoli. Due to the popularity of these meeting, his regular addicts in the audience had to reserve their seats. According to the Duc de Lévis, Métra 'had nothing remarkable in his whole person except his inordinately sized nose . . . gradually people of good standing became curious about what was said in this circle . . . M. Aranda [the Spanish Ambassador], who lived close to the Tuileries and who walked by often, did not scorn his conversation . . . he used to repeat exactly what Métra had read out without adding or subtracting a word and, like many members of the diplomatic service, sent him news which he wanted to circulate.'[2] Some of the less professional journals contained falsehoods, many of which were malicious and derogatory. In a nation denied a free press, the most effective means of defence against malice was to counterattack with wilder falsehoods in a rival journal. By comparison to the French, the British public were deluged with news; London alone possessed fifty-three newspapers and in 1767 the annual sale of papers was estimated at 11.5 million copies. It was not until 1779 that France had it first daily newspaper.

There were three Jesuit colleges in the Limousin. They were established to educate the children of the bourgeoisie. The local priests provided a basic education for poor children in villages. These children were removed from school as soon as they were able to contribute to the struggle for survival against nature, poverty or the seignorial lord.

'The excessive ignorance of the country people in this province', observed Turgot,' is a continual source of administrative confusion and difficulty; it is impossible to have any confidence in the syndic, for the majority will not know

---

[1] A. Young, *Travels in France*, entry of 8/8/89.
[2] Lévis, *Souvenirs et Portraits*, 1815, pp. 183–4.

how to read and write.'[1] Infant mortality was as high as one in four and only half the survivors reached the age of ten; puberty only occurred in girls after the age fifteen and in boys after seventeen.[2]

The most remarkable thing about the towns was the stench of bad drainage, primitive sewage and animals reared in backyards. This was common in towns and cities throughout Europe but Arthur Young was so struck by the condition of Brive that he described it specially in the diaries of his travels: 'The view of Brive from the hill is so fine that it gives the expectation of a beautiful little town, and the gaiety of the surroundings encourages the idea, but on entering such a contrast is found as disgusts completely. Close, ill-built, crooked, dirty, stinking streets exclude the sun and almost the air from every habitation.'[3]

Such is a brief sketch of the nature of the office and of the actual intendancy accepted by Turgot. Shortly after taking it, he declined the chance to transfer to Lyons and to Rouen, which were among the richest and most coveted in France. He had taken the Limousin on the understanding reached with Bertin, the *contrôleur-général*, that in this backwater he would have a great deal of freedom to reform taxation; a freedom which he would not enjoy in the more prominent intendancies. He may have realised that here, in one of the poorest regions of France, would be the hardest testing ground for reform. Yet here the need for reform was most evident and urgent.

---

[1] Schelle, op, cit., vol v p. 673.
[2] M. C. Keiner, *Quand Turgot Regnait en Limousin*, 1979, pp. 132–7.
[3] A. Young, *Travels in France*, entry in June 1789.

5

The Injustice of Taxation

One of the worst features of the *ancien régime* in France was the unjust and oppressive system of taxation. Louis XV asserted that, 'all the property of his subjects belongs to him and in taking it he is only taking his own'.[1] Letters of nobility and the cloth of the cleric were generally sufficient to win exemptions from the burden of taxation. The municipal bourgeoisie were quick to follow their example. Thus the main weight of taxation fell upon the poor peasants; they were too weak to resist the tax collectors, and too poor to contribute much revenue. The main beneficiaries of this injustice were the privileged and powdered folk at Versailles, who needed an income exempt of taxation to reward their various duties of state, such as holding the king's shirt or handkerchief for a few moments each day. The imposition of taxation was not uniform throughout France and depended on the whim of the *contrôleur-général*.

The principal taxes in the Limousin were the *taille* and the *vingtiéme*. The *taille* was levied on personal wealth, consisting of the taxpayers' earnings or possessions, in the greater part of France, though in a few places such as Brittany, Burgundy, Artois and Languedoc it was assessed on land belonging to the taxpayer. It was introduced by Charles VI in 1439.

> It was on that day, [wrote Tocqueville], when the French people, weary of the chaos into which the kingdom had been plunged for so many years, . . . permitted the king to impose a tax without their consent and the nobles showed so little public spirit as to connive at this practice, provided their own immunity was guaranteed. It was on that fateful day that the seeds were sown of almost all the vices and violent abuses which led to the violent downfall of the *ancien régime*.[2]

The nobility claimed exemption from taxation because of the feudal obligation, under which they were bound to render military service to the state. However, many centuries earlier the feudal obligations of the nobles had been dissolved. Yet

---

[1] Garet, Les Bienfaits de la Révolution p. 6.
[2] A. de Tocqueville, *The Ancien Regime and the French Revolution* [1969 edn.] p. 123.

they continued to claim exemption owing to the indignity of a nobleman paying taxes. They pretended that taxation had been devised in earlier times for common folk. The Church claimed exemption by virtue of their divinely appointed role. The bourgeoisie of the towns, which resembled loosely an urban middle class, had bought their immunity from the *taille* from kings, who were always in need of revenue. Sometimes towns had to repurchase that immunity several times over.

The *vingtiéme*, which is discussed further below, was levied on personal wealth but its main distinguishing feature was that it did not permit the range of exemptions which had become attached to the older *taille*.

Turgot proved that the burden of taxation ultimately came out of the *produit net*, that is the surplus enjoyed by landowners. In the poor regions, where there was no surplus, the whole burden fell upon the peasant, for there was no other value or person to tax Though the peasant proprietor held a greater acreage than the nobles, Church or bourgeoisie throughout France, he held the poorest land.

The *taille* was not regulated by rules of assessment. The collector was expected to preserve a rough sense of justice between taxpayer and state and also between taxpayers themselves. Thus, persons, liable to the *taille*, had no means of knowing what their liability to the tax might be. This uncertainty compounded the injustice of the *ancien régime*.

In early summer the Council of Finances apportioned the burden of the *taille* among the provinces. In each, the *bureaux des finance* and the intendant apportion the province's assessment among the *elections*, or districts. In July officers of the elections submit detailed report of crops to the intendant. The intendant submitted his advice to the *contrôleur-général*. The Council then settled the final assessments and grant rebates. The annual assessments of the *taille* were made on detailed reports, submitted by the intendants to the *contrôleur-général* on the state of the crops in his province in early summer. The burden of the *taille* between the prosperous regions and the poor was based entirely upon his decision. The intendants then apportioned the liability of their province between the different parishes of which there were 976 in the Limousin. Finally, an appointee of the parish, the collector, apportioned the liability among the parishioners. By this cumbersome procedure was the taille assessed every year from 1 October.

The collector was encouraged to collect from his neighbours, by being held liable to seizure of his goods and even his personal liberty could be forfeit for any shortfall in his collection. Moreover, he was unpaid for his labours. 'A collector', wrote Turgot, 'is one of the most unhappy individuals that can be imagined; liable to seeing himself dragged off to prison, continually obliged to advance money, the recovery of which will be gradual, and by dint of difficult and expensive law suits. He spends two or three years running from door to door, to the neglect of his own business. He gets into debt and is usually ruined.'[1] It was one of the worst

---

[1] Schelle, op. cit., vol ii p. 265.

servitudes under the *ancien régime* and sufficient in itself to persuade any one equipped with the skills of reading and writing to live in a town exempt from the *taille*.

The richer folk had the power to defend themselves against the syndic in the Cours des Aides, the court dealing with fiscal matters. A collector had to be aware that in future years his richer neighbours could be elected syndic, so he would be unwise to squeeze them too hard in the year when he happened to be the syndic.

The only protection of the poor lay in their poverty; they had to manifest complete privation in their homes and work places. Rousseau told of how, once when he had been dying of hunger in the country, he had begged a meal from a peasant. At first the peasant maintained stoutly that he had insufficient food even for himself. But Rousseau was desperate and persisted. The peasant agreed to feed him and fetched wine, meat and bread, explaining that, if it became known that he lived so well, he would have been ruined. Concealment was necessary to avoid assessment and seizure by bailiffs. Another ruse of the poor to minimise their liability to the taille was to pay the collector such paltry instalments, that it was hardly worth his trouble to make repeated journeys to collect them.

In the 1730s, Tournay, the intendant of the Limousin, tried to end the arbitrariness in the assessment and collection of the *taille* by introducing a *taille* assessed on land. Instead of searching and valuing the personal possessions of the peasant, the collector would look instead at a map of landholdings. Such a *taille* demanded at first the valuation of land. This *taille* was known as *taille tarifée*. Tournay had actually surveyed and valued two-thirds of the Limousin. Therefore, in the greater part of the province the collector of the *taille* was governed, and the taxpayer was protected, by agreed assessments. It was probably the existence of the *taille tarifée* which had attracted Turgot to the Limousin, because it seemed to provide a basis for the reform of the taille into a tax on the *produit net* of land; a reform which Bertin also favoured.

Unfortunately, in April 1761, a few months before Turgot was appointed to the Limousin, the Cours des Aides had regained its right to hear complaints against the *taille*. Previously, complaints had been heard by the intendant. As the Cours, like the parlement, was opposed to reform of taxation, it was doubtful whether they would tolerate the *taille tarifée* in parts of the Limousin for long, before reverting to the traditional form of the *taille*, under which the collector was free to extract money by whatever means existed to hand.

In order to prevent this happening, Turgot appealed to his friend Malesherbes, who was the president of the Cours des Aides, and explained to him the merit of fixed assessment over the demands of a collector. The Cours agreed that in the Limousin its judgements would be based on valuation sheets supplied by the intendant. In effect, the Cours had given their conditional recognition to the *taille tarifée*. But the assessment sheets, produced twenty years previously, had been drawn up without consistent principles and the original assessments had not been kept up to date, so that the changes of ownership and value had not been recorded. Furthermore, the workings of the surveyors, which would have explained their assessments, had been destroyed. A register had not been maintained. In short, the valuation records of the *taille tarifée* were a shambles.

Turgot recruited a number of commissioners to supervise the assessment of the *taille*. He himself entered the task of surveying the unsurveyed third of the province and of perfecting the original assessments with great zeal.

His immediate task was to gain the co-operation of the inhabitants of the Limousin, which was an arduous task in a region where every action of the state attracted habitual hostility, even if the purpose was to improve their situation. ' You must arm yourselves with courage,' he wrote to the first commissioners, 'if you are to overcome the obstacles which multiply in front of you . . . One of the most sacred duties of those who take part in public administration is to succour the weak and the feeble . . . Never should you miss the opportunity of promoting among the people the greatest confidence in your office by showing patience in listening and by the moderation of your actions . . .'[1]

Again he wrote:

> The more the public can become convinced of the utility [of the *taille* assessed on land], the more it will be disposed to work towards this and success will be that much more certain. I propose, therefore, to give as much publicity for my campaigns as possible in order to dispel, if I can, the people's distrust. I cannot urge you too strongly to work in step with me in order to inspire this confidence in the public by being totally just in the exercise of your duties and by putting me in a position to ease their burdens.[2]

He also appealed to the priests to use their powers in order to win their parishioners' co-operation, 'No one', he wrote, 'is better placed than priests through your vocation and excellent education, which the state prescribes and the trust which their ministry inspires in the people, to understand their situation and also the means by which it may be improved.'[3]

When the commissioners moved around the province the priests announced their coming and encouraged the parishioners to co-operate with them. On the day of their arrival church bells rang out. The commissioners heard the people's arguments about taxation. Assessments were then made and any appeals were heard on the spot. Priests were asked to keep the commissioners supplied with the details of the changes in ownership, deaths and also of losses of animals and crops which would afford grounds for relief from the *taille* assessment.

Turgot decided to compile a new register for the *taille*, as the task of updating

---

[1] D.Dakin, *Turgot and the Ancien Regime* [1939] p. 53.
[2] Schelle, op. cit., vol ii pp. 153–4.
[3] Ibid. pp. 169–70.

the previous register was too problematic. In 1762 he requested the sum of 60,000 livres to finance this project. His request was refused and work towards this progressive reform could not even begin. In November 1763 Bertin was replaced as the *contrôleur-général* by L'Averdy, who had no particular interest in tax reform in the Limousin. From then on Turgot had to content himself with operating the *taille* within the parameters which had already been agreed above.

He wanted to appoint paid collectors and to give receipts to taxpayers for tax liabilities paid. He was unable to attract collectors in the rural districts. However, he did succeed in having rotas of collectors drawn up by the commissioners rather than by corrupt parish officials.

In his *Avis sur les Impositions* of 1763 Turgot set out the case for removing the *taille* from persons and imposing it on the rent of agricultural land. Such a tax would grow in step with the wealth of nations and the increase in wealth would accompany an increase in the needs of the state.[1]

Moreover, in the place of tedious negotiations every year there would an objective foundation of assessment. In his annual reports to the *contrôleur-général* Turgot was continually demanding a reduction of the liability in the Limousin, which always seemed to bear a disproportionate share of the national *taille*. In 1766/67 he produced a detailed report to show that in the Limousin the surcharge was two or three times greater than in the neighbouring provinces. He also argued that the only means of preserving justice between one region and another was by a valuation of land. Turgot believed that the establishment of taxation on land value would indicate how much tax could be levied without depressing wages or discouraging productive work. But appeals to Paris were useless.

The *vingtiémes*, or twentieths, were introduced in 1749 by Machault, the *contrôleur-général*, as an alternative to the *dixiémes*, or tenths He wanted this new tax to be imposed on the land owned by privileged and unprivileged alike. After the conclusion of the wars of the Austrian Succession, Machault needed to replenish the revenue. The Church protested against this new taxation which was levied upon them. The bishops organised a campaign of prayer to obtain the king's grace, in granting them the traditional immunity from tax. They threatened to abandon their churches. The nobility refused to pay the tax and the *parlements* were prepared to repeal the *vingtiémes*. In 1751 Machault was dismissed for making such a bold attack on privilege. Thereafter the traditional exemptions were awarded. Great hopes had been raised that the *vingtiémes* would replace the *taille*. But in 1763 the parlements renewed them on condition that it was to be kept at its existing rate and with its existing exemptions. In other words it became an additional taille on the poorest people. The capitation tax, known as the *dixiéme*, fell heaviest on the poor like the taille.[2] It became merged with the *taille*

---

[1] Ibid. p. 306.
[2] Schelle, op. cit,. vol ii p. 611.

by the eighteenth century. The indirect taxes and custom duties, the most notorious of which was the *gabelle*, were collected in most regions by tax gatherers, known as farmer-generals. Towns and provinces, such as the Limousin, had purchased their exemption in earlier times. In addition, several towns levied indirect duties on goods called the *octrois*.

If taxation was assessed on public property, by which Turgot meant the value of land, the distribution of wealth would be just, work would be encouraged and rewarded, inflation would be avoided and prosperity would ensue. Unfortunately, politicians preferred to superintend the world of privilege and poverty which accompanied the taxation of goods and incomes.

6

The *Milice* and the *Corvées*

Milice

In 1691 Louis XIV introduced a system of compulsory military service, called the *milice*. It was introduced as a temporary expedient to recruit soldiers of the lowest rank, without public expenditure – the men taken into military service under the *milice* did not receive wages or compensation. In time the *milice* became a permanent institution. Liability for the *milice* concerned only men of sturdy build, at least five foot in height and between the ages of sixteen and forty. Naturally the clerics, nobles and privileged were exempt together with a number of lesser folk, as for example, the owner of a hundred sheep or the tenant of a farm worth over a certain amount. Allowing for the exemptions, out of the 160,000 men who were eligible in France, 10,000–12,000 were recruited annually. The intendants had to assemble the eligible males and lots were drawn for the places to be filled; those who drew the marked lots were liable for service for up to six years.

The *milice* was not only objectionable because it violated individual rights, but because it led to serious public disorder. The eligible candidates used to hide in the woods, in order to avoid assemblies of eligible candidates. The law allowed anyone to pursue these fugitives with firearms. Indeed murder was incited by these regulations, the public peace was violated and cultivation of crops was interrupted, and the young men were given a further powerful inducement to flee the countryside. A customary way of avoiding the *milice* was to cut off the trigger finger or inflict some other disabling injury. Turgot, mindful of public order, soon prohibited individuals from pursuing fugitives and handed that task to the police.

Turgot raised the case of Pierre La Saigne with the chancellor. La Saigne had been a former syndic – an unpaid 'volunteer' who collected taxes. One night in 1756 La Saigne had set out with an armed gang, as the law allowed him to do, to hunt down a fugitive in hiding. They arrived at the house where he was concealed and, in the ensuing confusion, someone was shot dead. The hapless syndic had been blamed for the killing. He had been condemned to the galleys for eighteen years.Turgot argued that he had been the victim of a bad law. La Saigne was restored to liberty shortly afterwards.

Turgot wrote to the Minister of War in 1762:

> Of all the [obligations] that different governments have imposed on their people, there is none which directly attacks all the rights and even the persons of the citizens and none which makes the people feel so keenly their degradation and servitude. All that a man holds most dear his attachment to his place of birth, the ties of blood and friendship, the paternal and filial attachments, the liberty of man, his life, all is put at risk by this lottery . . . the kingdom doubtless needs people to defend it. But there is a method of procuring it without forcing anyone.[1]

Turgot introduced two practices, which removed the compulsive force of the *milice* in the Limousin, even though both had been forbidden by an enactment of 1765. But a loophole in the enactment, allowing substitution in the case of illness, enabled him to remove the compulsive element. He instigated the practice of the collection of money by eligible candidates. The total sum could be awarded to a candidate, who volunteered to take the place of person chosen by lot. He had reduced the rigour of the regulations under his own authority, but in 1773 Turgot appealed to the Minister of War, Aigullon, to reform the system. The minister commissioned Turgot to draft the necessary edict of reform. But, alas, the minister was dismissed before Turgot had completed the task. A year later he wrote to the new minister to urge reform of the *milice*. In addition to proposing the repeal of the enactment forbidding the voluntary collection of money and the substitution of willing candidates, he proposed that the *miliciens* should form their own regiments, which could be maintained on a territorial basis during times of peace with meetings only for annual camps and essential training. These ideas were not accepted.

Corvées

The word *corvée* was derived from the Latin cura via, or care of the roads. They signified servitudes concerned principally with road building, which were rendered by the unprivileged without remuneration. However, there were lesser *corvées* concerned with military servitudes, which likewise fell upon the unprivileged.

(I) Military *corvées*

The military *corvées* were of two types. The first obliged townspeople to billet troops stationed near a town or passing through it. The Limousin was particularly suited for pasturing horses. Consequently detachments of cavalry were stationed regularly there and troops often in need of quarters. They tended to stay

---

[1] Schelle, op. cit., vol ii, pp. 206–7.

habitually in the same billets, with the result that the communal *corvée* was discharged by a few people.

Turgot remedied this injustice at first by hiring rooms from local innkeepers and charging the whole population as an addition to the *taille*. Later, in order to accommodate regiments permanently in the Limousin, he arranged for barracks to be constructed and, again, defrayed the cost as an addition to the *taille*, so that the charge was shared by a greater number of people.

The second military *corvée* required farmers to supply carts and animals to transport stores and baggage of troops moving through the province. The burden fell on the farmers bordering the roads and, as this could occur at any time, it might interrupt sowing or harvesting. In addition, their equipment and animals were often overloaded and maltreated by the troops. In 1766 Turgot received permission to employ professional contractors, as was done in the provinces of Franche-Comte and Languedoc.

(II) The road *corvée*

At the beginning of the eighteenth century the cost of road building would require much state expenditure. But as there were meagre public resources available even for the most important needs of state, road building, being relatively unimportant, was neglected.

During the late 1730s the intendant of Soissons, M. Orry, devised a system of road building without cost to public funds, which became known as the *corvée des chemins*. This system obliged the communities bordering the roads to supply the labour, materials and tools for their construction and repair.

In 1740 Orry became *contrôleur-général* and his system was introduced nationally under the supervision of the board of the *Ponts et Chausses*. His scheme obliged the syndic of every community to draw up the lists of those liable for the *corvée*. Naturally the nobility, the priests, the farmers and the urban bourgeoisie were not included in these lists; the peasant alone was eligible for this opportunity to render further unpaid service to the state.

The concept of the road building *corvées* might have appeared an elegant expedient to the rulers of the *ancien régime*, because the corvées provided roads without any expenditure by government. 'I would rather the government taxed the arms rather than the purses of men,' wrote Rousseau. 'This tax is fundamentally the least onerous and above all the one that can be abused least, for money always disappears when it leaves the hands of the payer.'[1] The purpose of such a society was, after all, to load burdens on the poor and lavish privilege upon the rich.

In the Limousin there were two roads running south from Paris through Limoges to Toulouse and one through Angoulême to Bordeaux. The first was in a

---

[1] Schelle, op. cit., vol iii p. 294.

poor state and the second was completed only as far as Angoulême. The secondary roads were in such bad repair that no distinction could be made between negligent upkeep and defective construction. The roadside parishes were often sparsely inhabited and the peasants had to be brought from a distance of about eighteen kilometres from their homes. The farmers in the Limousin used oxen rather than horses and, therefore, loads had to be lighter and journeys were appreciably slower. The terrain was hilly and crossed by numerous rivers and streams. The local syndics, who were responsible for the operation of the *corvée*, were incapable of administering the many details and the synchronisation of different operations, because many could neither read nor write.

As an experiment, Turgot arranged for the *corvée* to be conducted according to official regulations and discovered that it was impossible for the *syndic* to carry out his task. He had to enforce the attendance of those eligible, to verify the reason given to him for the many absences, to punish the shirkers, to arrange for the provision of tools, materials and transport. For these heavy responsibilities the syndic received neither remuneration nor even reimbursement of his expenses.

Turgot opposed the corvées on two principal grounds: they inflicted an injustice on the roadside parishes and they were the least efficient method of road building He also complained that the main beneficiaries of the roads were landowners, who contributed no direct assistance to the building or maintenance of roads. The value of land was enhanced by the existence of roads. Plainly, roads were essential to the land value of towns and the pretence that the peasants bordering the roads gained most from the roads, was absurd. Roads drew communities closer together. Growers in the country were linked by roads to their consumers in towns and villages. Consumers no longer had to fear for their supply of food. They could live in towns and villages without having to rear or grow their food supply. Towns were connected to other towns. Regional markets arose in commercial centres. Roads served society as blood vessels serve the human body; making it function as a whole. The capital was in communication to regional centres and they were in touch with the smallest communities of the region, just as blood capillaries were involved in the same system of circulation as the arteries of the body. In short, roads allowed society to develop beyond the village. Man is a gregarious being and prefers living in communities to living in the wilds. Towns became the natural locations for many trades and the professions and people were enabled to specialise in their work and skills.

Everybody benefited, but Turgot considered that the benefit to landowners was an unearned benefit. For while society provided amenities at public expense, the landowner reaped the benefit of that expenditure. Rural landowners gained access to markets, to larger numbers of workers and to skills available in towns. Urban landowners gained from specialisation and from the concentration of activity.

The value of land in town and country began to rise in step with the greater demand for the use of land, following communal expenditure on roads.

Landowners had not been required to contribute to these developments and yet they reaped the reward through increased rents or increased value of land.

Turgot thought the separation of the burden of building and repairing roads from the increase in land value was unjust. His main idea of reform was to recover through taxation the increase in land value and use the proceeds to finance the whole operation.

Within four months of his appointment Turgot wrote to Trudaine, who was a friend and the director of the *Ponts et Chausées*, proposing that wages be paid to those engaged on the corvées throughout France and that the cost be borne by the whole province. Trudaine certainly considered himself a liberal thinker, but he clung to the institution of the corvées, because, despite their disadvantages, they allowed the *Ponts et Chausées* to get on with the construction of roads without being impeded by lack of money. He asked Turgot to submit a memoir outlining his reform, so that it could be presented to the *contrôleur-général*.

Turgot proposed, first, that payment should be made for the labour, materials and the equipment. Second, that the roadside communities should be allowed to avoid the physical burden of the corvée, if they agreed to pay the monetary equivalent of their liability as an extra sum under the *taille*. Third, the intendant should then grant a rebate in the *taille* to those communities who had agreed to pay the monetary sum and charge the actual cost of the corvée among the whole province. Fourth, the construction of roads should be contracted to professional contractors.

This rather complicated manoeuvre of adjusting liabilities through the *taille* was a deliberate attempt to elude the intervention of the *parlement*. As a matter of law the *parlement* could say that an addition to the *taille* was an illegal addition to taxation. But they could not attack an intendant's reasonable apportionment of the *taille* between communities in his province. 'Up to this point', Turgot wrote to Trudaine, 'the *parlements* have always sought to present themselves as the defenders of the people against the crown and the crown would do well to unmask this role, if need be, by showing the *parlements* to be the enemies of the people. But I doubt they would want to attack an operation which can only be popular with the people.'[1] The *parlement* had battled with Fontette, the intendant of Caen, over a similar scheme.

These proposals achieved a number of desirable improvements. They removed the basic injustices of the *corvée*, they reduced the administrative burden on parochial and provincial government and they allowed for more professional construction of roads. But they were not acceptable to Bertin, *the contrôleur-général*. For he planned to replace the whole *corvée* system with tolls after the conclusion of the Seven Years War [1756–63]. Turgot wrote immediately to point out that tolls were just another tax on trade which would be paid, like the others,

---

[1] Schelle, op. cit. vol ii, p. 221.

by the consumer. There would have been no essential difference between financing the roads by tolls or by, say, a tax on sugar; both would reduce earnings and put an unequal burden on marginal regions.

In order to introduce reforms to the *corvée* system, Turgot had to battle with Trudaine and Bertin, while upholding the interest of the country people. 'There are parts of the province,' he wrote, 'where I have encountered all the problems imaginable to make [parishioners] understand their own interest; they could not imagine that I would keep my word . . . Their parochial assemblies are always presided over by three or four bourgeoisie, who do not have to suffer the *corvée* and who very often reside in exempt towns, prefer to see their whole parish crushed rather than pay five additional *sous* and would not fail to persuade the peasants that they are being deceived . . .'[1]

The longer his correspondence with Trudaine dragged on over minor points concerning the *corvée*, the more difficult it became to retain the trust of the country people that reform was imminent. When Trudaine admitted in December 1762 that the *contrôleur-général* would probably permit wages for work on the *corvée*, Turgot paid the wages for the *corvées* and also took upon himself to raise the *taille* on those parishes, which elected to buy their way out of the *corvée*. He later spread the cost among the parishes. Turgot explained to Trudaine that if he was running the risk, by taking matters into his own hands, of losing his position, he would do so without second thoughts. Finally in 1776, the Council validated Turgot's reforms of the *corvée* retrospectively.

Turgot took a direct interest in the planning and construction of roads, visiting sites in every weather with his chief engineer, Pierre Tresaguet. With line and level in hand he conducted surveys planning the gradients and the lie of the roads. He travelled several miles a day on horse. It has been said that 'Under the direction of Pierre Tresaguet the highways of France became the best in Europe. He followed a modified Roman method by laying a foundation of stones on the flat, then a thick bed of large stones followed by small stones. Later he set his foundation stones on edge and then reduced the thickness of the upper layer.'[2] Tresaguet was one of the first to build roads round mountains and he tapered gradients so that the steepest part was at the foot and that the rise thereafter to the summit was less steep, in order to spare the horses and the oxen. He designed cambered surfaces about fifty years before John McAdam, the celebrated Scottish road engineer. By 1774 Tresaguet and Turgot had built about 960 kilometres of major roads in the Limousin, linking with Paris, Lyons, Bordeaux, Poitiers and La Rochelle and linking towns within the Limousin, particularly those such as Bort and Etymoutiers, situated on the edge of the Massif Central. During his travels in 1787 Arthur Young commented, 'The noble roads we have passed [in the

---

[1] Ibid p. 348.
[2] A. G. Wolf, *A History of Science . . . in the Eighteenth Century*, 2nd edn, 1952, p. 558.

Limousin], so exceed[ed] any others I have seen in France, were among [Turgot's] good works; an epithet due to them because they were not made by the *corvées*.'[1]

Turgot had done as much as he could within the limited powers available to an intendant. He spread the cost of the road building among all those liable to the *taille* – in a word, the peasant – and he had provided the Limousin with excellent road communications to the rest of France. But he was not satisfied with these measures; they did not link the benefit of the roads directly with the cost of construction and repair. Roads increased the value of rural and urban land and it was just that the costs should be levied directly on these values. Yet this was a radical reform which only a minister could introduce. As a mere intendant, Turgot had to be content with the limitations of his power. As in many fields, the demands of equity, which linked benefit and burdens, were clear and simple and the clamour of selfishness was contrived and complex.

---

[1] A. Young, *Travels in France*, entry for 6/6/1787.

7

Réflexions sur la formation et la distribution des richesses

Turgot did not write a lengthy economic work. He planned such a work, but did not begin it. However, he did write one essay on economics. In 1766, two Chinese students, Ko and Yang, educated by Jesuits in France, had been befriended by the *économistes* in Paris and, had asked for a concise summary of their economic ideas. They wanted something to take back with them to China. Turgot obliged by writing an essay, entitled *Réflexions sur la formation et la distribution des richesses*, of about sixty pages.[1] It did not contain Quesnay's 'algebra' and nothing about the *tableau économique*.[2]

The essay did not come light until December 1769. In a letter, dated 12 December 1769, Turgot explained to the duchesse d'Enville, 'This poor boy [Du Pont] wrote so touchingly in order to rebuild the circulation of his journal, in arrears for several months. He beseeched me so urgently to come to his aid, that finding this manuscript to hand, I sent it to him.'[3] This essay had a wider purpose that being a gift to two Chinese students. In a letter in September 1770 Turgot explained to Dr Tucker, to whom he sent a copy, that there was nothing new in the essay but he was persuaded could spread elementary ideas.[4] The essay was prized out of him by Du Pont who published it in three installments in issues of *Ephémérides du Citoyen*, between November 1769 and January 1770.

Du Pont made some alterations in order to bring it more in line with the doctrine of the Physiocrats. The alterations incensed Turgot, for he detested the sectarian spirit of the *Physiocrats*. He loathed their readiness to speak with a collective voice. He wanted to make economics self-evident by the use of simple steps of reason. Within a month, however, Turgot had remorse for the vehemence of his anger and wrote to make peace with Du Pont.

His essay began with the state where man is dependent on the advances of nature for his immediate needs; that is fruit, berries, wood, animals, fuel and the like. He described the natural working of the distribution of wealth as population

---

[1] See *The Formation and Distribution of Wealth, Turgot's Reflections on Capitalism 1766*, trans. and edited by K. Jupp.
[2] Schelle, op. cit., vol ii p. 519.
[3] J. Ruwet, *Lettres de M. Turgot à la Duchesse d'Enville*.
[4] Schelle, op. cit., vol iii p. 621.

grows and skills and demand become more refined and diverse. Though Turgot was writing before the industrial revolution, he described the development of the commercial and financial system to a point when it becomes recognisable to modern experience. He described money and the circulation of money as a powerful catalyst in matching the limitless desires of individuals to their incalculable skills of production. He concluded in the last part of the essay by examining the effect of taxation on the economy of a society. He stated that a tax on the *produit net* of land is the only form of taxation which falls on a value created by a whole society, without violating private property. Such a tax secures justice in the distribution of wealth without disturbing the natural working of the economy of nations.

There is not much in the field of Western economic literature dealing with the natural working of society, the distribution of wealth and taxation levied according to justice. There is not much enthusiasm in this discipline for creating basic conditions in which liberty and prosperity will arise for a whole society. By contrast, this essay is a masterpiece of rare wisdom in political thought.

The essay projects the development of a capitalist society from the earliest stages of cultivation. Usage, economy and culture are interwoven in the essay. The blending of similar ingredients in history had been evident in several works after his Discourses at the House of the Sorbonne.

Turgot had projected a taxation system for an economy that was still predominately agricultural. He favoured a tax on urban land, but his reasoning was slightly different.[1] But the development of industry at the beginning of the second half of the eighteenth century in France was so primitive, that Turgot did not really have to trouble himself about a system of taxation for an industrial society. It was only later, in the early decades of the nineteenth century, that raw materials such as ore and coal were mined in sufficient quantities to enable industry to develop a base. As towns filled with factories urban society was created and the thinking he had outlined in his essay needed extension. In addition to the munificence of nature in the provision of raw materials had to be added the consequence of the gregarious nature of man, which created towns and cities. When the industrial revolution had transformed an agricultural economy into an industrial and commercial economy then land value would be created as public property according to the demand for the use of land.

Turgot concentrated exclusively on agriculture as the source of wealth and did not appreciate the future importance of the extractive industries, like mining, building and fishing, also produced raw materials. Although he was not a *Physiocrat*, in this respect he was heavily influenced by Quesnay.

Though Turgot's ideas were related to society in France during the eighteenth century, they had a universal application and with simple extension could be

---

[1] Schelle, op. cit.,vol ii pp. 314 & 647.

formulated for a society after the industrial revolution. It is often fondly assumed that the eighteenth century was a time of pre-industrial simplicity. There may have been no aeroplanes, cars, faxes and the like; but technological inventions do not render redundant the principles of justice and humanity, which Turgot believed formed the foundation of political thought.

Nothing in this essay caused quite such a reaction and quite so much misunderstanding as Turgot's explanation of how wealth was distributed and earnings were fixed in society. The late Professor Cobban stated: 'Turgot has developed something like an iron law of wages as a justification for keeping these down to the minimum necessary for existence.'[1] This censure is similar to a criticism made by Necker, an ambitious politician but no economic thinker. Turgot was not formulating an 'iron law' or justifying its operation. He put forward a number of simple propositions: namely, that someone with only his labour to sell, sells it in competition with others of the same skill; that this competition between them reduces earnings to a level of basic requirements; that an employer pays the least he can. In effect, he was stating that earnings were set not by a person's talent or production but instead by the minimum earnings an unemployed individual of comparable ability would accept as earnings.

Thus a world heavyweight champion, a natural monopolist, can almost name his price, whereas a workman can only demand what an unemployed man, would accept for his position. However once defeated, the heavyweight has to compete once again with his fellows. The earnings of both are set by competition. What Turgot discountenances altogether is the notion that an employer can fix the level of earnings for his employees. The level of earnings has a market rate for every skill and, if an employer pays less than the appropriate rate, he will soon lose employees and, conversely, if he pays above the rate, he will have queues wanting to join him. Skills, which are not generally beyond the ability of an intelligent person command earnings related to a general rate. Sometimes there will be a temporary shortage of, say, nurses and teachers or a new skill will arise, like computer programming, and for a time wages will rise until adjustment is made.

In short, wages are settled in every occupation by the competition for work. To pretend that wages are fixed by employers cannot be sustained by reasoned argument.

The divergence between Turgot and Necker on the question of taxation becomes apparent when ideas are applied in practice. Turgot believed that one of the prime purposes of society was to safeguard the private property of the individual. This required government to respect private property when levying taxation. The only tax Turgot considered in his essay was a tax on *produit net* of land, which meant in his time almost exclusively agricultural land. However, the concept of *produit net* would have been able in the following centuries to be

---

[1] A. Cobban, *Social Interpretation of the Revolution* [1964 edn.] ch 6, p. 63.

applied to land of every usage. This *produit net* was the product of the land net of all claims, like earnings, expenses and the profit. *Produit net* was the free gift of nature; no individual created it by his labour. If no individuals had created it, it cannot be considered as private property. It was, therefore, regarded by Turgot as a gift of nature to man and a perfect example of public property, belonging to everyone equally and to no-one in particular. Furthermore, a tax on this natural surplus could not be passed on by landowners. If landowners became subject to a tax on the value of land owned by them, the only means of paying the tax, without working the land himself, would be to rent the land to a tenant. If the landowner attempted to recover rent *and* tax from a tenant, he would find himself with no tenant, for they would move to land leased at the market level. In other words, Turgot was proposing a tax on a form of public property in place of taxes on private property, such as taxes on income or on goods and services. The effect of such a switch can be imagined; it would allow earnings and prosperity to keep in step with production and invention. It would also remove taxation altogether from marginal land which Turgot estimated comprised four-sevenths of land cultivated in France.

Necker, on the other hand, did not bother with establishing his thoughts on just principles and argued that wealth should be redistributed by taxes, levied according to political judgement. People go along with this unprincipled thinking and do not complain that the fruits of their labour excite the full force of tax. Taxpayers acquiesce in the confiscation of their private property; they allow government to make private property public and to make what is plainly public property [the value of land] private. The effect of this perversity has an incalculable effect on the distribution of wealth and mass poverty.

Turgot's essay was not intended to be a complete statement of his economic ideas. It was only a brief sketch of the more profound principles. Therefore, it must be read in conjunction with his letters and state papers if these ideas are to be developed to any extent. Voltaire thought that the French *économistes* took their ideas too seriously and he attacked their idea of the *produit net* in an amusing story, called *The Man with Forty Crowns*. His hero was a wicker-basket maker who owned land worth 40 crowns, about £6 per annum. During a war, whose origin and progress remained unknown to the wicker-basket maker, he refused to pay a tax of 20 crowns on his land. He was gaoled and later released as a wreck of skin and bone. On his way home he met a man with a coach and set of six horses.

He had six footmen to each of whom the wages were equivalent to more than twice my revenue. His head steward . . . received a salary of 2,000 a year and robbed him of 20,000 more. His mistress cost him 40,000 over six months. He told me smugly that he enjoyed an income of 400,000 per annum. 'I suppose', said I, 'that you pay 200,000 of this income to the State to help finance this worthwhile war . . .' 'I?', he retorted. 'I contribute to the needs of the State! You must be joking my friend. I have inherited a fortune of eight million livres; I own not a foot of land; my estate consists of government bonds and stocks. I owe the State nothing.'

This attack would have amused Turgot. He was ready to appreciate wit of all types. What Voltaire was really attacking was the unbearable spirit of sect which had engulfed the essential ideas of Dr Quesnay. Turgot would have readily agreed that such an attack was well merited.

In 1766 when he was writing the *Réflexions*, Turgot was corresponding with David Hume, the Scottish philosopher. Hume was a close friend of Adam Smith whom he had met around 1750 and with whom he remained friends for life. When Smith withdrew to Kirkcaldy in Fife to write *The Wealth of Nations* between 1766–76 and became an infrequent visitor to Edinburgh. Nevertheless, Hume kept a room vacant for him.[1] Turgot had known Hume well while the latter had been acting as Secretary of the British ambassador in Paris from 1763 to 1765. In his first letter of 23 July 1766 to Hume, Turgot compares the state of economic thought in both countries: 'English writers are a long way from appreciating accepting principles of economic thought, and it is difficult to reconcile such principles with the ambition of monopolising the commerce of the universe . . . It would augur well, however, if Mr Pitt and all others who govern nations would think like Quesnay on [economic questions]'. Hume replied on 5 August: '. . . why limit so much of the memoir by taking it for granted as a certain Truth, that all taxes fall upon the proprietors of land? You know that no government in any age or country of the world, ever went upon that supposition. Taxes have always to rest upon those who pay them by consuming the commodity; and this universal practice joined to the obvious appearance of things at least leaves room for doubt' [that tax fell ultimately on land].[2] Two months later Turgot returned in a further letter to Hume with the principles which might form the foundation of taxation: 'The fiscal system of every nation was set down in times when no one thought about [economic] matters. When it will come to be understood that it is built on ruinous foundations, it will still require much effort over many years before the present running machine is replaced by another. You know as well as I do the twin goals of all governments: subjection and cash. One strives, it is said, to pluck the chicken without making it squawk too loudly.'[3] Turgot argued that taxes, direct and indirect, cannot reduce the level of real earnings, for competition has already reduced them to a minimum; during hard times, when unemployment is high and a job is hard to come by, the minimum falls to its lowest. Thus when a tax is increased, there will be an immediate fall in the purchasing value of earnings. This will be followed by a general demand for increases of nominal wages, so that the purchasing power of earnings are restored.

Hume replied: 'You will own that, as the public revenue is employed for the

---

[1] E.C. Mossner, *The Life of David Hume* p. 561.
[2] J.Y. Greig, *Letters of David Hume*, p. 76.
[3] Schelle, op. cit., vol ii p. 503.

defence of the whole community, it is more equitable that it is raised from the whole . . . it appears to me that where a tax is laid on consumption, the immediate consequence is either that the tradesman consumes less or works more. No man is so industrious that he may not add some hours in the week to his labours; and scarce any is so poor but that he can retrench some of his expenditure. What happens when corn rises in price? Do not the poor live worse and labour more? A tax has the same effect.'[1]

Turgot had opened the correspondence in the spirit of serious consideration of taxation. But Hume replied with satisfaction as to the continuance of the present order. It may seem a reasonable proposition to spread taxation so that all members of society pay. But such a simplistic solution ignores the fact that people's capacity to pay is different, depending on whether, for example, they live by their own labour, which Turgot considered to be private property, or off a species of public property. Suppose that taxation is spread equally, it will bear hardest on the poorest and most marginal. A tax on a landowner of good land, is not the same burden as the tax of the same type levied upon a peasant in the country far from the capital. While Turgot agreed that everyone had the capacity to work harder than their normal rate, he likened it to straining a rope continually or to running a machine without any margin of slack.

Turgot also accepted that every individual could probably reduce their consumption, but pointed out this would be counterproductive, as it would diminish trade. Turgot also cited the gross invasion of private property perpetrated by customs officers and the great encouragement that taxation of goods and persons gives to smuggling.

Turgot replied on 25 March 1767 by setting out what he meant by a tax on the *produit net* and how this was distinguished from a tax of earnings and what different results would flow from either form of taxation.

But Hume showed no interest in pursuing the question. He expressed surprise to Morellet that Turgot 'was herding' with the *économistes*, whose ideas appalled him. Hume encouraged Morellet to denounce them in his economic dictionary: 'I hope that in your work you will thunder, and curse them and pound them and reduce them to dust and ashes. They are indeed the set of men the most chimerical, the most arrogant that exist.'[2] Hume was referring to the Physiocrats who were assuming a sectarian and didactic air. Turgot had warned repeatedly that these attitudes would put off intelligent people. But in one of his letters Hume showed his attitude and instincts were anything but liberal and philosophic. He attacked libertarianism, which the French *économistes* and Turgot espoused unquestionably. 'In Britain', Hume wrote to Turgot, 'the people were thrown into disorders . . . merely from abuse of liberty, chiefly liberty of the press;

---

[1] D. Hume, *Letters to Eminent Persons*, Letter no. 351, Sept. 1766.
[2] Greig (ed.), *Letters of David Hume*, vol i p. 205.

without any grievance, I do not say real, but even imaginary . . . they roar liberty though they have apparently more liberty than any other people in the world; a great deal more than they deserve and perhaps more than any man ought to have.' He also believed that the idea of the perfectibility of government was dangerous: 'There is too little between the governors and the governed.'[1]

Turgot had shown that the claim of government to be able to impose tax upon the specific people selected for tax and on no one else, was nothing but an illusion. The idea that tax can be targeted to particular taxpayers, apart from the landowner, is fantasy.

Some years later Turgot wrote to Benjamin Franklin, the leader of the American colonies, to persuade him not to introduce indirect taxes on goods. 'The consumer, when buying these commodities', began Turgot,' seems to pay [indirect] taxes by his own choice and many people, even quite well-known writers being seduced by this appearance, have not hesitated to prefer all types of tax which are levied on different goods and on imports and exports of goods . . .' He went on to say, '. . . if a new tax increases the expenses [of wage earners], by causing a rise in the price of the things consumed by them, it is necessary that their earnings increase in step.'[2]

There were two consequences of switching the burden of tax onto things other than the *produit net* of land. First, during a time of high and rising tax levels, the shifting of tax liability on to prices and individuals caused a rise in prices and inflation was bound to follow the attempts of the state to increase taxes and that of individuals to increase wages. The process was started not by the demand for increased earnings but rather by the imposition of tax, which effectively reduced their value. As inflation sets in, it feeds upon itself. As the value of money falls, government collects reduced revenue and, consequently, taxes have to be increased. Second, there were many parts of France farthest from the fertile lands and the centres of population where agricultural land was too poor to yield a *produit net*. The land was so marginal as to furnish only a bare living. In such places, therefore, the new tax could fall only on earnings; and as this caused them to fall below the minimum levels acceptable, production would cease and unemployment and poverty would result.

It is for this second reason, that Hume's idea of spreading tax evenly over a whole population is both unjust and inequitable as between taxpayers; it does not relate the true ability to pay tax to the liability to pay. Indeed Turgot reckoned that if tax were restricted to the *produit net* two-thirds of agriculture in France would revive.[3] 'Indirect taxes', he had written, 'reduce the earnings of the poor . . . until they can reimburse themselves [by demanding higher monetary wages], increase the expenses of cultivation inevitably, which is the most burdensome

[1] D. Hume, *Letters to Eminent Persons* p. 180.
[2] Schelle, op. cit., vol v, p. 510.
[3] Schelle, op. cit., vol ii, pp. 307–8.

way of eventually imposing the tax on landowners and is most destructive to capital where land is leased, and causes the immediate abandonment of marginal land, which diminishes inevitably the subsistence of the people. This leads the nation very quickly to misery.'[1] 'These inevitable consequences of taxes on consumption', concluded Turgot, 'always tend to weaken the ties which bind an individual to his country and to render the duty of all citizens to contribute to the corporate expenditure of society into an odious obligation.'[2] Unfortunately, Franklin raised superficial objections based on a fear of change and he preferred to attach his thinking more to appearances than to reality. Indirect taxes on the European model were imported into the American colonies, with the inevitable results predicted by Turgot: namely, unemployment, poverty, regional imbalances and periodic inflation.

Turgot no more favoured direct taxes on individuals than indirect taxes, for whilst the incidence of tax was different, the results were the same. The taxes would depress the value of earnings, giving rise to the payment of higher monetary earnings. Ultimately the impact of the taxes would be on the residual *produit net* and, in those regions where there was none, on earnings giving rise to unemployment.

---

[1] Ibid. p. 641.
[2] Schelle op. cit. vol v, p. 516.

8

The Grain Trade

The ancient order of protection

'About 1750', wrote Voltaire, 'the nation which was satiated with verse, tragedies, comedies, words, operas, romantic stories and with even more romantic moralising, began to discuss the question of corn.'[1]

The grain trade in France in the eighteenth century was oppressed by regulations, through which the government attempted to interfere in the natural operation of price and supply of grain. These regulations stipulated that:

(1) Producers and sellers of grain had to sell in official local markets – private sales outside these market were illegal.

(2) Producers and merchants were not allowed to store corn for periods in excess of two years. They had to disclose their yields of grain to officials on oath.

(3) Grain had to be sold within three market sessions after delivery grain to a market.

(4) Once a seller had fixed his price, he could not increase it during the sale of the whole consignment; markets were open for individual buyers or sellers until midday and the merchants and bakers could only buy up to regulated amounts during the afternoon.

(5) Individual buyers were not allowed to store more than a fixed amount of grain and police were empowered to search any premises for excess stocks.

(6) Merchants had to be licensed in order to deal in grain markets.

(7) International exports were forbidden.

(8) A multiplicity of taxes and seignorial charges were levied on grain.

The intended aim of these regulations was to protect the consumer, though its real purpose was to afford power and profit to the state and magistrates. The

---

[1] H.Taine, *The Ancien Regime* [1876], p. 294.

combined effect of these regulations was to suppress a free national market in grain, which would have given the consumer a reliable source of grain at the cheapest price in the world. As a result, variations in supplies and prices existed throughout France; there could be bumper harvests in one region and in another famine.

A region such as the Limousin, which was largely unsuitable for the cultivation of grain, might suffer a grain shortage or, even, a famine, whilst another region, such as the Paris basin, which was especially favourable for grain, could enjoy a surplus over local demand. In such a situation consumers in poor areas might not be able to afford the local price of grain which would be high due to the scarcity, whereas the producer in the fertile region would be limited to selling it locally at low prices on account of the excess of grain. Thus in the poor regions grain seed, usually stored for sowing in the following year, would be consumed; yet in the fertile regions the farmers would plant less than they might have, had they been selling in a free national market. In the Limousin when grain prices rose, the country people would substitute for grain in their diet by using rye, chestnuts, root vegetables and potatoes.

The grain regulations fragmented the French grain market into a medley of local variations. By suppressing a national market, these regulations eliminated the mechanism that would have smoothed out local differences. For example, a high price of grain in the Limousin would have attracted supplies of grain from low price markets throughout France and abroad. The effect of a market free of regulations would have been to harmonise the price differential between poor and rich regions, as well as between good and lean harvests.

The consumer was dependent on domestic supplies of grain, for no international merchant would dare to add to the existing risks of trade the possibility that the local market prices at the port of arrival might plunge, as a result of the regulation that grain had to be sold within three market sessions.

The *parlements*, who presided over the enforcement of the grain regulations, presented themselves as the defenders of the peoples' interest, though, plainly, the regulations worked against the people.

Turgot believed that a market free of regulations harmonised the different interests of the consumer, who wanted to buy at the lowest price from the widest selection; those of the producer, who wanted the highest price in the widest market; and those of the merchant, who wanted a market free of regulations. While a free market balanced these interests, regulations distorted the balance.

If the regulations did favour the producer by increasing the price of grain, consumption of grain would fall. Conversely, if the consumer was favoured by a fall in price below the market price, production would be discouraged. Once a balance has been re-established between production and consumption, the producers and the consumers contend against each other to wring out of government increasing measures in their favour. The cumulative effect is to persuade government that more interference is required.

The introduction of free trade

Immediately on Turgot's appointment in 1761, he received a request from Bertin, the *contrôleur-général*, asking the intendants for their opinion on the introduction of free trade in grain. Bertin was proposing to sweep away those regulations, described above, which the state had imposed upon the domestic grain trade in France over several centuries.

By an edict, or enactment of the Council of Ministers, of 1763, Bertin abolished searches for grain stocks. During the following year he issued a declaration to allow corn to be transported from place to place and to be sold outside local markets, except in Paris, where protectionist opinion was overwhelmingly in favour of grain regulations. In other words, Bertin had swept away the oppressive regulations in the greater part of the domestic market. The successor of Bertin, L'Averdy, was prepared to go further and he asked Trudaine to draft a new edict. Trudaine asked Turgot to help. In July 1764 the official edict appeared. It represented a timid step towards the creation of a free market; it allowed exports of grain, but only when the domestic price remained below 12.5 livres per quintal, or hundredweight, and provided the shipments were made only from designated ports and in French vessels.

The year 1764 was good for the grain harvests, but the markets were swamped with grain and prices tumbled. In the Limousin many farmers were ruined by low prices. Though the harvests of 1765 and 1767 were poor, farmers in the Limousin were unable to benefit from higher prices before protection was reintroduced.

The restoration of protection

The high prices of 1765 caused a number of riots in several towns of the Limousin, merchants were abused and magistrates ordered houses to be searched in contravention of the edict of 1763. The rioters were demanding an end to the transport of corn out of the province and the restoration of the former fixing of prices in local markets, both of which would discourage production and tend to isolate the Limousin. It was not sufficient for Turgot to order the magistrates and the people to observe the law. Habitual attitudes prevailed. The ancient order of protectionism had depended greatly upon the intervention of the magistrates and their *parlements*, who were proud of their public role. They were determined to resume their interventionist ways. The people did not understand the arguments in favour of freedom and fell like easy prey to the magistrates' protectionist prattle. They believed what the magistrates told them without question. Turgot had to change their attitudes and inspire hope in the experiment of free trade. In February 1766 he instructed the police to uphold the recent edicts and 'to reply to the popular complaints, which you hear everyday, with kindness and in detail and to speak with more the voice of reason than that of authority, to engage the priests and all who by estate and intelligence are in a position to influence the thinking of the people'.[1] He attached an essay on free trade in grain written by a friend, M. Le Trosne.

The introduction of measures of free trade in 1763/4 had not in itself changed appearances immediately. Time was required to show the consumers that a free market could work well, to persuade the *parlements* to give up their traditional prejudices and time was also required to show merchants that a free market did exist and would continue.

The poor harvest of 1765 did not strengthen the argument for protectionist regulations. On the contrary, poor harvests demonstrated the opposite need. Turgot argued constantly that, where prices were highest, there was the place of greatest need of a free market. For the purpose of a free market was to attract grain to satisfy demand.

The harvest of 1767 was worse than that of 1765 and it was not only grain which was affected. For the vines had not propagated well, the rye crop had been reduced by a half in a severe hailstorm at Easter and the spring drought had deprived the fattening cattle of grass and hay. In December 1767 the *parlement* demanded that the king should relieve the shortage of grain. He replied that the cause was poor harvests which he was unable to rectify. In March 1768 they repeated the same demand and the king again rejected them. The *parlements* were using the poor harvests as a pretext for regaining the protectionist powers taken from them by the edicts of 1763/4.

In October 1768 the *parlements* addressed the king once again: 'Instead of prosperity, happiness and increase of population, which should have ensued on the introduction of free trade, we have witnessed – famine threatening several regions . . . a people's wretchedness increases, their tears flow and mothers fear and deplore their fertility.' They expressed a fear that, 'unlimited freedom might descend into the licence of monopoly'.[2] The king replied, 'that he had taken effective measures for stabilising markets . . . The shortages had been occasioned by the circumstances of the seasons and had been aggravated by the fears of the people.'[3] The *parlements* had also attacked the speculation by merchants as one of the undesirable features of a free market. In fact, speculators always contribute to the operations of a market. Their intervention increases the number of bargains, whose multiplicity assist in determining a keener price.

Turgot wrote to Du Pont towards the end of 1768 about the attacks of the *parlements* on free trade. He called them 'les boeuf-tigres' [beef-tigers] to highlight their fierceness and their stupidity. He also criticised the leading ministers for being butted by these 'stupid animals'.

He was keen to see Du Pont's reply to the *parlements'* appeals in a pamphlet entitled *Lettre du Conseiller*. The *parlement* condemned the pamphlet to be burned

---

[1] Schelle, op. cit., vol, i p. 470.
[2] Ibid p. 53.
[3] Ibid.

and were deterred from proceeding against Du Pont personally because he was being protected by the Council of Ministers. Turgot advised Du Pont to be wary of supporting a government whom he did not trust. 'They recommend moderation', warned Turgot. 'Strange politics! Moderation is all right at times of even-tempered discussion, but, when knaves are active in pleasing the people with fallacies and lies, it is better to unmask them and show them to be liars.'[1] Sadly, he admitted to Du Pont, he saw 'nothing good to hope for; intelligence and goodwill are reduced almost to the same significance as ignorance and ill-will. It is necessary to weep on Jerusalem and to console oneself for a time of enlightenment which we shall never live to see.'[2]

The attitude of the *parlements* disturbed Turgot and he wrote some notes to express his concern.

> Public affairs have an inherent character which lends itself to all sorts of deception through the use of vague and uncertain principles, which are far less settled and are much more susceptible to the vagaries of public opinion than to law and justice. One becomes accustomed to weighing and balancing issues, sacrificing some to others; ... to saying, like politicians, that it is necessary to take circumstances into consideration and to bend principles to circumstances ... Few are wholly and resolutely corrupt and even fewer are wholly and resolutely committed to their duty. The majority are mediocre souls, poised between their petty interests and the fear of public opinion and they become preoccupied with reconciling these two as best they can. They are quick to limit the boundaries of their duties and to overcome their scruples of honour ... Whenever magistrates are limited to their original functions – to render justice, to bring the quarrels of their fellow citizens to an end through the application of law, to maintain public order by punishing those who disturb it – their integrity will not be exposed to dangers superior to ordinary strength and it would almost never happen that they could be tempted by an interest capable of outweighing the loss of reputation, which would be the punishment for such a lapse. The most powerful and richest individual is not sufficient to frighten an independent judge ... All this changes when a magistrate wishes to join the functions of judges with the cares of a politician ... The discussion of individual cases becomes tedious; one regrets time given to this boring and mechanical role; one burns with ambition to get out of such a small circle in order to display oneself in more exciting theatre. The great objectives of political policy, the conservation of fundamental laws, the defence of the

---

[1] Schelle, op. cit., vol iii p. 24.
[2] Ibid p. 27.

rights of the Prince and the liberties of his subjects absorb all one's attention; friendships with those in difficult or sensitive situations are neglected and they only cultivate the brilliantly talented people, who excite the admiration of the multitude and secure votes. The slow analytical progress of the mind which discusses step by step, which considers all sides of a question, which weighs carefully the means and the objections, this patient cool and impartial examination, which brings to bear on a subject a quiet mind and which gives birth to conviction, seems to be a manner proper to a judge. But it is no longer any use when it is a question of persuading a multitudinous assembly. The moderate tone of reason is not sufficiently imposing to succeed in that. In the multitude of events everything affords everyone the prospect of distraction; triviality and impatience, natural to all men, increases like an epidemic. Attention becomes wearisome and rare.[1]

It was a frustrating experience for Turgot to watch the argument for free trade being neglected and the specious platitudes of the magistrates, who were more interested in regaining their protectionist powers than in relieving the people's famine, being publicised.

In October 1768 Turgot wrote to L'Invau, who had succeeded Averdy as *contrôleur-général*, asking to be considered for the position of prévôt des marchands, or mayor, in Paris – the position his father had held thirty years before. He explained that he did not desire a change for the sake of it, but because he wanted to be in closer touch with his friends in Paris and, no doubt, he wanted to play a more effective role in opposing the rise of protectionism. Isolated from intelligent company, thwarted in his desire to reform the *taille*, opposed by the *parlements* in Paris and in Bordeaux, and seeing the Council allow the protectionists to cease the initiative over the issue of free trade, it is little wonder that he sought a change. L'Invau replied to his letter, but without referring to his request.

In the following winter of 1769 L'Invau was replaced as *contrôleur-général* by Terray. If L'Invau had been a weak supporter of free trade in grain, Terray was, as might be expected of a former magistrate, a thorough protectionist. In 1773 he had advised the *parlement* of Paris to bear with Bertin's liberal edict, 'For if freedom does not yield the results expected of it, one can return to the old laws.'[2]

The Neapolitan ambassador in Paris, Galiana, who described himself 'as a sort of Plato or Machiavelli with the mind and the action of a harlequin . . . having no faith in anything, on anything or about anything', published his attack on free trade in his *Dialogues*. It had provoked a strong reaction among the *économistes*,

---

[1] Schelle, op. cit., vol iii, pp. 29–33.
[2] Schelle, op. cit., vol ii p. 61.

who wanted to refute the fallacious arguments of the ambassador on free trade. Fearing the appointment of Terray had terminated the favourable climate for free trade, Turgot advised Du Pont 'not to commit the folly of refuting Galiana. One should laugh at this work, which is very witty and full of spirit, but leave the refutation to someone who does not have a journal or an intendancy.'[1] Turgot had in mind the *Journal de l'Agriculture, du Commerce et des Finances* which had been the forerunner of Du Pont's journal before it was suppressed in the mid-1760s. But Du Pont joined with Morellet and Mercier de la Rivière to publish a reply to Galiana. Terray, acting under the clever persuasion of Galiana, suppressed Du Pont's reply, prohibited the press from considering commercial policy. In 1772 Terray suppressed Du Pont's journal, the *Ephémérides du Citoyen*.

The replacement of a weak man, L'Invau, with some sympathy for free trade by a strong man, Terray, with none, occurred at a critical time for the Limousin. The crops had been seriously damaged by hail and storms in the spring of 1770. The situation was so desperate that Turgot feared a famine. The *parlement* of Bordeaux issued an *arrêt*, as regulations of the *parlements* were called, in January 1770 to compel farmers and merchants to supply the local markets and prohibit sales outside it. The *arrêt* contradicted the edict of 1763; it seemed the prelude of the restoration of the whole protective order, which obliged each province to live off its own resources. Yet it was just at this time that the Limousin needed to import grain from outside, and merchants had to be sure that their operations would not attract the attention of the police or the magistrates.

Turgot sent the Council a copy of the *parlement*'s edict together with a copy of his own draft edict quashing it and the Council enacted Turgot's draft promptly, in order to re-emphasise the edicts of 1763/4. The magistrates in Turenne forbade grain to be transported out of the district. The lieutenant of the police in Angoulême sought to reintroduce protectionist regulations by prohibiting the hoarding of grain above certain levels and forcing sellers of grain to sell in the local markets. Turgot immediately quashed these measures and stressed the importance of a free market, in order to relieve shortage.

The first supplies of grain to arrive in the Limousin were plundered en route and civil disturbances occurred in towns where grain was being sold. Turgot confirmed the edicts of 1763/4 and fixed imprisonment for those found guilty of disturbing the public peace or causing seditious assemblies.

In October 1770 Terray asked the intendants to let him have their reactions to his idea of repealing the edicts of 1763/4 and, thus, ending the short experiment of free trade in grain. Turgot received this request as he was setting out to review the effects of a famine throughout the Limousin. According to Condorcet, he travelled about 450 kilometres by horse during November in wet and wintry conditions and during the evenings he wrote seven letters to clarify his ideas on

---

[1] Schelle, op. cit., vol iii, p. 373.

free trade for Terray. Years later he lent copies of three letters to Louis XVI which unfortunately have since been lost. The remaining four letters run to 100 pages and in them he examined the case for free trade from the point of view of the consumer, the farmer and the state.

He exposed the French distrust of international trade. It was, he argued, 'a veritable chimera to imagine that by allowing the export of French grain, foreigners will be able to make off with the entire French harvest. Indeed, all France had to hope or fear from international trade is to participate in supplying French shortages in competition with England, Poland, Muscovy, the Low Countries, the Baltic states, Barbary, Sicily and Egypt.'[1]

He showed that during the famine of 1740/1, during a time of protectionism when France was at peace and the seas were open, the price in Angoulême for a *setier* of wheat was 15–16 livres while in Paris it was 31–43 livres and the capital had suffered more than was necessary on account of the regulations. 'It is therefore the want of freedom and not freedom itself which causes famine. This want of freedom caused the famine of 1740. It is not freedom which is the cause of shortages of 1768 and 1770.'[2]

He went on to demonstrate that the land between Poitiers and Angoulême and around Berry, La Tourriane and Périgord, around the border of the Limousin, was as fertile as that in the Paris basin. A reason for the marked difference for the large-scale farming around Paris and the miserable subsistence farming around the Limousin was accounted for to a large extent by the fact that the market price in the Limousin was much lower than around Paris. Indeed the prices of grain in the Limousin did not even support proper cultivation. The central theme of his argument was simple:

> Free trade follows [every] variation without any inconvenience. All the changes which free trade brings become gradually imperceptible. Negotiations between individual buyers and sellers are a kind of groping which reveals to both parties the true price of everything with certainty. Surpluses and shortages are shared by all, gains and losses are also shared by everyone, so that there is no injury, and if there was an injury arising from the unavoidable course of things, it would be borne by all. L' Invau could be accused of having engineered it and the peace would not be disturbed.[3]

These letters amplify the subject of free trade which he had only touched on in his *Réflexions*. They were, however, of no interest to Terray.

On 23 December 1770 Terray repealed the former edicts of 1763/4 and made

[1] Ibid, p. 294.
[2] Ibid, p. 300.
[3] Ibid, p. 326.

the move which Turgot had feared for several years. Free trade was outlawed in France and the position reverted to the position as it had been in 1763.

When Arthur Young, the English traveller, heard of the food shortages in France during 1792 and the talk about the backward state of French agriculture, he exclaimed, 'There is but one plan: *ABSOLUTE FREEDOM* . . . .Proclaim a free trade and from that moment ordain that an ink stand be crammed into the throat of the first member [of the Assembly] who pronounces the word corn.'[1] Indeed, freedom of trade is like breathing: effortless and beyond control.

International trade

In fighting for free trade in grain Turgot had been combating the domestic protection of grain. But he was well aware of the international dimension of trade. Writing to M. Trudaine in 1766 he accepted that unlimited freedom of trade and removal of 'every sort of tax' would encourage trade at home and from abroad. Indeed, he believed foreign trade would enliven domestic trade. In December 1773 he wrote to Dr Tucker whom he regarded as one of the few English writers to grasp free trade: 'My principles on this question are the complete freedom to import, without distinguishing between goods shipped on vessels of this or that nation, and similarly complete liberty to export in every type of vessel without export duties or limitations, even in times of famine.'[2]

Turgot developed these two principles at length in a paper on the protection of iron masters. Almost a century and a half later Richard Cobden once heard Napoleon III describe the French iron masters as 'the masters' of France. This paper is as clear as anything written on free trade and as damning as anything written against import controls:

> The only means of stimulating any trade of which I am aware is to give it the greatest freedom and to free it from all taxes, which have been multiplied by the misconceived interest of the Revenue . . . If, after complete liberty has been secured by the removal of all taxes on manufacture, transport, sale and consumption, there remains anything more for the government to do in order to encourage a trade, it can only be the means of educating [craftsmen] . . . It is worthwhile for the government to send young men to foreign countries in order to study processes neglected in France and to make their discoveries public. This is useful, but liberty and the removal of taxes are more effective and definitely more necessary . . .
>
> There is no entrepreneur who does not desire to be the only seller of his goods, there is no trade of which the participants do not attempt to

[1] A.Young, *Travels in France* [1929 edn.] p. 355.
[2] Schelle, op. cit.vol iii, pp. 614–5.

ward off competition and find false arguments to delude people that it is in the interest of the state at least to stifle foreign competition, whom they can represent more easily as enemies to national trade. If entrepreneurs are listened to, and they have been too often, every branch of trade will be infected with the spirit of monopoly. These half-wits do not realise that the same monopoly is exercised, not as they deceived government into believing against the foreigner, but against their fellow citizens, consumers of goods and in their turn the sellers to the monopolists. They do not realise that all associations of men in the same line of business will not fail to equip themselves with the same pretexts in order to obtain from a deluded government the same exclusion of foreigners . . . They do not realise that there is a real loss to the whole of the national economy, or rather for the state, who, by buying less from abroad, sell less to him. The consequent and artificial increase in prices for all buyers necessarily reduces the standard of living. Whatever sophisms the vested interests of certain entrepreneurs can dream up, the truth is that all branches of trade must be free, equally free, entirely free; that the policy of some modern politicians, who imagine themselves to favour national commerce by forbidding the import of foreign goods is pure illusion; that this policy does not end until it has made every branch of trade an enemy of every other branch, until it has nurtured among nations a seed of hatred and war, whose most harmless effects are a thousand times more costly to the people, more destructive of wealth, of population, of happiness than all the paltry mercantile gains that can be imagined to accrue to the nations who have allowed themselves to be deluded. The truth is that in wishing to harm others, one harms only oneself, not only because the reprisals for these measures are so easy to make that other nations will not fail to make them, but still more because we deny to ourselves the incalculable advantages of free trade; advantages such that, if a developed state like France wished to adopt them, the rapid progress of its trade and industry would force before long all other nations to imitate her in order not to be impoverished by the complete loss of its trade . . .

Thus our policy should be to surrender to the course of nature and of trade, which is no less necessary or irresistible than the course of nature, without pretending to direct it. For in order to direct it without deranging or harming it, it would be necessary to follow all the variations in the needs, interest and the industry of man and to know all these in such detail as could not be gathered. Government of the most able, assiduous and dynamic kind will risk always being wrong in at least half the cases . . . If one did collect all these details, this voluminous knowledge which cannot possibly be collected, the result would be to let things go exactly as they go of themselves in accordance with the actions of men's interests, which create the equilibrium of a free economy.[1]

The duty of government in regard to trade is to protect the consumers' freedom to trade as they wish freely in both the domestic and international markets. Freedom is the natural balance which favours consumers and producers alike. To consumers free trade makes available to them the widest markets, and, thus, the lowest prices; to producers it opens the widest markets in which prices must reach the highest obtainable levels. In peacetime every sort of government interferes with this natural harmony and the consequences are impossible to predict. In the protectionists' vocabulary one of the most frequently used phrases is 'national interest'. There is a supreme interest during peacetime in maintaining freedom of trade. This interest shows that state regulation of trade in peace achieves nothing for a nation. Governments have to learn that power and control are ultimately defeated by the accumulation of powers.

Protectionists appeal on behalf of some group or body, usually of producers. Government owes a duty to society and should learn to detect partial demands; these may be put more insistently, but they are all ruinous to the liberty of the individual and society which government should uphold.

This much Turgot considered as the basic grammar of political thought; something which politicians should ponder rigorously before entering public office.

Turgot had seen the protectionist tradition set aside by Bertin in 1763, a limited amount of free trade enjoyed for a decade and protection restored by Terray. France, which was the Western birthplace of free trade, had become the veritable Bastille of petrified protectionism.

---

[1] Translation by W.W. Stephens, *Life and Writings of Turgot* pp. 249–55.

9

Famine

Throughout the eighteenth century many regions of France experienced shortages of food and in every decade there was at least one famine in France. Paris, however, remained an exception because it was surrounded by abundant supplies of grain. The apparent causes of these periodic disasters were severe frosts, extreme cold, drought or floods, incessant rain, hailstorms and thunder in every season and to this woeful list was added crop diseases. The real cause, however, lay in misgovernment: the heavy burden of taxation falling on the poorest, the protectionist shackles thrown over economic activities and the lack of communication throughout the nation. The natural elements provided only the *coup de grâce*.

In the Limousin the peasant proprietor, after discharging the *taille* and seignorial dues, had little wealth to put aside for tools and for future expenditure of cultivation. What incentive had the peasant proprietor to sow for a local market, to which he must take his grain personally with all the risks and trouble involved and in which he must sell within a matter of three markets whatever the price happened to be? What incentive had he to overcome these difficulties if the wary eye of the *taille* collector would light upon the fruits of his success? By limiting his endeavours and his existence to a narrow compass, however, the peasant maintained himself and his family on the level of mere survival. Thus he made himself prey to the storms, frosts and diseases. When they took their periodic toll, he had to consume his seed for the next year, in order to survive. The peasant diet tended to include the most basic foods that people in towns and in châteaux would not contemplate eating.

What need had a peasant of roads, bridges, ports, newspapers, parlements, powdered courtiers, palaces or the urban bourgeoisie? All that mattered was survival; nothing was as important. There were many areas of inferior fertility with wetter and colder climates, in which a better living was to be had, than was reaped by the peasant in the Limousin. But these peasants were not dispossessed of the fruits of their labour though the *taille* to the same extent as in the Limousin and other poor regions.

Underlying the rigours of climate in the Limousin was a chronic condition of poverty, with the consequence that good growing conditions would not have made the peasants in the Limousin prosperous. For the fruits of any good harvests would have been stripped of them by greater liability to the *taille*. The harvests in 1765 and in 1766 had been poor and in 1767 there was a general crop failure. Many vines had not survived three severe winters; rye, the staple crop, failed for the third year in succession as a result of a severe frost at Easter; and the pastures for fattening animals, which abounded in the Limousin, had suffered during the spring drought, so that cattle had to be sold in the Paris market for depressed prices. The harvest in 1768 offered a good prospect of recouping the losses of previous years but a violent storm in mid-August ruined many unharvested crops and incessant rain thereafter, prevented winter sowing of cereals for the following year.

The outlook for 1769 was bleak. During the winter of 1768 the ground had become waterlogged through continual rain and the few crops that had been sown in the autumn germinated. In the following spring a drought prevented the tilling of the spring-sown crops. Heavy rains in the late spring and early summer prevented the ears of the cereal crops ripening. At the harvest in 1769 the grain yields proved to be poor, as had been expected.

The inhabitants of the Limousin had become accustomed to relying on vegetable crops, such as radish, buckwheat and chestnuts whenever the price of grain rose. But even these hardier crops were severely damaged by torrential rain in August and September and, finally, all but destroyed by a violent storm in October. Consequently the harvest of these vegetables was delayed until late in the autumn.

As prices of foodstuffs rose during the autumn of 1769, theft and riots occurred in rural districts. In the small town of St Léonard, near Limoges, crowds of 200–300 gathered every night to demand bread and threatened to burn down the houses of the bourgeoisie.

'I have just given orders', reported Turgot, 'to collect together several brigades in order to arrest these disorders at their beginning, but the mischief is too widespread. The prejudices of the people are still too ingrained and the police are too few to allow much hope of checking the mobs by fear, if at the same time one does not offer the hope of immediate and effective help in this unhappy situation.'[1]

The only resort for the province was to bring in food from other regions which had not been affected by the famine and from abroad. But this resort was not readily available. First, the grain merchants were not prepared to move grain around when they feared civil disorders and the arbitrary interventions of the magistrates and the police. Second, the money market in Angoulême, the financial centre of the Limousin, had been eclipsed by trials on charges of usury

[1] Schelle, op. cit., vol iii, p. 115.

and fraud. Thus credit was no longer readily available. Third, when grain arrived from the west coast ports or down the Charente to Angoulême, the supplies had to be moved by mules across the province, for there were no roads running west to east, so the transport of grain to the interior of the Limousin was impossible. Finally, the cost of transport would price the imported grain above the means of most rural inhabitants. It was, therefore, impossible to rely on the free market after centuries of protectionism to bring in supplies.

Had free trade existed, there would have been trust in the grain markets, roads built to outlying regions and the most efficient forms of transport to convey goods and people to market. For these features depended on the existence of freedom and justice. Under protectionism the individual was reduced to impotence. He was, in fact, the natural mainspring of economic activity. In a state of impotence, he looked to the state to avoid famines, build roads and improve transport. The state could do these things, but only at the expense of the individual.

'In default of the resources of commerce', Turgot advised the *contrôleur-général*, 'it is essential that the government take measures to assure provisions.'[1] He admitted that the provision of assistance by the government brought with it the danger that if it operated in the grain and the food markets through its official agents, it risked being defrauded. This might discourage merchants operating in markets in which they feared sudden price movements on account of government intervention.

Turgot proposed to Terray three kinds of relief, which would avoid these dangers. He proposed, first, that merchants should be offered subsidies for grain brought into the province before the following August, by which time the harvest of 1770 would be available. For this purpose he requested the sum of 100,000 livres. Secondly, the government should pay money to the disabled, the aged and to mothers of young families for, he believed, the King is father of his people. For this expenditure he asked for 50,000 livres. Thirdly, he proposed that the government should finance an increased road building programme to employ able-bodied people in ditching and earth moving. For this work he asked for 100,000 livres. In sum, he had requested a sum of 250,000 livres, compared to the provinces' annual *taille* liability of 1.9 million livres. Terray granted 150,000 livres and stipulated that 50,000 was to be used as loans to the merchants, 20,000 for buying rice and the balance of 80,000 to be employed in road building. The idea of trusting the discretion of the man on the spot was not a French tradition.

By February 1770 the situation was desperate and Turgot asked for more money and for more authority to act as the circumstances required. Priests were reporting deaths by starvation, landowners said that they had less food than they needed to feed their own families and retain seed for the following year; a cargo of rice ordered by Turgot from Hamburg was icebound in the Baltic until May; and the

[1] Ibid, p. 118.

price of grains of all kinds had risen far beyond the means of country people. Furthermore, the police, with the backing of the magistrates, were enforcing the old regulations covering hoarding, house searches and sales in public markets. In the town of Tulle these regulations were introduced on the pretext that there was no corn in the markets, when the actual reason was that all roads into the town were blocked by snow.

Turgot wrote to Terray in early March 1770, 'Every day adds new details to the moving picture of misery of which I am the witness, and I am very grieved because I cannot effectively relieve it.'[1] He wrote to Condorcet, 'I am harassed continually by letters from every part of the province and still more by the sight of the misery which cannot be remedied by all the work in the world.'[2] During the spring he had to use troops, stationed in the Limousin at that time, in order to put down civil disorders, for they only compounded the difficulties of the situation.

He estimated that both to relieve the able-bodied who needed work and to buy beans and subsidised grains would together require a sum of 800,000 livres. He had been allocated only a tenth of that amount. With that he was able to start wool-spinning in the villages rebuilding the ancient walls around Limoges and to make monthly payments to the road contractors on condition that they employed a stated number of inhabitants. The road contractors 'have given themselves to this business . . . with zeal that cannot be praised too highly . . .,' reported Turgot. 'Indeed far from securing a monopoly in this business I have discovered that they have helped other contractors who wished to participate in all manner of ways.'[3] The supplies imported by merchants greatly relieved the famine up to the harvest of 1770.

In addition to arranging work programmes and the imports of food, Turgot appealed to the rich inhabitants to contribute both money and service. In December he and the Bishop of Limoges had appealed to the nobles and the richer people to form assemblies of charity which might render a contribution in several ways. This appeal evinced no response; it was widely reported that landowners were dismissing their domestic servants and failing to support their *métayer* tenants, who depended on them for their seed, tools and cattle. He had, therefore, to procure from the *parlement* of Bordeaux an *arrêt* ordering the nobility, the leading bourgeoisie and the Church to convene regular committees in their parishes in order to advise how work could be provided for the able-bodied and food for everyone up to the next harvest. The *arrêt* was not coercive, as Turgot wanted to encourage a voluntary response from the richer inhabitants. He wanted them to share and to lighten the suffering of the poorer people; just as he wanted, through a policy of free trade in grain, the rich regions of France to share their surpluses with the less fortunate provinces suffering starvation.

---

[1] Ibid, p. 137.
[2] Ibid, p. 418.
[3] Ibid, p. 437.

The practical measures instituted by Turgot included house-to-house visits to list people in need, the institution of charitable works for the destitute. Groups of women made clothing and taught sowing and aided the formation of Charity Bureaus in each district. In February 1770 Turgot addressed the Assembly of Charity in Limoges:

> The misery which has caused the food shortages in this province is only too apparent. It would be superfluous to sketch a picture of it, since it meets the eye on every side. One is persuaded that all those that are in a position to help the poor need only to consult their hearts in order to readily discharge a duty which humanity and religion prescribe. But when the needs are so extensive it is important that help is not distributed in a haphazard, careless way.[1]

He directed that beggars should receive only sufficient food to return home and that alms were not to be given. His address covered every detail concerned with the operation of the charitable workshops and the details of the road building schemes which were to run in tandem with the private contractors. He took care to protect donors of charity from waste and corruption.

The money which financed charitable committees and their workshops was provided by the rich. In order to prevent fraud and meanness, the assessment sheets were circulated to the donors to record their contributions and records were maintained of expenditure. He proposed, however, to give sums to the clergy on trust that they reserved these sums for those in need who were too proud to claim, and he required no accounts or details of these transactions to be maintained. The work done by the charitable workshops was matched to skills and desires. It has been estimated that between 2000–3000 people were employed on ditching and earth moving.

During the spring of 1770 he enacted several important measures on his own authority: he ordered that landowners should support their *métayer* tenants and their families until the harvest; he broke the bakers' monopoly in Limoges by opening the market to all comers, because he believed that they were over-pricing their bread; he procured an *arrêt* quashing a law which allowed money linked to the price of grain to be collected during the famines; he quashed all attempts by the police to contravene the free-trade edicts of 1763/4 and he framed new regulations for dealing with beggars.

The harvest in 1770 was as bad as that of the previous years and the outlook for the next winter and spring was worse. Buckwheat and chestnuts yielded more than the previous year but the rye yield was worse, yielding sufficient for only

---

[1] Ibid, p. 205.

about three months. The rye crop in the mountainous regions of the east side had a small grain with no protein content. It had been attacked by maggots and when the infected stocks were eaten, it caused gangrene to develop in the limbs, which fell from the body with their own weight. Two things were needed: food and the means to pay for it.

The harvest of rye throughout Europe had been similarly poor, except in Poland, where unfortunately a plague threatened to delay shipments until after the thaw in the following spring. In October 1770 there was talk of war between Britain and Spain, which would prevent any imports from abroad reaching the west coast. At the very moment that it was crucial for the Limousin (and about a third of France reckoned to be in a similar situation) that internal free trade was preserved, the *parlements*, intensified their campaign to regain their ridiculous powers to fragment the grain trade in France by protectionism. It was at this point that Turgot wrote his seven letters on free trade to Terray.

He requested an additional cash grant of 200,000 livres to be used for paying for the transport of grains in the province and to relieve the liability under the *taille* for the mountainous eastern regions. He added a postscript to say that incessant rain threatened to spoil the harvest of buckwheat and chestnuts. But the gloom began to brighten in the autumn. The following harvest turned out to be much better than had been predicted, the grain prices began to fall, peace prevailed between Britain and Spain and grain and rice was shipped through the Baltic Sea before the ice set in. Yet in the mountainous region the famine continued in all its rigour.

In April 1771 Turgot appealed to the *contrôleur-général* for a reduction in the *taille* as a means of allowing the province to recover from the famine and to pay arrears amounting to 900,000 livres. He had been asking for a reduction annually on the grounds that the province was already surcharged. He asked for a complete waiver of tax for the mountainous region and a reduction of 480,000 livres for the rest of the province. Without this relief Turgot feared that farmers would not save sufficient stocks of seed for the following year. The famine had been prolonged by the depletion of seized stocks and by the sowing of seeds with little protein content. After the next harvest in 1771 he allowed the farmers to take loans for seeds purchased from outside and did not require the loan to be repaid until after the next harvest.

In August 1771 Turgot wrote to Du Pont to tell him that his gout had been worse than he had experienced in the summer. He hoped that he could complete his task in Montagne, though he confessed that, having exhausted every means available to him, he did not know what more could be done.[1]

By the end of 1771 he presented his financial account of the famine. He wrote to the *contrôleur-général* in order to explain the deficit on his operations:

---

[1] Ibid, p. 493.

It is with much regret that I present you with such a large deficit. I think, however, it is fair to point out that it is less great when compared with the operations I have carried out, rather than merely with the sums received. I have financed the import of various grain, rice and beans valued at 890,248 livres, I have executed public works worth 303,400 over two years, I have distributed alms of 47,000. I dare to imagine that a deficit of 90,000 livres on operations exceeding 1,240,000 livres will surprise you less and that you will think less unfavourably of my economy, perhaps even that I merit some approval; this is the principal recompense that I desire for my work.[1]

He omitted to mention that often he had taken initiatives without the backing of law, because the needs seemed to him more urgent than they did to the *parlement* in Bordeaux.

The cause of famine Turgot believed was to be found in injustice. He believed that the condition did not arise from nature alone.

---

[1] Ibid, pp. 458–9.

10

Turgot's Friends

After leaving Paris in 1772 at the end of his summer vacation, Turgot admitted in a letter to Condorcet that he 'was sad to leave Paris and that [he was] still sad. I do not have to fear the disappointment of my ambition; but any fears that I might have had for that end have been redirected to my friendships and when I leave my friends I feel like an exiled minister.'[1]

Life in the Limousin was frustrating for Turgot. His zeal for reform was blunted by Terray, and his ideas disregarded. He was making no progress on the solution of the economic ills which afflicted the people of the Limousin. There was no justice in taxation, no humanity in the *corvées* or *milice*, no freedom in trade nor reform of the causes of famine. Turgot was aware that in Paris he could enjoy the company of friends, discussion of ideas, the diversity and life of a capital city. He could pursue his love of science by study and experiment. He was at home there.

He spent at least four months of the year, usually in the summer, in Paris and after the famine had passed in 1771 he spent almost as much time there as in the Limousin. For the duties of an intendant did not occupy him fully once the chance of reform had disappeared under Terray and the famine had come to an end. He needed to escape serving under Terray, who was one of the most corrupt politicians of the *ancien régime*. His term as an intendant had begun under Bertin with so much promise. He had seen the reforms which were desperately needed, but he was powerless to do anything; to persuade even his superiors, who had little idea of conditions outside Paris or Versailles, had become a waste of time and effort.

While in the Limousin, one of Turgot's consolations for solitude was correspondence with his friends. One, Du Pont, claimed to have received more that a thousand letters from him, but only a few hundred have survived. He met Du Pont in 1764 after being impressed with his work on free trade. Du Pont was enthusiastic about political ideas and possibilities for political change in France. He was completely sincere in his enthusiasm, but he was also something of a fanatic, reckless as to his own safety and unsympathetic to those who did not

---

[1] Schelle op. cit., vol iii, pp. 571–2.

agree with him. He became one of Dr Quesnay's younger disciples and was a leading publicist of his ideas through the journal entitled, *Ephémérides du Citoyen*, of which he was the editor until it was suppressed by Terray in 1772. He coined around 1767 the name *physiocrat*[1] for the body of économistes and he worked as hard as anyone to impart the scheme and detail of Quesnay's theories. Turgot never regarded himself as a member of the *physiocrats*. He was, said de Tocqueville, 'a man of quite another stamp' from the *physiocrats*.[2] He feared their spirit of sect, which offended many opponents whom were interested in their field and many who were not.

Du Pont understood Turgot's thinking well. He wrote, '[Turgot] detested sect and that esprit de cours because experience had shown him that it is very difficult with even the most worthy of men, for the inevitable fanaticism of sect does not become to some extent the love of truth and justice which M Turgot preferred above everything. The morality of the most scrupulous body is never equal to that of the honest individual.'[3] Historians who group Turgot with the *physiocrats* do him a great injustice and make a profound error.[4]

In many letters Turgot admonished Du Pont for overstating his case, for his polemical style of writing, for his didactic tone, for neglecting the simple ideas in favour of the contrived and for editing articles of his contributors' articles, in order to show that their ideas conformed more closely to those of Dr Quesnay. Once Turgot contributed two articles on the price of bread and the interest of money to a journal which had been the forerunner of Du Pont's. The articles had questioned Quesnay's ideas. When Du Pont protested Turgot urged him continually to be tolerant of opponents, mistrust enthusiasm and to advance only facts which were certain. In a letter dated 29 March 1765 he confessed his doubts about Dr Quesnay's reasoning: 'I am not entirely satisfied on the foundations of our algebra.[5] I am like the disciple of Leibnitz who ... arrived at truths without being satisfied on the continuity of reasoning that had led them thither.' Du Pont once rejected Turgot's reproach for being too sectarian. Turgot replied that the rejection showed more and more that his original reproach had been just. On another occasion Turgot asked, 'Is it true that the Doctor is to publish his geometry? That would be the exposure of all exposures; the sun will go rusty.'[6] Refuting Quesnay's attack on usury Turgot wrote, 'As to his [Quesnay's] disciples their admiration of the genius of the master and the spirit of school held them in a rut.'[7]

---

[1] Meaning *'those who follow the rule of nature'*.
[2] de Tocqueville *The Ancien Regime and the French Revolution* Fontana edn. [1969], p. 181.
[3] Du Pont *Mémoires sur la Vie de M Turgot* [Philadelphia 1788] p. 42.
[4] See Gide & Rist, *History of Economic Doctrine* p. 65; and J. Schumpeter *History of Economic Analysis* [2nd Imp 1955] pp. 243–44.
[5] As Turgot called Quesnay's complex thinking.
[6] Schelle, op. cit., vol iii, pp. 77.
[7] Du Pont, *Mémoires sur la Vie de M. Turgot*, p. 82.

Once while writing a comic play about Joseph II of Austria, Du Pont had sought Turgot's advice. Turgot thought he should concentrate on educating the public with simplicity and reason. Writing fables for Emperors as if they were children and addressing the public by harangue were the evidence of sect. Repeatedly, he encouraged Du Pont to write for the public reader.

He took a close interest in Du Pont's young family and in his economic journal, *Ephémérides du Citoyen*. He was always encouraging Du Pont to write on free trade and protectionism; a book, he believed, would settle the argument in favour of freedom, by showing how inadequate and illusory was the case for greater state control.

The greater part of their correspondence was taken up with the events of the political world. It was written in a code designed to conceal the meaning from the state censors, who intercepted letters and even diplomatic bags. During the battle over the restoration of free trade between 1763–70 Turgot was advising Du Pont to lie low, in order to preserve his liberty. At length, Du Pont's patience broke. He accused Turgot of failing to influence events on account of his timidity and reserve.

> I have a great defect,' conceded Turgot, 'but it is not that of timidity. This defect is to take upon myself too much work and to be lazy, more through wantonness of mind than through actual inertia . . . It would be necessary, in order that I act , that I would have to be the absolute master, because then I would only have to see something and then act accordingly, whereas I need to persuade others to make them act and sweat blood in order to supply with clarity thousands of details which require a long time to substantiate and which are evident to me after only a glance.[1]

Du Pont seems to have tried to persuade Turgot to follow a social life in the Limousin, for when he was away from Paris he lived as a recluse being frustrated in seeing none of his ideas implemented in daily administration.

> My position and still more my character, being removed from ordinary life, and consequently from enquiry and choice in this matter have not enabled me to discover whether your ideas are crazy. Furthermore my compulsory duties, my habit of missing dinner [in order to ease his gout] and the impossibility of giving myself to gambling at my age, distance me still further from the societies in which I would be able to put your ideas to the test.[2]

---

[1] Ibid, p. 491.
[2] Ibid, p. 562.

After the suppression of his journal in 1772 by Terray, Du Pont became frustrated. He wanted a position in which he could influence government. In the same year, when offered a position as tutor to the children of the Prince Czartoriski, Du Pont emigrated to Poland and signed a seven-year contract.

In 1813 Du Pont remembered Turgot with deep emotion in a letter published by *Mercure de France*. '(T)he glory of my life is to have closer than anyone to profit from (Turgot's) intelligence . . . I loved him for himself and for the nation. I loved the nation in him'.[1]

Another correspondent of Turgot was the duchesse d'Enville, the daughter of the duc de La Rochefoucauld. She was almost ten years older than Turgot and had been widowed. She was interested by the practical problems of government and by political and economic ideas. She followed his advice about political and historical reading and sought his opinion on such men as Sully, the seventeenth-century French statesman, whom Turgot described as a thinker who did not rise above the general notions of his time, and Colbert, whom he regarded as a vintage protectionist. Turgot persuaded her to judge the quality of statesmen more by their ideas and principles than by their actions. The duchesse was also interested in scientific experiments in agriculture. On her advice Turgot made a number of experiments including the breeding of various strains of grain and pasture seeds, the growing of potatoes, the introduction of silk worms, the use of a new rat trap and the drying and storage of grain.

Once in 1768 Turgot had been ordered to arrest a Catholic who, in preparation for his marriage to a Protestant, had renounced his religion. After three months of imprisonment, Turgot could not get him released and he wrote to the duchesse d'Enville, 'Imagine', he declared, 'that a man must become a Catholic in order to gain his liberty! This will be a great victory for the Catholic Church.'[2]

From 1770 Turgot began writing to Condorcet, the marquis de Caritat, a writer and mathematician, on a wide range of subjects including law, politics, physics, chemistry, astronomy, algebra, geometry and literature. The first of these letters were two lengthy arguments about the jury system in criminal trials. Condorcet supported the jury as used in England, which was an unprofessional body of individuals who were chosen for a trial or series of trials. Turgot preferred investigating magistrates, who were, unlike jurors, professional. His main reservation against juries in general were their partiality and their tendency to acquit, even in the face of compelling evidence of guilt. He preferred a preliminary hearing, at which the accused would be represented by counsel, and a later trial, if necessary. The questions of law and fact should be determined by a panel of judges drawn from a tribunal selected every three years by the people. If a crime carried the death penalty, Turgot believed that the first trial should be

---

[1] Schelle, *Du Pont et L'École Physiocratie*.
[2] *Lettres de Turgot à la duchesse d'Enville*. Letter dated 29 Nov 1768.

held in the locality of the crime and that, if the death penalty was invoked, there should be a review of the trial by a higher tribunal, and, if they confirmed the sentence, the mitigating circumstances should be considered by a committee of pardon. Turgot also thought that juries were particularly inappropriate when the offences involved civil unrest and religious protest, for, on these occasions, when it was necessary to identify and punish the leaders, there was widespread sympathy for the disturbances.

Turgot shared Condorcet's views *on lettres de cachet*, or arrest warrants, and the injustice of the *parlements*. Turgot admired the English practice of printing judicial judgements and of informing the accused of the charges alleged against him. However, the one reservation Turgot had of English practice was that of starving a jury into unanimity; he thought they should be isolated until they reached a decision.

They exchanged twelve lengthy letters on subjects of science, such as the phlogiston theory, the constitution of water, the theory of combustion, calcination of metals and the elements, ether, air and fire, the phenomenon of crystallisation, as well as logarithms.

In June 1772 Condorcet wrote to Turgot, 'You are very fortunate to have a passion for the public welfare and to able to satisfy it; it is a great solace and of a higher order than study.' Turgot replied, with uncharacteristic haste, within a week:

> Whatever you may say, I believe that the satisfaction from literary studies is far greater than any other. I am quite convinced that by literature we can be a thousand times more useful to mankind than we can be in any official position, in which we strain ourselves, often without success, to effect some slight benefits, while we become the instruments of the greatest evils. All these small benefits are ephemeral, but the light that a man of letters can shed must destroy sooner or later all the artificial evils of mankind and enable man to enjoy all the gifts offered by Nature . . . I promise you that gout has not prevented me in any way from believing in final causes and . . . that the complete system is not and cannot be known to us. To shed blood [gout sufferers were bled often], to cough, to have gout, to lose one's friends, are all details of the execution of a decree of death against all that is born. If we die only to be reborn, it is still true that the sum of good is greater than the sum of evil, excepting always those evils which men bring on themselves. I believe the former evils are transient for the individual who develops both his thinking and his feeling.[1]

Condorcet's biography of Turgot's so impressed Lord Shelbourne, the British

---

[1] Schelle, op. cit.,vol ii,p. 573.

Prime Minister, that he arranged for it to be translated into English. Shelbourne thought the biography might teach young politicians a few essential principles.

Another friend whom Turgot visited frequently in Paris was Julie Lespinasse, who held a lively salon. Among her most ardent supporters were Alembert and Condorcet, or 'le bon Condorcet', as she called him. She was interested by political ideas and discussion. When inwardly convinced of an argument or motive, she gave it powerful and dignified expression. In a letter from Turgot to Julie the publication of Galiana's *Dialogues* were discussed and an interesting point was made:

> He [Galiana] possesses the art of those who muddle things that are clear ... This art consists of never starting at the beginning, in presenting a subject in all its complexity either by some fact which is only an exception or by some event, which being unconnected, extraneous or of secondary importance does not bear on the subject and counts for nothing in its resolution ... I do not like to see him always so conservative, always so hostile to enthusiasm, so strongly in accord with all the *ne quid nimis* and with all those who enjoy the present and who are quite happy to let the world go on as it pleases, because all is well for them. As M. Gournay used to say, having had their beds well feathered, they do not want them disturbed.[1]

During his leisure in the Limousin Turgot was free to devote himself to the classics. In particular, he was unsatisfied with his translations of Virgil. His secretary, Caillard, knew Voltaire and Turgot was able to send some translations through him under a pseudonym to Voltaire to seek his unbiased opinion. Voltaire was then over seventy. He replied four months later. 'The decrepitude of age and a long illness are the reasons [of my delay] ... Here is the first translation with any spirit. The majority of the others are as dry as they are unfaithful. I note in your work an enthusiasm and a style peculiar to yourself ... I applaud your merit as well as I appreciate your courtesy.'[2] Turgot was not entirely satisfied that Voltaire had really considered the harmonies of the translation and he wrote to him on this point. But he only drew the reply from Voltaire that old age and illness prevented further consideration of his work.

During the mid-1760's he wrote to David Hume about his celebrated quarrel with Jean Jacques Rousseau. He tried to persuade Hume that despite Rousseau's absurd behaviour and his ingratitude, he merited consideration as a writer. Turgot had met him once at the home of Holbach and learned of his manners as a piece of general knowledge. 'Are we to reckon as nothing', Turgot asks Hume, 'his *Social*

---

[1] Ibid, pp. 420–1.
[2] Ibid, p. 414.

Contract'. In truth this book boils down to the precise difference between sovereignty and government. This distinction yields a most important truth and one that appears to me to determine ideas on the inalienability of the sovereignty of the people under governments of every description.'[1]

Diderot, the *encylopédiste*, wrote to Catherine the Great of Russia during the winter of 1773 about Turgot:

> M. Turgot is one of the most honest men in the country and to be sure, perhaps, the most able in every way. He will never leave Limoges, and if he does, I will let out a cry of joy, for it is necessary for the spirit of government to be totally changed and improved in almost a miraculous way ... But is this man known to the ring? Without doubt, but as a hothead who upsets everything; as kings are told when it is necessary to brush aside a man of merit.[2]

Fortunately for the underprivileged people of France, Louis XV died the following year, in 1774, and Turgot was called from the Limousin to be appointed a minister in the Council. His long political apprenticeship was over at last. The frustration at serving a series of *contrôleur-générals* gave way to the hope that he be able to attempt reforms, which were long overdue.

When the news of his elevation reached the Limousin 'joy and sadness swept through the province', wrote an inhabitant. 'The clergy announced that they would celebrate divine service. On the appointed day work was abandoned, country people were to be seen on their knees upon the paved stone of the basilicas, and priests, in the midst of vapours of incense, called for divinity to choose to smile on the worthy projects of the minister.'[3] The author added that Turgot's memory was handed down in the Limousin from parent to child some forty years later.

Several decades later Du Pont mentioned Turgot's intendancy to Thomas Jefferson, the third President of the United States. 'In the Limousin', wrote Du Pont, 'we do not know whether to admire most the comprehensiveness of his mind or the benevolence or purity of his heart. In his essay on the distribution of wealth and other general works and in the large principles developed in his shorter works, we can admire the breadth and stature of his mind. But when we see that mind thwarted, harassed, maligned and forced to exert all its powers in the details of provincial administration, we see a Hercules put his shoulder to the wheel of a bullock's cart. The sound principles set down in both types of writing are a valuable legacy to ill-governed men and they will spread from their provincial limits to the great circle of mankind.'[4]

---

[1] Ibid, p. 660.
[2] M Keiner, *Quand Turgot Régnait en Limousin*, p. 289.
[3] M. Tallander, *Éloge de M. Turgot* p. 28.
[4] *Correspondence between Thomas Jefferson and DuPont de Nemours*, 1930, p. 146.

11

Louis XVI's Council of Ministers

The historical background of French government must be considered before pursuing Turgot's career beyond this point. To gain some idea of the legacy bequeathed to Louis XVI in 1774, it is necessary to start with the *grand siècle* of Louis XIV, whose reign began in 1643 and continued to 1715.

If the greatness of a monarch is reflected in monuments, military adventures, clever diplomacy, splendour at court and the opulence of the royal personage, then Louis XIV has every claim to be called the Sun King, for in all these achievements he excelled. If the quality of his reign is measured in terms of the people's liberty, then the reign of Louis XIV bears the indelible stamp of tyranny. Criticism of the government was punished and, therefore, silenced; municipal government was discarded; Protestants were outlawed as the great Edict of Nantes [1598], which had given them their freedom, was reversed; the costs of war and play at Versailles were recovered from the poor by a multiplicity of taxes, commerce was ordered in the most trifling particularity by Colbert; the police were armed with considerable power – and there was no shortage of prisons.

In 1715 Louis XIV died and was succeeded by his grandson, Louis XV, then aged only five. For twenty-eight years the government was carried on by regents. It was a period of weak government. The *parlements* and the Church, which had been suppressed in the previous reign, quarrelled for supremacy with each other and with government. In 1743, at the age of thirty-three, Louis XV began his personal rule and was determined to rule without rivals. As a child he was brought up to shun the company of women and to observe religious pieties. Later, however, he reacted against his rigid upbringing and sank into shameless sensuality, adultery and threw aside the constraints of religion. He was undermined gradually by his own debauchery and feebleness. From 1745 France was governed by the whim of Mme de Pompadour, his mistress: she wound the king and his nation around her little finger. In 1756 France was joined with Russia and Austria in the petticoat coalition of Mme de Pompadour, Catherine of Russia and Marie-Thérèse of Austria and entered the Seven Years War against Britain and Prussia. France suffered serious defeats at Rossbach in Germany, at Plessey in India and at Quebec. The terms of peace in 1763 were humiliating for France.

The crown and the *dévots*, the religious party, vied with the parlements, who swooped onto the political stage whenever they detected a weakness in government. The *philosophes*, or intellectuals, were always a danger to the crown and the established order, simply because they thought. In 1764 Mme de Pompadour died and Louis XV found Mme du Barry suitable for the vacancy. She brought her favourites into power and among them were three ministers: Maupeou, Aiguillon and Terray. In 1770 this troika provoked a quarrel with the *parlements*, in order to obtain a reason for exiling the magistrates. For the *parlements* constituted an obstruction to their tyranny, which was unleashed during the latter years of Louis XV's reign.

In late April 1774 Louis XV contracted smallpox. His condition was serious. Upon his life depended the fortunes of Mme du Barry and her friends and favourites, ministers of the Council and their friends, the standing of the ranks of the court at Versailles, or 'the anthill', and Turgot himself. The Archbishop of Paris had been warned that the irreligious king would not survive the shock of the last sacraments. On 14 May 1774 Louis XV died and his grandson, Louis XVI succeeded to the throne of a nation of over 22 million subjects at the age of twenty. His own father had died earlier. He was unprepared and, on hearing the news, exclaimed that it was as if the whole weight of the world had descended on him.

'The accession of Louis XVI to the throne, [observed a contemporary], caused a widespread joy to sweep through the whole kingdom'. The long reign [of Louis XV] had been remarkable for the scandal of the king's life and the degradation of his administration. In peace the nation was crushed by taxation, while gold and silver were lavished on the favourite courtiers who paraded in 'the most ostentation and the revolting opulence in life, in pavilion and in furnishings'.[1]

In war, too, the picture had been one of defeat and the loss of territory.

Louis XVI was neither a scholar nor a statesman. Yet he could speak German, Italian and English. His interests were physical labour, clock making, hunting and eating. However Viscount Stormont, the British Ambassador in Paris, reported that 'The strongest and most decided of the king's character are a love of justice, a general desire of doing well, a passion for economy and an abhorrence of all the excesses of the last reign.'[2] His young Austrian wife, Marie-Antoinette, was not a women on whom he could depend in this critical time. Her mother Marie-Thérèse, the Empress of Austria, had surrounded her with tutors of every description in Vienna, but she had succeeded in learning so little, that she could barely write when she had married Louis XVI. During her marriage she 'lived in a continual agitation of pleasures, raced in horse-drawn gigs, pageants on donkeys and parties with the princes and her friends'.[3]

---

[1] Georgel, *Memoires*, p. 702.
[2] *State Papers*, 7, p. 292.
[3] E Lavisse, *La Régne de Louis XVI*, p. 3.

The king's late father, who had died while dauphin, had left a list of ministers suitable for office and this list assisted the first decisions of the young king. The leading contender for a position in the government was the duc Choiseul, but his name was not on the list. The duke had been a leading minister for thirteen years up to 1770 and was by far the most experienced politician around. He had arranged the marriage of the king to Marie-Antoinette and was supported by the Austrian Party. But he was opposed by the *dévots* for the role which he had played in the suppression of the Jesuits and for his unconcealed amorality in politics and in his publicised love affairs. To his great astonishment, Louis XVI did not summon him. The king demonstrated his desire to break with the degeneracy of the last reign, by exiling Mme du Barry to a convent at Pont-Les Dames, near Paris. But after six months he released her and pensioned her with 60,000 livres per annum.

He consulted his aunts, Mme Adélaïde and Mme Narbonne, about the appointment of the ministers and they suggested the name of Maurepas, the unfortunate minister who had been exiled in his provincial château by Mme de Pompadour for twenty-five years following the incident of the defamatory sonnet. Maurepas was seventy-three and, despite a long exile, had considerable experience as a minister, having made his debut when he succeeded his father as minister of the navy at the age of fourteen. Furthermore, his name did appear on the dauphin's list. He had a clear memory for people and for events and he knew something interesting about everyone of importance. He and his forbears had been *parlementaires* and his allegiance was to the magistrates rather than to the other institutions of state. He and his wife had a great number of relatives and friends, several of whom held positions of power. He was accurately described as 'well shaven, well powdered, well rejuvenated [and] had the appearance of thinking profoundly of nothing'.[1] The king appointed him the senior minister, but not prime minister.

The position suited Maurepas, who wanted to be a personal adviser and enjoy confidential weekly meetings with the king.

> Without having superior genius, [observed the duc de Levis], he was a man of ordinary sense and wit; but he had skill in affairs, he had experience and discernment. What he lacked was more in the nature of character than of talent and know-how . . . he was completely submissive to the wishes of his wife, who herself was a very mediocre person. But the greatest of his faults was an indifference for public welfare, which derived less from age than from egoism: provided that his personal credit suffered no setbacks and his position, to which he was attached as to life itself, was secure, everything else was of secondary concern. In short he was a

---

[1] Chronique Secrète de Baudeau, *Revue Rétrospective* [1834], pp. 29–96.

passenger on the vessel of state, rather than a pilot, letting it go its uncertain course according to chance and events, of which he should have made himself the master.[1]

Another contemporary stressed Maurepas's talent when he stated that, 'He did not distinguish himself with his views or his act, rather he acquitted himself with great quickness of mind and by the use of pleasing and felicitous words.'[2]

The king chose Vergennes, whose name was on the list, as minister for foreign affairs in preference to Breteuil, who was a follower of Choiseul. Vergennes was noted for his tenacity of office and it was said that only death would part him from his position. Du Muy was appointed the minister of war. He was a *dévot* and was honest, though he lacked the ability to form a large view, to lead a ministry or distinguish between details and principles. Maurepas was unable to retain his nephew, Aiguillon, in the Council. The king was adamant that Aiguillon should go in order that the Council be cleansed.

For a short time, the king retained the troika, Maupeou, duc de La Vrillière and Terray who had 'Terrified the nation, rather than oppressed it.'[3] He was perplexed by finance, particularly when Terray showered him in papers and explanations of the financial situation. The king did want to separate himself from the harshness, extortion and bad faith of Terray's administration but finance did not appear as straightforward as the other departments of state. 'I have stated', wrote Véri, the former fellow student of Turgot at the Sorbonne, 'that if in the whole of France there were two people (with the exception of his accomplices and immediate subordinates) who did not know that he was a well-known crook . . . then he could be kept on as *contrôleur-général*.'[4]

The duchesse d'Enville recommended Turgot to Maurepas's wife as a candidate for the Council. Véri, who had spent several years with Maurepas during his exile, gave the same advice to Maurepas. By June, Turgot was being tipped as the successor to Terray and this gave rise to considerable anxiety among the farmers-general, or tax gatherers, and the courtiers, who marked him as a reformer. They circulated the fact that he had been disliked in the Limousin. Indeed, he had been disliked by some, as a contemporary explained:

The Limousin nobility was accustomed to enjoy the fruits of greater injustice under the guise of privilege, gentlemen of lowly title were able to procure reductions in the assessments of the *taille*, the *vingtièmes* and the capitations on their dependents and the burden fell on the unfortunate without protection. Besides the intendancy had been a fine

[1] Lévis, *Souvenirs et Portraits* [1815], p. 4.
[2] Sénac de Meilhan *De Gouvernement* . . . [1795], p. 145.
[3] Condorcet, *La Vie de Turgot ch. V.*.
[4] Véri, *Memoires*, vol 1 p. 129.

inn where they found a sumptuous table, women and gambling. M. Turgot, an industrious bachelor who dines more often than not alone,[was] not their man.[1]

But the king was showing signs of prevarication and Terray, who was retained, warned the king against the dangerous principles of Turgot.

Maurepas pressed the king to consider Turgot for the ministry of the Marine, which included both the navy and the colonies. The king interviewed him for that post, but was more interested to discuss with him finance, the grain trade and taxation. On being warned that Turgot was an *encyclopédiste*, and, as such, an opponent of the Church, the king replied, 'He is an enlightened and an honest man and that suffices for me.'[2] Turgot was appointed Minister of the Marine on 20 July. 'I do not imagine that he is more a mariner than I am', wrote Voltaire to Mme Deffand, 'but he seems excellent on land, full of enlightened reason. He loves justice as much as others love their own interests and he loves truth almost as he loves justice.'[3] Condorcet was overjoyed by the news of the appointment and wrote ecstatically to Voltaire:

Nothing more fortunate could have happened to France or humanity. Never has a man entered any council of monarchy who combines in himself virtue courage and disinterestedness, love of the public welfare, enlightenment and the zeal to spread these qualities. Since his appointment I sleep and wake as peacefully as if I was under the protection of the laws of England.[4]

---

[1] Chronique Secrète de Baudeau, *Revue Rétrospective* vol 3 [1834] 5 June 1774.
[2] Voltaire's *letter to Condorcet*, 12 August 1774.
[3] Schelle, op. cit., vol iv p. 79.
[4] Ibid pp. 78–9.

12

Ministerial Office

The Marine was not the ideal department for Turgot and hardly one that his training in the land-locked Limousin had equipped him for. But he proved himself to be an exceptional minister. He obtained the king's permission for two naval expeditions. *M. Saint-Edmond* went to the East Indies to collect plants and to observe rice growing but, unhappily, this vessel went down with all hands; with better fortune *M. Ombey* went to Peru and returned in 1785 with a rich collection of plants and minerals.

Turgot laid plans for nautical surveyors to chart little-known parts of the oceans and he encouraged an existing experiment on the desalination of sea water. He paid naval dock workers in Brest their wages, which had been overdue for eighteen months, and checked the bureaucracy of the navy, which was rotten with venality and *pensions*. He decided to commission battleships from Sweden, whose excellent timber and building skills enabled them to underquote French prices by a fifth. He had Euler's book on navigation, which had been published in St Petersburg, republished for use by the navy.

Turgot held liberal ideas about the role of the colonies. He regarded them as refuges for excess populations of the mother countries and for the victims of political and religious oppression. He was keen for them to develop their own prosperity and place in the world and, therefore, he rejected strongly the commercial and political ties which Britain was wrapping blindly around her colonies. He thought that the French colonies should be allowed to trade freely with the whole world in the vessels of any flag. He planned also to convert the isles of France and Bourbon off the east coast of Africa into free ports, through which trade would flow without state control. This would eventually attract Indian and Chinese traders to Europe.

During the late 1760s he had opposed the state support of the East India Company, which had received a monopoly of the French trade in India, as a counterpart to the British East India Company. The French Company had encountered financial problems and was rescued by the state under plans devised by Necker. Turgot had chided Du Pont for agreeing far too readily that 'fortified trading places are required against the Indians in order to trade there; this supposed necessity is one of the pretexts with which the spirit of monopoly clothes itself, but it is far too shallow as a pretext and one which it is difficult to substantiate.'[1] Turgot believed that trade was a natural tie between nations and that fortresses were unnecessary and ruinous of the smooth flow of trade. Turgot did not agree that the state should bail out bankrupt monopolies.

He looked beyond the narrow view that colonies could be run as possessions and demonstrated that both the mother country and the colony had a similar interest in the freedom of trade. The reasons for binding a colony by exclusive trading arrangements and by political government during its infancy have often been the pretext for holding on to misconceived trading and territorial advantages, which harm not only the mother country and the colony, but also excite the enmity and the envy of the rest of the world. In 1770 he had written to Dean Tucker:

> I confess that I cannot disguise my astonishment that in a nation [Britain] which enjoys a free press, you are almost the only writer to understand the advantages of free trade and not to be seduced by the puerile and cruel illusion of trading monopolies. Let the influence of enlightened and humane policies destroy this abominable notion, which lingers after the mania of conquest and religious intolerance which the world is beginning to come to terms with. Millions of men have been sacrificed to three monsters (trading monopolies, conquest and religion)!
>
> I am glad to see, as a citizen of the world, an event approaching which will dissolve the phantom of commercial jealousy more than all the books of the philosophers. I refer to the separation of your colonies from their mother country, which will be followed in a short time by that of the whole of America with Europe. Then the discovery of that part of the world will become really useful; it will increase our enjoyment much abundantly than in the days when we bought it by drops of blood.'[2]

Turgot considered that were Britain to form an empire, it would achieve one benefit after such an enterprise came to an end: the spread of the English language over a larger area of the globe.[3] This one benefit, he asserted, would be incidental rather than intended. It might be added that, as a result, the British would be, as a consequence, poor linguists.

Unfortunately Turgot's tenure of the Marine was for a month only, too brief, to develop his liberal ideas on colonies.

Through the summer of 1774 there was a general idea that the corrupt instruments of Louis XV's reign needed to be purged; namely Terray, the

---

[1] Schelle, op. cit., vol iv, pp. 69–70.
[2] Schelle, op. cit., vol iii p. 422.
[3] Schelle, op. cit., vol ii, p. 512.

contrôleur-général, Maupeou, the chancellor, and La Vrillière, the minister of the king's household. Terray was advising on the need to cut government expenditure, to reduce taxes and to restore credit, in order to correct his earlier recklessness. La Vrillière was proposing ambitious savings in the expenditure of the royal household, which he had allowed to grow over several decades without demur.

The king was aware of the necessity of ridding himself of these three, but was unable to decide upon their successors and so he postponed their dismissal. Finally, the issue was forced upon him by the circulation of a rumour that Terray had renewed a contract with the corrupt state grain company and had secured a profit for himself and his cronies. In order to preserve trust in the government, the new king had to act immediately. For nothing could have more effectively linked the new administration with the past reign than the renewal of this disreputable contract.

In early August Louis XVI wanted to dismiss Terray and Maupeou but to retain La Vrillière, who was the brother-in-law of Mme Maurepas. A few weeks later Maurepas recommended to the king that Turgot should replace Terray as *contrôleur-général*. After delaying for three days, the king summoned Turgot. They discussed the grain contract and general financial questions. The next day the king told Maurepas that he had decided to replace Terray with Turgot and Maupeou by Miromesnil, a loyal parlementarian recommended by Maurepas. Again the king requested that the announcements be withheld for a further three days. Maurepas insisted that the announcements should be made immediately, in order to kill speculation in the Council. The king summoned Turgot for a second audience.

He offered Turgot the ministry of the *contrôleur-général* but Turgot asked for a further meeting before he would accept. The reason for this further meeting was explained by Véri: 'The morning before Turgot went to the king, Turgot met the abbé Vermond, the confidante of the queen, in my office. The three of us discussed the rumours and the appointment of Turgot to the finance, on the difficulties of that position, on the greed of the court, on the weakness of the king and, consequently, on the slight hope of saving of expense. 'I know of only one bond', volunteered Vermond, which can restrain the weakness of the king against the importunities of his companions – 'that is to secure his word.' His word, duty and above all his promise are the most powerful bonds and perhaps the only that I know him to acknowledge. Therefore, M. Turgot, if you are offered the finances, furnish yourself with his word in all important matters.'[1] Turgot accepted this advice and the purpose of the second meeting was to secure his word. The meeting ended with Turgot saying to the king: 'It is necessary, Sire, that you will permit me to put my general views in writing and, if I dare say it, my conditions,

---

[1] Véri, vol i, p. 187.

on the manner in which you must support me, in this task, for I confess to you, I am worried by the situation, even on the basis of the vague idea that I have of it.' 'Yes, yes', replied the king, 'you will have it. But I give you my word in advance', he said as he took Turgot's hands, 'to support all your views and to support you in all the courageous decisions which you have to make.'[1].

Turgot returned and penned the following letter to the king:

> Having just left Your Majesty's chamber, full of anxiety on account of the great burden you place upon me, and overcome by the kindness with which you have deigned to reassure me, I hasten to convey my respectful gratitude and the unreserved loyalty of my life.
>
> Your Majesty has been good enough to allow me to put in writing the promise which you have made to support me in the execution of those plans which are always, and now particularly, of absolute necessity. I would have preferred to give my opinions on the present financial state, but time has not permitted. Therefore I refrain from a fuller explanation until I have obtained more accurate information. Sire, I confine myself to emphasising to you three precepts, †No bankruptcy; no increase of taxes; no borrowing°. No bankruptcy; either open or disguised by arbitrary reductions of interest (on public borrowings). No increase in taxes; the reason lies in the circumstances of your subjects and still more in Your Majesty's heart. No borrowing; every loan diminishes the available revenue and necessitates at length either bankruptcy or an increase in taxes. In peace it is permissible to borrow only in order to liquidate existing debts or to redeem other loans contracted on less advantageous terms.
>
> There is only one way of fulfilling these three aims: that of reducing expenditure below the receipt sufficiently to secure an annual saving of 20 million livres for the redemption of long-standing debts. Failing this, the first canon shot will bankrupt the state. One may ask on what can savings be made. Every official, speaking for his own department, will maintain that all items of expense are indispensable and they will be able to advance very good reasons. But since one cannot perform the impossible, all must yield to the absolute necessity of economy. It is essential for Your Majesty to insist that the heads of all departments should act in concert with the Minister of Finance. It is imperative that he should discuss the importance of proposed expenditure in the presence of Your Majesty. Above all, it is necessary, Sire, that as soon as you have determined the expenditure of each department, you should forbid the officials ordering new expenditure without first obtaining the

---

[1] Ibid. p. ?.

permission of the Treasury. In default of this regulation each department will load itself with debts, which become Your Majesty's debts, and your Minister of Finance will be unable to balance the income and expenditure.

Your Majesty is aware that one of the obstacles to economy is the multiplicity of demands by which you are constantly assailed and which have been sanctioned too readily by your predecessors.

It is necessary to arm yourself against your generosity by greater kind heartedness, by considering whence comes this money which you are able to distribute to your courtiers and by comparing the misery of those from whom it is extracted by the most rigorous measures with the condition of those people, since all abuses attract secret and powerful protectors.

It may be hoped by an improvement in agriculture, the suppression of irregularities in the collection of taxes and more equitable assessments of taxes, substantial relief may be obtained without greatly reducing the revenue. But unless economy is the first step, no reform is possible, because every reform involves the risk of some interruption in the collection of the revenue and because increasing difficulties, caused by the manoeuvres and protests of those interested in maintaining abuses, are only to be expected, since there is no abuse on which somebody does not depend.

So long as the finances of the nation are continually subject to expedients to provide for public services, Your Majesty will be dependent on the financiers, who will be able to defeat the most urgent operations by their manoeuvres. No relief will be possible either in taxes in order to relieve the tax payers or in any arrangement relative to domestic government. The government can never feel at ease because it will never be popular and because the discontent and the anxieties of the people are always used by intriguers and disaffected persons to excite trouble. It is then upon economy that the prosperity of your reign, the tranquillity, its reputation among other nations and the happiness of the nation and yourself depend.

I must stress upon Your Majesty that I take office at a serious moment with general anxiety over the subsistence of the people having been fomented in the public mind for several years by changes in the principles of administrators, by imprudent operations on their part and above all by a harvest which seems to have been mediocre. On this matter, as upon others, I do not ask Your Majesty to adopt my principles without first having examined and discussed as well as by yourself and by your trusted officials in your presence. But should the justice and the principles be acknowledged, I entreat you to support their application without fear, for the clamours which are certain to arise, no matter what policy you adopt.

These are matters which Your Majesty allowed me to recall to his mind. You will not forget, Sire, that in accepting the office of *contrôleur-général*, I have felt to the full value of the confidence with which you honour me. I have felt that you have entrusted me with the happiness of your people and, if I may be permitted to say so, the office of promoting among your people the love of your person and your authority. But at the same time I am aware of all the danger to which I expose myself. I foresee that I shall be alone on fighting against abuses of every kind, against those who profit by them, against the multitude of prejudices, which, opposed to all reforms, are such powerful levers in the hands of persons interested in perpetuating disorder. I shall have to struggle against the natural goodness of Your Majesty and of persons most dear to you. I shall be feared, hated even by the majority of the court and by all who solicit favours; they will attribute all the refusals to me; they will call me a hard man because I advise Your Majesty not to enrich even those you love at the expense of your people's subsistence. And the people themselves, to whom I will sacrifice myself are so easily deceived that perhaps I shall arouse their hatred by the very measures designed to save them from their troubles. Appearances being against me, I shall be subject to calumny with sufficient force to deprive me of Your Majesty's confidence. I shall never regret losing an office which I never sought. I am ready to resign it into Your Majesty's hands as soon as I can no longer be useful in it. But your esteem, reputation for integrity, desire to promote the common good, all of which have lead you to favour me, are more precious to me than life and I run the risk of losing my own reputation even though meriting, in my own eyes, no reproach.

Your Majesty will remember that it is my faith in your promises that leaves me to undertake a burden perhaps beyond my strength and that it is to you personally, to an honest, just and good man rather than the king, to whom I give myself. I venture to repeat what you have been kind enough already to hear and approve. The touching kindness with which you have taken my hands in yours, as if accepting my devotion, will never be effaced from my memory. It will sustain my courage. It has inseparably united my happiness with the interests, the glory and the welfare of Your Majesty.[1]

Turgot was fully aware of the injustices of the *ancien régime* and of the vehemence of the outcry which would follow reform of them. He was also aware

---

[1] Condorcet, *La Vie deTurgot* pp. 84–94.

that the king, by whose will ministers held their office, was inexperienced and had no idea either of the injustices or of the protests which their reform would cause.

Turgot described the discussion with the king to Julie Lespinasse, who recorded that the meeting was opened by the king who enquired, 'You do not want to be the *contrôleur-général* then?' 'Sire', Turgot had replied, 'I would have preferred the ministry of the Marine, because it is a more secure place and one where I am certain of being able to do good, but at this moment it is not to the king that I surrender myself, but to an honest man.' Then the king took his hands and promised, 'You will not be deceived in any respect . . .' This soulful action of the king', reported Lespinasse, 'filled M.Turgot with every hope.'[1]

At the news of the appointment joy spread through Paris and the provinces. In the Limousin a holiday was declared and, after a civic ceremony, a fireworks display was staged in Limoges. The carriages of Terray and Maupeou were mobbed as they left their homes in Paris and after their departures their effigies were hanged and burnt on bonfires. Marie-Antoinette wrote to her mother in Vienna, 'The people have made an extravagant show of joy at the dismissal of the chancellor and the *contrôleur-général* . . . I have already told you, *chère maman*, that Turgot is a very honest man; an essential quality at the ministry of finance.'[2]

Vermond confirmed that Turgot was keen from the outset to win the confidence of the young queen, for in some ways she was a more determined and a more powerful character than her husband. It is probable that Turgot was referring to the queen among 'those most dear' to the king and he was trying to avoid the opposition of the queen by involving her as much as possible in government.

'There will be no ostentation', predicted Julie L'Espinasse, . . . 'in a word there will be the greatest simplicity; that is to say, the style of M. Turgot himself'.[3] He reduced his own salary as *controleur* from 142,000 livres to 80,000 livres, he waived his right to installation expenses, which could have amounted to as much as 150,000 livres, and he suppressed the gift paid by the farmers-general to a new *contrôleur-général* of 300,000 livres, because it was a traditional bribe. While he preferred simplicity, there was probably more to Turgot's decision than that; he was mindful of the miseries of the poor, who shouldered the burden of taxation and he thought that acceptance of these presents was to submit to the first instalment of bribery.

The *contrôleur général*'s responsibilities were wide. Véri described them succinctly: '[His] influence extends even to the least branch of government; the whole interior depends on it; everything abroad is depended on it.'[4] At the centre was finance. Maurepas wanted Turgot to concentrate on this alone, but Turgot

[1] Schelle, op. cit., vol iv, p. 103.
[2] Ibid. p?.
[3] Ibid p. 121.
[4] Véri, vol i p. 157.

saw this as only one facet of his responsibilities. The *contrôleur* had a staff of 350 officials housed in the *palais Mazarin*, occupied today by part of the Bibliothèque Nationale.

The head of this central office was the chief clerk and Turgot immediately dismissed the incumbent, Leclerc, who had accumulated a fortune under Terray. He replaced him by Vaines, who had worked on his staff in the Limousin. Apart from what might be called the administrative staff, numbering seven permanent officials of the ministry, the *contrôleur* was assisted by several junior ministers. These seven intendants of finance included the Trudaines and the two Ormessons. Turgot invited Du Pont to return from Poland under official letters of recall. Though Du Pont lost financially as a result of breaking a contract, he returned to become an inspector of commerce. In fact, he became Turgot's private secretary. Condorcet was appointed a general inspector of commerce with special responsibilities for the mint. He insisted on forgoing remuneration until it was possible to place a value on his work. Outside his ministry Turgot appointed his friends: Suard as the official historian, the comte d'Angivillers as the director responsible for public buildings, Morellet was given a sinecure in the department of the post to help him complete his economic dictionary, and Baudeau became editor of the *Nouvelle Ephémérides*, which received government recognition.

For thirteen years Turgot had been dealing with country people, who for the most part could neither read nor write. Now he found himself dressed in a morning coat and armed with a ceremonial sword, in the midst of the powdered folk congregated at Versailles.

Shortly after his appointment he received a demand from the comte de Provence, a brother of the king, who had a reputation for unbridled greed. After their meeting the comte wrote to Turgot in order to press his demands of which Turgot seems to have taken too little cognizance:

> I do not want to leave you with the impression that when the king granted me the duchy of Alençon, I would have only a rental income of 400,000 livres. You did not examine the charges on this income with as much scruple as the receipts and if you think, as you intimated to me in line with the intention of the late king, that I should have 500,000–600,000 livres, I leave you more than 300,000 on your conscience. The concern and justice of the king and of your honest character are my guarantees that this will not be forgotten. I completely forgot to mention my other demands.

He listed the inadequacy of a bereavement allowance, expenses of 50,000 livres in respect of stables built by him for the comte d'Artois, and arrears of income due since his marriage of 150,000 livres, which could have been claimed at the higher figure of 300,000 livres. 'It is in the last matter', he concluded, 'that I anticipate the effect of goodwill, for the rest depend on justice. I insist, however, on receiving a reply on all these matters.'[1] Such was the language which one might expect, if a prince had been writing to a mere cashier. There is no record of Turgot's reply, but doubtless it would have not have conceded to such outrageous demands.

Montyon, a fellow intendant and acquaintance of several years, described this picture of the new *contrôleur-général*:

> The face of Turgot was handsome, majestic, with something of the dignity noted in antique heads. His countenance, however, was neither sweet nor agreeable, lacking a resolute expression and had a somewhat distracted air . . . out of place everywhere but in his study, his elocution laboured, diffuse and obscure but sometimes he delivered profound and luminous ideas . . . His mind had the nature of genius; he perceived everything in a broad perspective of relationships by examining the elements and penetrating the essence of things. But unfortunately he saw everything in abstraction, disdaining to bring his attention to bear on facts, paying no attention to the country he was governing, to the century in which he found himself living, to the established institutions, to accepted usages, to prejudices or interests.[2]

Turgot found it difficult to indulge in social conversations or to lubricate his sentiments with charm. He also found it difficult to discuss a serious matter with people who had no regard for reason or for clarity, stating the prejudices by which their judgement had been altogether displaced. His opponents found him cold, bigoted, distant, self-absorbed. Condorcet described how Turgot reacted to certain emotions which explains to some extent the reason why he attracted personal dislike:

> As he could not dissemble his hatred of the wicked and his contempt for cowardice and meanness, these sentiments painted themselves on his face and upon his whole countenance . . . As his hatred of the vicious was a consequence of his love of human nature, he never inspired a sense of vengeance. It did not influence his judgement. He praised his most inveterate enemy, when their actions merited praise, and defended him against any unjust imputation, allowing for the good qualities which he possessed.[3]

Viscount Stormont informed his superiors at the British Foreign Office that:

[1] Schelle, op. cit., vol iv p. 117.
[2] Montyon, *Particularities sur quelque ministres de finance*, pp. 75–92.
[3] Condorcet, *La Vie de Turgot*, ch 10.

No man can have a larger, more liberal way of thinking upon political points. No man ever came into such employment with a higher reputation of ability and honour, yet notwithstanding all these advantages, I think there is doubt whether he is enough hackneyed in the ways of men to know how to struggle with all that artifice, fraud, corruption and rapacity which a *contrôleur-général* must expect at every turn, and which, perhaps, are not to be subdued merely by sense, honour and truth.[1]

Stormont was especially supportive of Turgot because his thinking was so opposed to even the idea of war.

---

[1] *State Papers*. Letter 14 Sept 1774.

13

Minister of Finance

A week after his appointment, Turgot gave the *contrôleur-général*'s traditional address to the Cours des Comptes, which was the court of *parlement* with fiscal jurisdiction. His speech was heard with customary respect. He promised to relieve the burdensome taxes of the people, to restore faith in the dealings of the government and repay the national debt. Though these three aims might be relevant to almost every age and place, they were particularly relevant to France in 1774. The reply was made by the president of the court, Nicolai, who, amid hollow and effusive flatteries, delivered a veiled threat to the minister who appeared dangerous. Turgot was reputed to be a thinker and a liberal thinker at that. 'You will find', assured the president of the court, 'in the magistrates at this gathering intelligence, zeal and disinterestedness. They are involved in your work. Every time attempts have been made to strip them of their powers, or inflict injury to their jurisdiction, harm has been stirred up.'[1]

'Legislation in fiscal affairs ', wrote Condorcet, 'has long had but one principle; a desire of augmenting the revenues of the sovereign without exciting clamours which are too dangerous to the government. The consequence of adopting this principle was that the regulations which were enacted bore hard upon the people and particularly upon the country people, who, being scattered, could neither force an audience nor inspire terror.'[2]

The financial administration was a decentralised network of unravelled complexity and it was permeated by the customary venality. It was operated, moreover, by self-interested officials, who were keen to deduct their fees and claims from the moneys received by them. There was no central national account into which receipts, or from which payments, were paid. The direct taxes, such as the *taille* and the *vingtième*, were collected in each parish by the unfortunate syndic who then paid the *receveurs-généraux*, or receivers, of the election – a group of parishes. They paid these sums, after deducting their charges, to the receivers of each province. In the small number of border provinces, called the *pays d'état*,

---

[1] Schelle, op. cit., vol iv, p. 107.
[2] Condorcet, *La Vie de Turgot* ch 5.

Paris in mid-eighteenth century

The Palace at Versailles

Les Jardines de Tuileries

Voltaire

Condorcet

Malesherbes

Necker

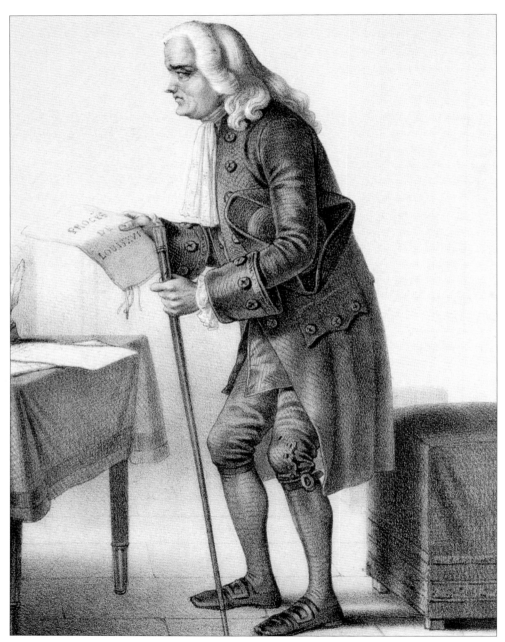

Dismissal of Turgot

the receipts were paid direct from the collector to the *contrôleur-général*. The receivers paid the local *trésoriers*, or treasurers, who operated a *caisse*, a till, out of which they paid various local expenses and other local and national treasurers were responsible for defined headings of expenditure. 'The privilege of the [receivers and treasurers], low in the social scale but high in the national [financial] system, was to remain independent and unorganised; the privilege to engage in a wide range of public and private ventures for personal and family advancement; and the privilege to manage his own *caisse*. Thus the [receivers and treasurers] stood as a bulwark against rational – indeed almost any – organisation of the national system.'[1]

Thus both the receipts of direct taxes and payments therefrom passed through the hands of several independent individuals, who had purchased from the crown the right to deduct certain fees and charges. Though not accountable to the crown as agents, they were subject to the audit of the *Cours des Comptes*, who like the receivers and treasurers, had also purchased their positions; in 1771 the presidency of the *Cours* was worth 550,000 livres, vice presidency 300,000 livres and the ordinary auditors paid 72,000 livres. Their remuneration was in part paid in deductions from the revenue and in part from personal immunities from taxation. The *Cours* exhibited the general airs, interests and pretensions of the *parlement*. The whole inefficiency and corruption of this financial system was compounded by the fact that the government were heavy borrowers from the receivers and treasurers.

The indirect taxes were collected by the farmers-general. They were called farmers because they harvested the tax revenue for their own profit. They purchased the right to collect taxes from the state. In return for guaranteeing the state a fixed fee, the farmers collected as much as they were able to extract and the excess represented their profit on the contract.

The financial position facing Turgot was impossible to ascertain precisely. There were no national accounts, no budgets and no method of determining how much was owing to and by the state. Thus, the financial situation of the government could be estimated only to an approximate extent.

In 1748 France was at peace after the two Silesian wars earlier in the decade and after the war of the Austrian Succession. The *contrôleur-général*, Machault, had introduced a new tax, the *vingtième*, in a bid to break the privileges, which had the effect of shifting the burden of taxation on to the poor. As has been explained, the bid failed, Machault resigned and the *vingtième* soon became riddled with exemptions in favour of the nobility, the Church and the bourgeoisie. The situation deteriorated over the next dozen or so years. In 1759 the *contrôleur général*, Silhouette, defaulted on government debts. The Seven Years War [1756–63] was financed by increased taxation and by borrowings secured against

[1] J. F. Bosher, *French Finance* 1770–95 p. 73.

future revenue. Then Bertin, and after him Invau, tried to break the privileges and both were dismissed for having attempted to do so.

What was needed was a *contrôleur-général* who would restore the finances of the nation without tampering with established privileges. In 1769 Terray became the *contrôleur-général*. He had intense respect for privilege and a corresponding scorn for justice and morality.

The financial situation was alarming; 100 million livres of overdue debt; the revenue of 1770 and part of that of the following year committed as security for loans; a current deficit of 60 million livres and almost nothing in the till.

His immediate advice was that expenditure, particularly in the royal household, should be curtailed and financial administration should be tightened. The king could not have countenanced the reduction of the expenditure of his household, for that expenditure maintained his personal glory, secured the contentment and the favours of his mistresses, financed the 'anthill', as Turgot called it, at Versailles and held the devotion of the courtiers, whose idle attendance at court had to be purchased. So Terray chose default on state obligations and bankruptcy as the only resort.

In January 1770 he converted some of the borrowings, called tontines, into life annuities. The tontines, named after their Italian founder, were non-repayable borrowings in which the lenders were grouped in similar age brackets and interest was paid on the death of a borrower to the survivors of the same group; so that the last survivor received the interest formerly payable to the whole group of people. In other words, the death did not diminish the debt until the entire group of borrowers had perished. Then the interest and the original loan were expunged.

Borrowing by life annuities was the more common form of a non-repayable loan, whereby a lender loaned a sum in return for an annual annuity during their life. The use of annuity as a means of borrowing was much cheaper to the state than borrowings in the form of tontines, for the annuity ceased upon death. By converting the tontines into the annuities, and so defaulting on the liabilities of the state, Terray was reckoned to have saved 150 million livres. The damage to the credit of the state is not capable of measurement, but certainly the sum of 150 million was far less than the total damage.

His second measure was to reduce the interest payable by the state on certain other borrowings by half, the effect of which was to make another immediate gain at the expense of the nation's financial credit. While he reduced state pensions above 600 livres payable to former public servants, he increased the allowances payable to himself and his patrons, such as Maupeou and Mme. du Barry and his own friends.

Terray took an altogether bolder step of freeing the revenue from the charges created on it in favour of the lenders to the state. In other words, he had destroyed the security offered by the state to many lenders. This measure enabled him to use the uncharged revenue freely. This was a crude attack on the financiers, the farmers-general, the receivers and treasurers. There was a short-term arithmetical gain to the state, but there was lasting and unquantifiable damage to the credit of the government. The pretext was sought in an edict of 1763, which allowed the government to suspend payment of its debts in times of war; Terray merely stated that the time was worse than war.

In the face of such outrageous disregard for both the integrity of the state and the property of individuals, the *parlements* remained silent; partly because the magistrates were jealous of the financiers and partly because Terray, a former magistrate himself, had been careful not to rescind the obligations due to the magistracy.

'Although', wrote Edgar Faure, 'there had been talk of ruin, suicide, martyrdoms, the majority of the [dishonoured] bills remained in financiers' hands and became instruments of jobbing rather than of saving; the public at large were hardly interested in the measure.'[1] The statement is true in a narrow sense, but the inference, that it is possible to repudiate obligations of the state without bringing loss and penalty on the public, is false. When government bonds or bills are dishonoured, the reputation of that government and that nation are impaired and it is seen at home and abroad as a dishonest and irresponsible borrower. The dishonoured bills are traded among brokers, because they know that a government in default will have to redeem its obligations before it can borrow again. The damage to the public may not be felt directly, because comparatively few may have been holding dishonoured bills, but indirectly the public pay in the form of higher interest rates, caused by the loss of credit suffered. It is, indeed, astonishing that a former finance Minister [M. Faure was Minister of Finance in three French governments during the 1950s] should imply that the damage caused by Terray's actions was felt only by a small number of bill holders and not by the public at large. Financial honesty in national finance runs like a golden thread. It takes centuries to build, but it can be destroyed for centuries by just one measure of dishonesty.

In June 1771 Terray lowered the income from perpetual stocks and on life annuities by a fifteenth and a tenth respectively. Repayment of more debts owing by the state was suspended and Terray justified the measure to the king thus, 'more than half the public predict it everyday and this opinion, produced by lack of confidence, brings with it the necessity of its implementation'.[2]

Taxes were placed on such articles as starch, paper and books, a *vingtième* was imposed and indirect taxes were increased by two sols per livre [two shillings in the pound]. Municipal offices, which had been sold in 1694, were re-possessed and re-sold to the highest bidders. Terray withdrew the authorisation of the auctioneers, who had purchased them also in 1694, on the grounds that they had

---

[1] E Faure, *a disgrâce de Turgot* p. 156.
[2] Gomel, *Les Courses Financiers de la Révolution* [1892] p. 41.

then paid too little. In 1774 he entered a new six-year contract with the farmers-general and obtained an increase of 20 million livres in the price, after having allowed them an increase in both the rate and the number of taxes.

During the four years to 1774 Terray had increased the revenue by 60 million livres and reduced government debt by 20 million livres. 'In summary,' wrote Marion, 'the administration of Terray had been violent but effective.'[1] Faure finds much to praise in the achievements, the intentions and even in the methods of his administration. But the end of reforming the finances of a nation in an arithmetical sense does not justify the means, which, in this case, violated the interests of both the individual and the nation. The achievement that was measurable has to be weighed with the loss of liberty suffered by the taxpayer.

'L'abbé Terray', recorded Véri, 'reduced by necessity to effect a partial bankruptcy and to increase taxes, had been worthy of praise only if he had done it with a tone of decency, courage and honesty, instead of only bad faith, indecency and rape. It is impossible that any operation of finance is entrusted to him. The corruption of his heart is too manifest in thousands of occurrences whose details cannot be given here. They are unfortunately too well fixed in the memory of the citizens.'[2]

Neither bankruptcy nor partial bankruptcy, by wilful breach of the obligations of the state, were forced on Terray. It is the last resort to which a nation is forced when taxes cannot be increased, when expenditure cannot be reduced, when postponement of the obligations cannot be arranged and when the credit of a nation cannot procure any forbearance. This was not the case in France in 1769 when Terray came to office. No finance minister can claim to have been pushed into a situation of national insolvency or into a situation from which the only escape is through bad faith and repudiation of the obligations of the state. He is servant of the state first and of the sovereign and government second. If the government refuse to implement his plans to avoid repudiation of the obligations of state, then he must resign or accept full personal responsibility for betraying the credit of his nation: it is not possible to explain the action of Terray as that of a minister coerced either by circumstances or by his superiors. He was persuaded to act as he did by his own weakness and wickedness.

In 1774 when his personal position was in danger and when the new king was rumoured to be at the point of dismissing him, Terray began talking of reforms such as the reduction of expenditure, reduction of taxation, the taxation of all land and the repayment of creditors. None of this was prompted by more than a desire to stay in office.

The legacy of Terray was the destruction of France's credit abroad, and at home a people oppressed by additional burdens. M. Faure, however, contends that Turgot not only inherited a clean sheet from Terray, who had dared to brave the

---

[1] M. Marion, *Histoire de la France* [1927] vol 1, p. 277.
[2] Véri, op. cit., vol i, p. 116.

unpopularity and censure. He goes on to suggest that during Turgot's interview with the king before taking office 'he took care to link his position to that of the departing minister, without doubt out of a sense of courtesy and in order to give himself more weight by stating: 'Doubtless abbé Terray has already told you about the financial situation.'[1] Turgot had no desire or reason to link himself with the corrupt administration of Terray, though he had the courtesy to avoid attacking it. The suggestion that he might have given himself weight by leaning against Terray is as ridiculous as it is perverse.

The government debt was estimated at 313 million livres, representing long-and-medium term debt of 235 million livres and the remainder made up of short-term advances in anticipation of the revenue of the following year. The reform, which Turgot had been preparing, was the replacement of the multiplicity of taxes by one tax to be levied on the *net produit* of agriculture. But that move would excite a storm of protest, which would obstruct the compilation of a cadastral register. Though he was aware of the need to relieve the poor from the weight of taxation, he was also aware of the need to maintain the nation's credit, neither of which could be immediately secured by the introduction of so contentious a measure. His plan of fundamental reform had to be put aside during the immediate financial crisis.

It appeared, according to Véri, that Terray had given loan certificates to his friends who had advanced no moneys at all, in order to reward them without the need of pensions. Turgot, therefore, requested the holders of payment orders signed by Terray to present them to the ministry and to prove that they had advanced the sums alleged. He also suppressed the *ordonnances comptants*, or cash payments, by which a minister could make undisclosed payments without incurring the scrutiny of the *Cours des Comptes*.

Turgot needed to reduce the expenditure of the army and the royal household, which together amounted to 114 million livres, or just under 30 per cent of the gross expenditure, and the financial expense of 149 million livres, or just under 40 per cent. In September 1774, within weeks of his appointment he wrote to Du Muy, the minister of war, asking for economies in all but essential expenses. He suggested economies in the recruitment of officers, who, having purchased their commissions, were determined to exercise their full right to salaries, pensions and privileges. Instead Turgot favoured opening the rank of officers to merit alone. He proposed the closure of establishments on the old eastern frontier, which since the reign of Louis XIV had not even been the actual frontier. Turgot questioned whether economies could be made in the cost of provisioning the troops and in the commissions earned by the treasurers of the military *caisses*, or cash tills. Though the French army (190,000 men) was smaller than that of Russia (500,000 men), Austria (300,000 men) and Prussia (200,000 men), it absorbed more revenue than the others.

---

[1] E. Faure, *La Disgrâce de Turgot*, p. 162.

He ended his letter with the main reason in proposing cuts: 'The recovery of the nation's finances is the interest not only of the king and of the Kingdom, but also of those who have responsibilities for the departments of government. If the finances are not in order, nothing can be discharged properly and at every turn there will be constraints.'[1] Du Muy replied by asking Turgot to approach the matter like a statesman rather than a *contrôleur-général*; in other words, to stop quibbling. Turgot also wrote to Sartine, who had succeeded him at the ministry of the Marine, and enlisted his co-operation in saving expense and in dealing with the financial disorders in colonial outposts.

The minister of the royal household, the duc de La Vrillière, whom de Tocqueville called the 'last debris of the administration of Louis XV', had no interest in economy, even though the king himself would have welcomed it. Turgot did try to persuade the king to move the coronation from Rheims to Paris in order to save the sum of 7 million livres necessitated by this anachronistic tradition. But the coronation was the grand occasion for the Church to unfurl its colours and they observed tradition scrupulously. The uncrowned king did not want to anger the clerics.

In 1773 Terray sold the right of collecting rents and dues from the royal domain in the provinces of Rouen, Caen and Alenìon to some of his friends for the term of thirty years. The friends agreed to take on aged pensioners nominated by himself and by Cochin, an intendant of finance. The result of this unconscionable bargain was that the agents of these contractors combed these three provinces, searching for crown land and land which might be proved to have been unlawfully alienated by the crown. They offered the tenants of such land slightly more than their obligations to the crown. Having acquired their leases by paying a small premium, they set about evicting the sub-tenants on the grounds that there was some legal imperfection in their title, even in one case when the sub-tenant could prove occupation under a lease for centuries.

Despite the outcry, Terray detached the rights and dues over the domain in the other provinces of France from the farmers-general and awarded the right of collecting them to his cronies, who had created the disturbances in the three northern provinces. Such was the outcry that Turgot repaid the advances of these contractors and passed the supervision of the royal domain to a government board, which boosted the revenue from 1.6 million to 4.1 million livres per annum.

In 1774 Terray sold the right to collect duties on mortgages, the registration and the sale of land and buildings to a group of contractors, who had agreed to advance a repayable loan of 8 million livres. The advance was repayable in equal annual instalments, so that by the last year only 1 million would remain outstanding. The interest charged was fixed at 480,000 livres, representing in the

---

[1] Schelle, op. cit., vol iv, p. 483–7.

last year a rate of 48 per cent. The contractors were also awarded a management fee of 480,000 livres per annum. Again Turgot repaid the advance and terminated the contract. The supervision of these dues was entrusted to a government board from whom he demanded an advance of 12 million livres and to whom he allowed interest at 6 per cent on the reducing balance.

The last financial reform of consequence affected by Turgot in 1774 was the suppression of an additional supplement of eight sols per livres (eight shillings in the pound) added by Terray in 1771 to the taxes on tobacco, wine, water and cloth. They were an increment to the taxes, collected by the farm but outside their contract concluded in 1768; in other words a straight gift to the farmers, which Turgot quashed.

In September 1774 Turgot wrote to the intendants about the *octrois*, indirect taxes, levied in municipalities. The exact origin, the assessment and the collection of many of these municipal taxes was uncertain and, consequently, the authorities and the farmers general had wide discretion. In most case these taxes were a hindrance to consumers and retailers alike, and, as many of them were so small in amount, they served solely as irritants. The real complaint against these taxes, was, in Turgot's words:

> The injustice with which nearly all the bourgeois of the towns, whom one might have imagined could have borne these taxes, have devised ways of exempting themselves from contribution to communal expenditure at the expense of the weakest inhabitants, the small traders and the country people . . . If, for example, a tax has been put on wine, care has been taken to impose them on wines consumed in bars and to exempt those consumed by the bourgeoisie . . . thus those who profit most from expenditure in towns are precisely those who contribute almost nothing to them.[1]

He asked the intendants for their ideas on the reform of the *octrois*.

The Farmers-general

Immediately after his appointment Turgot considered the operations of the farmers-general. The sixty farmers were immensely wealthy and they earned the description of the 'sixty pillars of state'. They enriched themselves more by lending to the state than by collecting revenue.

The tax farms had been established in their modern form by Colbert in 1681 as a means of collecting additional taxes without increasing the *taille*. The indirect taxes comprising the tax farm included the salt *gabelle*, the *aides*, or taxes on

---

[1] Ibid pp. 180–1.

commodities, the *traites*, or customs duties, the *domains*, or taxes on the royal domain, and a host of variations and local taxes. Of all these the *gabelle* was the most notorious. It was levied on families according to the amount of salt which they were deemed to have consumed in a year. In different provinces the *gabelle* was collected at different rates and these differences gave rise to an active smuggling trade. One estimate was that as many as 60,000 people from all levels of society were involved in this illegal trade and, according to Lavoisier, the farmers employed 21,000 people to prevent evasion of the *gabelle* and most of the other indirect taxes. The annual profit in 1774 of the farms amounted to 18.8 million livres, with each farm producing about 312,000 livres each.

In 1774, before the appointment of Turgot, a new six-year contract with the farmers had been negotiated by Terray. The bond, or permanent loan from the farmers to the state, was increased to 93 million livres and the annual payment to be made to the state was set at 152,000 livres.

Turgot disliked the tax farm system for several reasons: the government were able to increase the farmer's revenue by merely increasing the rates of the taxes collected; the indirect taxes collected by the farmers fell most heavily on the poor; the taxpayers were oppressed far more by the farmers, motivated by profit, than by the servants of the state, tempered by lesser rewards and inevitably by bureaucratic lethargy.

There were rumours that the new *contrôleur-général* was intending to break the contract before its expiry in 1780. He had no such plan. He recognised the contract as a species of private property, created by agreement.

However, Turgot examined the operation of the farmers-general and a few weeks after taking office he presented a paper to the king on the tax farms. He drew attention to the fact that the farmers had brought a large number of sleeping partners, – pensioners and relatives – into the contract. Among these parasites, numbering the friends and relatives of the farmers, were found five members of Terray's family, his lawyer and several people who may have been his nominees. Terray wanted to remunerate his nominees without drawing attention to the fact, by disguising their remuneration in the expenses of the farms. Turgot estimated that the amount lost to the state was at least 2 million livres per annum. There was nothing that could be done as Terray had committed the state to a contract and, having decided to leave it in being, Turgot could not quibble about the terms. He proposed to the king that in a future lease with the farmers only competent partners aged at least twenty-five should be allowed to be a party to the contract. Turgot felt that a public contract to do with collecting public revenue should not be regarded by the farmers as a private transaction in which they involved their relatives, friends and infants. The king advised the farmers accordingly.

Turgot did, however, curtail an irregular practice of the farmers-general. It involved the exemption of the Auvergne to the *gabelle*. The province had won the exemption early in the sixteenth century by paying a higher *taille*. In 1773, however, Terray had allowed the farmers to supply two towns in the Auvergne with salt. The Cours des Aides declared that the permission was unlawful, but in July 1774 Terray quashed their decision. Turgot had no hesitation in declaring the exemption of the Auvergne in respect of the *gabelle*.

The contract of 1774 was due to expire at the end of that decade. It covered indirect taxes which Turgot wished to abolish. Thus it was inevitable that the contract would have to be rescinded and the farmers-general's deposit of 93 million livres would have to be repaid out of a loan specially earmarked for the purpose of repayment.

In November 1775 Véri reported that Maurepas, Malesherbes and Trudaine were anxious that Turgot had decided to rescind and that he would bring the financial community into hostile opposition. But their fears were ungrounded as Turgot had decided to postpone rescission until he could afford to suppress the notorious *gabelle*, or tax on salt. He did not plan to repay the deposit of 93 million livres all at once, for, even if he could have raised that amount, it would have wrecked many of his other financial plans. 'Must I be disabled', he asked Véri, 'by not being able to find all the money at once? Is the injustice of waiting for full repayment comparable to the harm suffered by the people? As to loss of revenue, I believe that vigilance and economy will be possible without resort to unlawful measures. If there is a loss because illegality is brought to an end, then it must be borne and means must be found to make it good'.[1]

---

[1] Schelle, op. cit., vol v, p. 315.

14

The Restoration of Free Trade in Grain

On 13 September 1774, within three weeks of taking office, Turgot drew up his edict to restore free trade in grain. The Council of Ministers assented. The edict reversed the protectionism which Terray had re-established in December 1770. It was necessary to sweep away the laws and the regulations, which Turgot had encountered in the Limousin, in order to allow a free market to arise throughout France; sellers and buyers could do their business without intervention by either police or magistrates.

The day after the edict was published, Turgot met the British ambassador to France, Viscount Stormont, and they discussed trade. 'In a conversation I accidentally had with him at Compigne on the subject [of free trade],' reported Stormont,' upon mentioning that principle as one that many men in England espoused, he said with vivacity if you [England] set that example you would do essential service to mankind.'[1]

The edict did not restore free trade in Paris, then with a population of half a million, nor did it allow exports, though it did reserve a ministerial power to do so in the future. The reason for stopping short of full restoration of free trade was to prevent raising implacable opposition at the outset. The essential reform was to remove controls operating outside Paris, which had cut the national trade into a patchwork of local markets.

The introduction of free trade at the outset of his administration in 1774 has attracted two misconceived criticisms. First, that Turgot had rushed into this reform against the tenor of his earlier statement that free trade in grain was a revolution which operated slowly by degrees.[2] Turgot had been referring not to the introduction of free trade, but instead to its acceptance by producers, merchants, consumers, police and magistrates after its introduction. He had insisted throughout the previous decade that government should introduce free trade in grain without delay, and that, following its introduction, they should hasten its acceptance by proclaiming its application in every season.

---

[1] State Papers.
[2] L. Laugier, *Turgot et le Mythe des Reformes* [1979], p. 37; M. Keiner & Peyronnet, *Quand Turgot Régnait en Limousin*, p. 287.

The reason why Turgot chose to wait only three weeks before taking this step was due to his desire to encourage producers to sow their winter crops with greater confidence, since they now knew that they could look forward to selling throughout France rather than only in a local market. Not only have the critics misled themselves about the introduction of free trade, but they demonstrated political ignorance by suggesting that free trade should be introduced gradually. History shows that, in a matter so contentious, the introduction of free trade must be effected as quickly as possible, if it is to have any chance of success.

The second criticism of Turgot's measure was that the harvest of 1774 had been so mediocre that he had not chosen his moment well, because he must have known that there would be shortages and widespread demands for controls.[1] Turgot had seen conditions of famine much worse than those in 1774 and he had then argued that free trade in grain was more necessary at a time of famine than in times of prosperity and ease. For it was then that a poor province, such as the Limousin, should be saved from famine through importing supplies from the richer provinces of France, who were holding a surplus of grain. The worse the shortage of grain, the higher the price would go and the greater was the need for a free national market.

Had Turgot delayed with this reform, people might have protested and the magistrates might have responded with their customary blindness by reintroducing their old protectionist measures, the only effects of which would be to intensify the shortages of grain. Should Turgot have delayed his action in order to placate the magistrates, whose intervention in the grain markets was largely a matter of the selfish pursuit of power and attention? To have delayed would have been to put the poor provinces in a precarious situation unnecessarily for another year.

Though Turgot's edict was agreed on 13 September it was not announced for a week and Baudeau reported that there were contentious debates in the Council. What probably caused the trouble was the nine-page preamble in which Turgot explained how a free market spreads surpluses and shortages among the greatest number of people. Turgot read the preamble to Véri, who complained that it was long and simplistic. 'It will be found', Turgot explained, 'diffuse and boring . . . I wished to make the matter so clear that every local magistrate could make country people understand it. It is a question on which public opinion can count for much. I wanted also to publish at the outset my replies to the representations that the tribunals, intendants and provincial judges can raise with me. Finally, I wanted to make this truth so commonplace that none of my successors may be able to contradict it.'[2]

'I have been reading edicts for sixty years,' commented Voltaire. 'They have deprived us of nearly all our national liberty in an unintelligible language. Here

---

[1] E. Faure, *Le Disgrâce de Turgot* 1962; p. 1226, Laugier, op. cit. p. 37; G. Rudé, *Annals Histoire. de la Révolution Français* vol 3 [1958].

[2] Véri, op. cit. , vol i p. 201.

STATESMAN OF THE ENLIGHTENMENT

is one which restores our liberty and I understand the words without difficulty. Here is the first time that a king reasons with his people. Humanity holds the pen and the king signs.'[1] Writing at the beginning of November 1774 Métra recorded that 'The edict on the grain trade which M. Turgot has issued and of which he was the author caused a sensation and it still has lost nothing of its impact . . . the nation has read with delight words in this edict of propriety and of freedom, terms long struck out of the dictionaries of our kings.'[2]

Turgot wrote to the intendants, the *procureurs-généraux*, the judges of the tribunals and the presidents of the chambers of commerce asking them to explain to people in their districts the reasons for his edict and he instructed them that in no circumstances was the movement, storage or sale of grain to be subject to any official control or intervention.

The *parlement* of Rouen registered the edict but added a clause obliging the magistrates and the police to continue their supervision of the grain markets, in order to ensure that they were provisioned with sufficient grain. The effect of this added clause was to nullify the purpose of the edict altogether. It fell to the Keeper of the Seals, or minister of justice, to quash this clause by a fresh edict. But he was a parlementarian and in sympathy with the views, interests and prejudices of the magistrates. He attempted to explain the merit of the clause to Turgot. He warned that:

> The *parlement* will remonstrate . . . the people of Rouen, always anxious about their subsistence, always excited by the fear of going without bread, liable to blind panic, will start murmuring and the merchants of Rouen, who fear them, will not be willing to undertake their trade in grain for fear of becoming the object of the people's hate, abundance will not arise and your principal object will not be attained . . . [the quashing of the edict] will alarm the people; it will be denounced in the *parlements* who delayed registering [the original edict] only through fear of popular feelings . . . the dispute will begin, merchants will undergo the attacks to which they are naturally prone and your main object will fail. Do not imagine, Monsieur, I beg of you, that all I have said is dictated by the prejudices opposed to your views. I share your view of the heart of this important matter, but my knowledge of the Norman character, fourteen years of administrative experience in that province and the sincere desire which I entertain for the success of your views have all led me to present these observations.[3]

Turgot's edict contained a clause that the government would not operate again in the grain markets. This marked the end of a contract which Averdy had signed

---

[1] Lavisse, *Histoire de France* vol ix, p. 35.
[2] Schelle, op. cit. vol iv p. 222.
[3] Ibid, p. 220.

in 1764, between the state and a grain merchant, called Malisset. The purpose of this contract was that Malisset and other merchants should buy a hoard of grain for the Paris market in order to quieten the fears of famine among inhabitants of the capital, who were too close to the seat of government to be ignored. The contract provided that the government put up the money and the merchants managed the operation, in return for a 2 per cent commission on sales and purchases. It became known as the *pacte de famine*, because it was widely believed to exist only to profit the crown and to impoverish the people by removing grain from the provincial markets. In 1770 Terray had brought the whole operation under direct control and entrusted the day-to-day management to M. Sorin and M. Doumerc. After four years of operations it appears that they had lost more than 10 million livres of public money. This came to light in 1774, after some fishermen found several paper sacks weighted with heavy stones in the Seine. According to Métra, Sorin had feared an enquiry after the fall of Terray and had tried to lose the documents in his possession. From an inspection of the waterlogged documents, it was plain that the two merchants had used the money supplied to the grain operation for their own account. Nothing could be proved, except that there was a considerable loss after liabilities had been paid.

Turgot was more intent on liquidating the company than in pursuing the agents, who had been empowered to defraud the state. Whenever the agents of the government had entered a provincial market private merchants would not risk competing against them, because, knowing that the agents were backed by limitless resources, the private merchants knew also that they could afford to incur unlimited losses in an attempt to control the market.

France was the birthplace of both protectionism and free trade. In 1774 the French nation experimented for the second time with free trade under a minister who showed that free trade preserved the balance between producer, merchant and consumer.

15

The Recall of the *Parlements*

When Turgot was appointed *contrôleur-général* in August 1774 the *parlements* were still banned after the magistrates had been exiled under *lettres de cachet* issued by the ruling troika in 1770. The magistrates had been hustled into exile during the night by armed musketeers. When the nation awoke next day, it was prostrate before the harshness of the ministers. They were hated: Maupeou for his ruthless autocratic manner, Terray for his abject corruption, and La Vrillière for his harshness.

La Vrillière was feared for his unsparing resort to the *lettres de cachet*, by means of which a victim could be arrested and imprisoned or confined to a nunnery without legal redress. According to Métra, even 'a simple workman could obtain a *lettre de cachet* for five louis [120 livres]'.[1] Métra told the story of how a woman obtained a *lettre de cachet* against her husband with the assistance from her lover, who was a senior cleric. The officer charged with the arrest tipped off the husband, who fled. The troops arrived some nights later and seized the amorous cleric from the wife's bed. They refused to listen to any explanation which would bring dishonour on the lady's reputation and bore him away to prison.[2]

When Turgot had come into the Council of Ministers in July 1774, the king was already inclined to recall the *parlement*. The king realised that he could win immediate popularity from many quarters by restoring the *parlements*; from his brother, the comte d'Artois, and his cousin, the Prince de Conti, a *parlementaire*. Both members of his family were deeply committed to the recall of the *parlements*; from the nobles, whose flank was exposed to ministers, such as Turgot, determined to attack the whole fabric of venality and privilege; from the people, who seemed hypnotised by the ceremony and the empty words of the magistrates; and from Maurepas and his wife, whose families had been parlementarians for centuries. Louis XVI loved the applause of the people. But he was also minded to hold power in his own hands and he was counselled by the *dévots*, the church folk, not to recall the magistrates. The king was not a church man, but yet, out of

---

[1] Métra, *Correspondance Secrète*, vol ii, entry 13, July 1775.
[2] Ibid., vol iii, entry 27 August 1775.

respect for his late father's friendship with the Jesuits, he remained sympathetic to their demands.

After the dismissal of Terray and Maupeou, the Council of Ministers was divided over whether to recall the *parlements* or not. Maurepas and Miromesnil, both inveterate *parlementaires*, were in favour of recall, Vergennes and Du Muy, an ardent *dévot*, were against. The views of the other ministers were not so definite. A committee was formed of Maurepas, Miromesnil, Turgot and Sartine. Nothing is known of the deliberations of the committee and neither Véri nor Stormont, who both had ears close to the ground, even knew of its existence. In early September Stormont reported back about the move to restore the *parlements* to Lord Rocheford of the Northern Department of the Foreign Office in London: His Lordship replied: 'I am persuaded Your Excellency judges right in supposing that the Parlement, if restored, will abound in the strongest professions of loyalty and submission, but I am mistaken if they forget to revenge the injury they have received, at least to put it out of the king's power to reduce them again.'[1]

In mid-October 1774 the *lettres de cachet* against the magistrates were rescinded amid public rejoicing. The recall was made subject to conditions: in future the *parlements* would operate the law courts without interruption, they could remonstrate for only a month after the publication of an edict and, if they issued *arrêts* to quash the edicts of the Council, they would lose this right to remonstrate. Turgot's attitude to the recall was not disclosed and it has given rise to conjecture since. Carre, a French historian specialising in the eighteenth-century, was the first to question the belief that Turgot had resisted the recall.[2] He relied heavily on the correspondence between Condorcet and Voltaire, whom he imagined was privy to Turgot's thinking. Since Turgot had become a minister, he had been deluged by Condorcet with ideas and papers on many subjects, whether they came within Turgot's field of responsibilities or not. In the middle of August Turgot had written to Condorcet to quell this outpouring and told him, 'I cannot reply to all your follies.'[3] Turgot was not in touch with Voltaire and there is no reason to suppose that Voltaire had any idea of Turgot's views. As he does not appear to have discussed the question with Véri, who was much closer as a confidant than anyone, it would seem that Turgot held his peace.

If the existence of the committee was kept secret, it would have been wholly out of character for Turgot to have discussed the recall, even with his friends. Though the basis of Carre's argument, that Turgot had actually canvassed a return of the old *parlements*, is thin indeed, Dakin, Faure, Cobban and Laugier have accepted his findings and with it the implication that Turgot was naïve in not understanding the character of the *parlements*, or careless in his conscious disregard of the danger which they would pose. How as a reforming minister, they

---

[1] State Papers.
[2] *Révolution Français*, vol XLIII 1902, p. 193.
[3] Schelle, op. cit., vol iv, p. 86.

ask, could Turgot have compromised his planned reforms by canvassing the return of the praetorian guards of the *ancien régime*? If there was strong circumstantial evidence that Turgot had actually canvassed this move, then this question would have to be addressed. But there is no such evidence.

Laugier not only accepts Carre's argument, but also wanders into fiction by trying to reconstruct the workings of Turgot's mind: 'Inner debate . . . between his conscience which inclines him to refuse all accommodation with this cast whose power to damage he well knows and his personal interest which commands him to deal with it in order to please those to whom he owed his place and honours. It remains only to appease his conscience, which is no less important by finding fallacious reasons, but reason nonetheless sufficient for a volte-face.'[1] To attempt to reconstruct history by fiction is perilous. In the absence of direct evidence, Turgot's attitude towards the recall must be deduced from his past views on the *parlements*, which were remarkably consistent from the early 1750s. Plainly, Turgot had never been in doubt about the obstructive character of the parlements; it is quite unlikely that upon becoming *contrôleur-général* his vanity should have prevailed over his reason. Knowing the character of the *parlements*, it is out of the question that he would have positively supported their return. He must have realised that the king was in favour of the return and that his leading minister was pushing for the recall; *the steps for the recall were already in hand before his elevation to the Council.* It is most likely that he would have accepted the majority view of the committee, for he could not have reversed it. Thus he could concentrate only on framing the conditions attaching to the recall.

Stormont reported in late October, just prior to the recall, that, 'I am assured that M. Turgot and M. Sartine are not fond of the share they had in this business, and like to have it known that their share has been a small one, and that the whole was in a manner determined before they were called in . . . There is no doubt that Maurepas and Miromesnil have formed the whole plan.'[2] Véri also predicted the rise of the *parlements* and explained how they managed to cow the officials of state. 'The intendants of the provinces', he stated, '. . . are exposed to these [mandatory] orders [of the *parlements*] like any other citizen. In times of trouble of even simple parlementaire unrest, none of these officials can safely follow their usual ways nor execute the king's orders if it is frightened of displeasing *parlement*. Everyone is afraid of an arrest warrant, banishment and a note of dishonour because as a consequence civil effects are terrible until annulled by a new *arrêt*.'[3]

On 26 November the *parlements* reassembled amid scenes of amazing adulation. 'One need not be a prophet', Lord Rocheford assured Stormont, 'to say that this is the end of royal authority. This, the French king will find out, when it will be too late to recover a Power, which in my humble opinion he voluntarily throws

---

[1] Laugier, *Turgot et le Mythe des Reformes*, p. 163.
[2] State Papers, Letter dated 26 Oct. 1774.
[3] Véri, vol i, p. 213.

away.'[1] Such an assessment agreed with that of Lecky, the eighteenth century English historian:

> The restoration of the *Parlements* [by Louis XVI] appears to me to have been a capital mistake. It raised up without necessity an opposition to the Crown of the most dangerous and embarrassing description and at the same time enormously increased the difficulty of accomplishing the equalisation of taxation and commutation of the feudal system which were the two measures most absolutely necessary if a revolution was to be averted.[2]

The king reminded the magistrates that they had been exiled for defying the crown and they would be exiled again, if they repeated their defiance. It was a strong speech. But the magistrates were not contrite; they viewed themselves as the constitutional partners of the crown, rather than as the subordinate components of the state. But speeches of mild and loyal submission were uttered only to be seen as shallow pretences by anyone of sense. Stormont certainly was not deceived and he predicted that the magistrates 'will avail themselves of circumstances as they arise and, whenever there are divisions in the ministry, they will be the engine which one minister will play off against the other, and in which an old and dying minister (probably a reference to Maurepas) might perhaps wield in such a manner to establish his own power on the ruin of the king'.[3]

Within three weeks of their recall, the magistrates of the *parlement* of Paris remonstrated against the edict which had secured their recall – claiming they had been created originally by 'fundamental law'; they had no need to be 're-established' by the crown; they believed their power to remonstrate had been too severely curtailed; and they protested that the elevation of judicial powers to provincial appointees was unlawful. Thus some of the predictions had been fulfilled and the *parlement* had soon reverted to its traditional grooves. No one must have sensed the omens more than Turgot, who alone among the ministers, had entered the Council in order to reform some of the injustices of the *ancien régime*. The others in the Council aspired only to save their positions, their privileges and the interests of their friends and, consequently, feared only that the *parlement* would harm their petty self-interests.

It was ironic that Turgot had suffered the harsh administration of the troika while he was an intendant in the Limousin and could not enjoy freedom to introduce reforms as a minister while the 'boeuf-tigres', as he had called the magistrates of the *parlements*, were in exile. Now he was able at last to reform protection the reactionary magistrates had been released again.

---

[1] State Papers, 9 August 1774.
[2] W. E. H. Lecky, *History of England in the Eighteenth Century* [1882] Vol v chp20 p. 442.
[3] State Papers,16 Nov 1774.

16

Stirrings of Opposition

On 3 January 1775 Turgot had a severe attack of gout and, by continuing to work from his sickbed, caused complications in his chest. For three or four days he lay, according to Schelle, completely incapacitated within 'two fingers' of death. Two days later Julie Lespinasse wrote to Vaines: 'M. Turgot is a little better. I have had three pieces of news of him since I saw you [this morning] and I will receive as much again before midnight – that satisfies me without calming me – I have not gone out and I will not see anyone who tells me about balls and dancing. I will listen to talk only of M. Turgot, not with animated interest but with an interest for virtue and for fear of his successor. For myself he ceased to be *contrôleur général* two days ago; he is simply M. Turgot with whom I have enjoyed a friendship for the past seventeen years.'[1]

Gout was described by James Robertson, a contemporary English doctor, as follows: 'the attacks, which are known by the denomination of regular fits of gout; one or more joints of the extremities, become inflamed, painful and tender . . . When the fit goes off, the joints . . . are always found to have become rigid and inflexible, in proportion to the degree in which the disease has existed in them; frequently remaining enlarged and incapable of free motion for a considerable time.'[2] The usual treatment was blood letting with the aid of leeches.

Fortunately, the worst of the attack passed quickly and within four days he resumed his duties, though it was not for three months that he was fully mobile. One of his continuing concerns was the outbreak of foot-and-mouth disease which Stormont was at this time calling 'a national calamity'.[3] Du Pont describes the scene in Turgot's bedroom as he grappled with gout and how he managed to issue an eight-page memorandum to the intendants: 'As soon as a page was ready he dispatched it to the printer in Versailles. He was dictating, the proofs were brought up to him and he corrected them. The instructions were drawn up and printed during the course of a day and a night. He then dictated the letters which accompanied the instructions. He was well aware that it was endangering his life.

---

[1] Schelle, op. cit., vol iv, p. 280.
[2] J. Robertson, *Observations on the Nature and Cause of Gout.*
[3] State Papers.

116

The effort brought the gout up to his chest. He remained almost four months without being able to stand up.'[1] In March Métra reported, 'So far he has the complete confidence of the king. As he is indisposed with gout, he is carried in a chair into the chamber of His Majesty, where they work together for three hours at a time. The king loves to learn and Turgot is the means by which he can learn.'[2]

The foot-and-mouth outbreak generated much correspondence and required many administrative decisions to be reached during the first three months of 1775. Even if he had been fit the outbreak would have imposed a strain. It consumed attention which could have been spent on a number of pressing reforms. He hoped to stamp out the disease before the warmth of the summer encouraged its spread. By April 1775 the worst was past but the outbreak lingered for some months.

On 2 February Turgot approved a request, which had been sent to him by the intendant of Rouen, from a wife of a poor and weak husband to engage in a needlework business. Women had been barred from this trade for centuries by the guilds, whose monopolies Turgot was determined to set aside. Among the thousand daily administrative acts, this must have been especially enjoyable to Turgot, for the case involved the plainest injustice.

Stormont reported in early January 1775 that Turgot 'had an infinite number of secret enemies, who are constantly at work and may very probably undermine him at last. This is the more probable because he is not qualified for such a struggle and is much better acquainted with administration than men. All the financiers are in open opposition to him . . . are constantly trying to stab him in the dark.'[3] Indeed after only a few months, it had become clear that he had attracted opposition from many quarters. Many critics of Turgot accuse him of deliberately attracting the opposition and blame him for that. His enemies believed it was a fault to contemplate reform, rather than enjoy the privileges of the *ancien régime.*

The magistrates did not thank him, a former magistrate himself, for having terminated their intervention in the grain markets by re-establishing free trade, because it was in this field of activity that they won the gratitude of the people. One of the leading magistrates was the prince de Conti, a prince of the royal blood and a descendant of a lesser branch of the Bourbons. In January the king had written asking the prince to stay out of the affairs of the *parlement* in order to prevent him leading the attack on the conditions attached to the recall of the *parlements.* Perhaps Conti saw the mind of Turgot directing the pen of the king, because from that time he began showing his dislike of Turgot.

The nobility distrusted Turgot because he, the descendant of nobility, was bent on fundamental reforms, which threatened their privileges. They imagined

---

[1] Schelle, op. cit., vol iv, p. 279.
[2] Ibid. p. 282.
[3] State Papers.

themselves to be a race apart from lower orders of society and entitled to the privileges awarded to them. Words such as liberty and justice did not find inclusion in their vocabulary. The condition or welfare of the people did not attract the focus of their thinking. The notion of reform was believed to be a sign of insanity. The proper task of a nobleman was to look after his fellows and their privileges.

The Church feared a thinking minister, a former theological student, who made a show of his religious tolerance – tolerance being deemed an attack on the Church – for it desired a monopoly of religious belief. The king was informed that his *contrôleur-général* never went to mass and this disturbed him sufficiently to mention it to Maurepas. He reminded the king that the abbé Terray, the hated minister, had gone to mass every morning!

The farmers-general and the financiers feared that Turgot might do without need of their loans and services. Their wealth consisted of their power to harass taxpayers. That power depended on Turgot while he remained *contrôleur-général*.

The courtiers, who feasted at Versailles like shrimps round a sewage pipe, were suspicious of a minister, who had no interest in their ways. They were concerned that Louis XVI was depending increasingly on Turgot. They were particularly troubled that he seemed able to bring forth a sentiment of justice in Louis which they regarded a most unkingly virtue.

In short, there was a general wariness of a minister in whom could be found no respect for privilege, no trace of the esprit of *parlement*, no reverence for religion nor scent of the court. Much of the fear of the magistrates, the nobility, the Church, the financiers and the courtiers was what Turgot was about to do, rather than what he actually had done. These various bodies depended for their existence upon injustice and corruption. Most were simpletons on stilts but, when defending their interests, they were vicious in their wickedness.

'The courage of M. Turgot, being reduced to face the complaints of all these people, has been found more than sufficient. He has strengthened the king in his principles by his letters and also in person,' recorded Véri.[1] In 'a country where abuses and corruption are so inveterate it is not surprising that a minister of integrity should attract opposition'.[2] The opposition to Turgot was general at the beginning of 1775, but it lacked focus.

During the spring, when grain prices rose after a poor harvest of the previous year, the people could no longer call on the intervention of the police and magistrates to deal with merchants and middlemen. 'The French nation has been so thoroughly disciplined over centuries to take no steps without crutches, that she no longer knew how to walk unaided.'[3]

In March there was a riot at Cherbourg where grain was being loaded for the

---

[1] Véri, vol i, p. 287.
[2] State Papers.
[3] P. Foncin, *Essai sur le ministere de Turgot*, p. 184.

navy and for other ports. Turgot had always acted swiftly to suppress public disorder and he instructed the intendant to use troops to arrest the ringleaders. A few days later he confirmed prison sentences on five rioters, ranging from two weeks to a few months. He was unhappy that the intendant at Cherbourg had taken no steps to publicise the reason for the edict on the freedom of the grain trade in his province. In La Rochelle the police ordered an inspection of stocks of corn and imposed a freeze on sales. On hearing of these measures Turgot quashed them immediately by an *arrêt*. In the last days of March and throughout April disorders occurred in Evry, Metz and Rheims.

On 18 April a larger riot broke out in Dijon over discontent at grain prices, but it lacked grounds of protest, direction and public passion. The governor was saved from the mob by the gallant intervention of a bishop, the property of a magistrate was invaded, the premises of a miller were ransacked, stocks of grain were pillaged and a certain amount was thrown into the river. On hearing that the rioters had destroyed stores of grain, Turgot suspected that the riot had been orchestrated by opponents of his policy of free trade. In fact there was evidence to show that the miller was suspected of mixing grain flour with vegetable flour and the mob had thrown away his adulterated supplies.

Days after the riots in Dijon, Turgot reduced taxes levied on grain sold in the towns of that area and he announced subsidies for grain imported into France for the next harvest. In the edict containing these measures, Turgot reminded the magistrates and the police that they were forbidden to intervene in the grain markets.

On 20 April Necker published a pamphlet on the grain trade entitled *La Legislation et Le Commerce des Grains* which became a best-selling success almost immediately. It attempted to present an alternative to the unpopular policy of Turgot. Necker repeated the exaggerated and empty verbosity, which he had employed in his *Éloge* of Colbert, to attack Turgot. In the introduction of his essay, he takes the reader off on what he believes is a glorious and noble pursuit of truth. Instead it was verbose, vain and empty:

> Everywhere truth seems to flee or to wish to tire him who follows her; she seems to refuse herself to all simple and general notions by surrounding herself with exceptions, reserves and modifications; it is in vain to seek her and seize her . . . Men who meditate in their office full of praiseworthy desire to enlighten the world, but too easily disposed to believe that it is always lack of intelligence that makes government imperfect, hurry to untie the gordian knot, establish a principle, generalise it, push it to the extreme and by this extending its authority, they weaken it, denature it . . . it is also a type of abstract courage which, far removed from the world of men, attacks and surmounts all difficulties by the force of reason and the power of truth . . . It is in the midst of this

continual clash; of interests, principles and opinions that the legislator must seek the truth.[1]

Necker argued that Turgot's edict of September 1774 showed 'that the king does not owe the provision of essential subsistence to his subjects ... if one intends that the sovereign must be insensible to the laws which can assure abundance in the kingdom and prevent the divergence between the price of goods and that of work; if one may counsel him to abandon blindly these matters to the pretensions of ownership and to the caprices of liberty; this may be in my opinion a great error and it may pretend that a sovereign must be insensible to the most essential circumstance of the multitude and to public order.'[2]

Necker was a protectionist who believed that the king should exercise, in addition to all the regulations of markets, his power to hold down prices. Having put Turgot's method of free trade to one side, as those of a heartless thinker, he called for a genius to balance the opposing interests of producer and consumer, insinuating that he was a man of that stamp.

Necker's actual proposals, which figure as footnotes to his flowing prose, were three: export should be allowed only when the domestic price had fallen below 30 livres the setier [in other words, when it was cheap]; in the towns bakers should be required to carry minimum levels of stock; and, finally, that when the price had passed 30 livres, grain should be sold only in the official markets, in order to prevent the price being driven higher by speculation.

It would seem that he had chosen a middle course between the extremes of free trade and protection; that is to say, enjoyment of free trade when prices were low and the security of the old protective measures when prices rose beyond acceptable levels. But, as Turgot had pointed out on numerous occasions, it was precisely when the price rose that the poorest required free trade to attract grain and, so, drive prices down. If the magistrates were hovering over markets, waiting for prices to meet intervention levels, merchants and growers would not risk undertaking substantial operations. Free trade and protection are not compatible systems, nor can they ever work, as it were, in parallel. But the real weakness in Necker's argument lay in the role he reserved for the enlightened and disinterested minister. He was thinking of himself in that role.

The minister, who intervenes in a market as a well-intentioned pragmatist, in order to balance the different interests of producers and consumers, is a fool, like someone putting his hand down his throat in order to supervise his digestion. For once the forces of protectionism have been unleashed, no minister can restrain them before they contaminate the life blood of commerce. But Necker was not preoccupied with the mere question of the grain trade; he was spurred on by

---

[1] M. Necker, *Les Oeuvres* vol 1 [1820], pp. 3–9.
[2] Ibid.

boundless resources of vanity and ambition. His heart was set on office: on the position of *contrôleur-général*. The attack on free trade in the grain trade was only a stepping stone to that coveted position.

Three days after the essay was published Turgot wrote to Necker: 'If I had written on this subject and had I believed it my duty to defend the opinion which you embrace, I would have waited for a quieter moment when the question aroused the interest only those in a state to judge the matter without passion. But on this point, as on others, everyone has his own way of thinking.'[1]

Necker replied to say that he had delivered his manuscript on 12 March 1775, when there had been no troubles, and he even stated that the official censor form proved this date. He would have been ready to postpone publication if he had been asked to do so. But, plainly, if Turgot had advised Necker to hold up the publication, his well-known belief in a free press would have been compromised publicly. According to Morellet, the essay had been finished in September of the previous year and when he offered to read it over to him, Turgot had declined to avail himself of that opportunity, he had advised Necker to put it before the public.

It may be that the outbreak of riots and the publication of this essay coincided accidentally, and there is no direct evidence to suggest that they did not. But both attacks on Turgot's policy of free trade were complimentary; one was mounted by the people with violence and the other with argument. They indicated the beginning of the conspiracy against Turgot. It achieved nothing but it threatened something more sinister and dangerous in the wind.

Condorcet described the marshalling of the forces opposed to Turgot. It was composed of those 'who have not been treated by him as they would have desired; those who feared his reforms; the financiers who see him with unease open eyes to the abuses of their administration; the magistrates large and small and the majority of the police whom liberty had deprived them a large part of a cherished influence on the people; those who would wish to have a share in government and finally those who would like to dismiss him. All these have come together to raise complaints.'[2]

---

[1] Schelle, op. cit., vol iv, p. 412.
[2] Véri, vol ii, p. 281.

17

La Guerre des Farines

Hardy, a French diarist, noted in his unpublished journal that, after the grain riot in Dijon in April 1775, strangers from the provinces had begun to linger at the grain markets in Versailles and Paris. Their presence spread disquiet. On 27 April trouble broke out at Beaumont-sur-Oise, about twenty miles north of Paris, and the riots, which broke out in the region around Paris during the next fortnight, have come to be known as *la guerre des farines* [the flour war]. This was the beginning of a serious protest against Turgot.

The movement in the price of bread since the last harvest provides an unlikely background for grain riots; from August 1774 to the first week of March 1775 the price remained static at 11 sous for a 4 lb loaf, in mid-March it had risen to 12 sous and by mid-April to 13 sous. After riots at Dijon the price reached a peak of 13.5 sous. Under the corrupt administration of Terray the price reached 16 sous, but at that time there had been no grain riots.

Beaumont-sur-Oise was an unremarkable location for the riots. It was not situated in a poor region. The town was near Paris, which was to be the rioters' destination. The town was also close to the country home of the prince de Conti, who was rumoured to have been one of the anonymous leaders.

Prince de Conti detested the liberal spirit of Turgot. Once a dog relieved itself on a carpet by a fireplace at the prince's home. As someone went to beat it, Conti stopped him saying, 'Liberty, liberty, complete liberty.'[1]

The rioters who gathered there were less ready to loot stocks of corn and property than they had been in Dijon, and they seemed intent on demanding bread and flour at 2 sous a pound, which was well below the market level. This demand, which might have seemed to provide immediate relief, would have destroyed the free market in grain. If the real purpose of the demand for cheaper bread was to wreck Turgot's policy, it was well conceived. For the demand appeared mild and uncontentious.

On 29 April a mob moved up the Oise to Pontoise where they frightened the authorities into fixing a price for flour below 2 sous per pound and threw the

---

[1] *Revue d' Historie Économique* vol 131[925], pp. 314–33.

cargo of two grain vessels bound for Paris into the river. Métra recorded a most interesting account on encountering a mob of 12,000–15,000 peasants near Pontoise: 'We observed that they stopped at each mill which they demolished in an instant and they threw corn, flour and bran into the river. I heard a small priest who exhorted them 'Loot everything, my friends, God wishes it. Destroy all so that we can have food' ... [After readily accepting a drink of wine the priest explained] 'My friends, I am more at home in the parish. Some of my colleagues and I are leading these dear people, we have received money for this worthy task; we are throwing away all the corn which we find for fear of starvation; we are going to cut the throats of the bakers in Paris in order to maintain the fundamental laws of the kingdom.'[1]

From there they moved slowly towards Paris looting grain supplies as they went through Poissy and St. Germain. They changed course from Paris to Versailles, where the king was in residence. At eleven o'clock on the morning of 2 May the king wrote to Turgot to describe the situation there: 'I am going to confer with [the minister of war] to decide what we are going to do. You can count on my firmness. I have just dispatched the guards [there were 10,000 at Versailles] to the market place. I am very happy with the precautions which you have taken in Paris. It was on account of these that I was most afraid ... You will be quite right to arrest those of whom you have spoken [the ringleaders]. Above all when you are holding them under arrest do not be in a hurry and question them thoroughly.'[2]

Three hours later the king wrote a second letter to Turgot: 'As for us here, we are absolutely quiet. The riots started being lively but the troops calmed things down and the rioters conducted themselves peacefully in their presence. M. Beauvau [the captain of the guard] questioned them. Some told him that they were from Sartouville and Carrière-Saint-Denis and others replied that they were from more than twenty villages. Most said that they had no bread, that they had come to get some and they produced some very poor bread made of barley which they bought for 2 sous ... The greatest error was that the market had not been kept open; for, when it was open, everything went extremely well. People bought and sold as if nothing was wrong ... I am not going out today, not through fear, but to allow everything to quieten down. M. Beauvau has just interrupted me in order to tell me about a stupid thing that has just happened; the rioters have been given bread at two sous a pound. He pretends that there was no choice between that and forcing them by bayonet to buy at the market price. The market here is over. But the greatest precautions must be taken to prevent them returning to lay down the law. Let me know what these should be. For this is very awkward.'[3]

Turgot had always been quick to assert the crown's authority and to pay

---

[1] Métra, *Correspondence* vol ii, p. 274.
[2] Schelle, op. cit., vol iv, pp. 416–17.
[3] Ibid.

compensation to those damaged whenever the public peace was threatened. For a demonstration or a riot usually attracted attention and bystanders were apt to be drawn in, thus strengthening it.

As the rioters worked their way to the capital, it became plain that the immediate aim of the rioters was to cause an artificial shortage of grain and flour in Paris, by frightening merchants and bakers into inactivity. If this aim had succeeded, then it would have been comparatively simple to blame the *contrôleur-général* for the apparent shortage of grain. Accordingly, Turgot prepared for their arrival. First, he consulted Biron, the commander of the army, and Lenoir, the lieutenant of police. He stressed to them the cardinal importance of keeping the bakers and the grain markets open. Second, he announced that a boat owner, whose grain cargo had been pillaged on the Oise, was paid 50,000 livres as compensation and that owners of grain in Paris suffering damage from rioters would be compensated in the same way. Third, he advised the king to write to the first president of the Paris *parlement* in the following terms: 'Stocks of grain had been pillaged, read the king's letter, in several markets around Paris in circumstances which give me good reason to believe that these riots have been fomented by persons with evil intentions. I have taken the most effective measures to assure the provisioning of Paris and the outlying markets by putting to an end the fears of those who supply the markets. As every step taken by my *parlement* would only increase alarm, I order you to instruct them that I am watching over everything . . .'[1]

The king feared the riots in Paris would pose a greater threat to order than those in Versailles and he asked Turgot to return to the capital in order to finalise preparations. Turgot's strategy was to keep the bakeries open at all costs. He dispatched a courier from Versailles to Maurepas in Paris with the instructions of the king. Maurepas was at the opera that evening.

During the night troops were patrolling the countryside around Paris, yet at about seven o'clock on the morning of 3 May a party of nearly 500 rioters including a large number of women, children and transvestites entered Paris, intending, according to Hardy, to break into the central market in order to steal or split open the sacks of grain being stored there. When they found that the market was heavily guarded they began looting the bakers' shops – there were about 1,300 such shops in Paris – and breaking into those which had been boarded up. Some bakers transferred their stocks to adjoining properties, but the rioters soon became wise to this manoeuvre. Sometimes bakers were offered the price of 2 sous a pound for bread, less for flour, and sometimes the stocks, together with any cash, were stolen. Even butchers and *pâttisseries* reported thefts.

'What was really very difficult to understand', reported Hardy, 'and was really astonishing to see was a mutinous mob doing absolutely whatever it wished

---

[1] Ibid, p. 420.

without hindrance and without any step being taken to prevent all that had been foreseen the previous evening. Several officials, having gone to the office of Lenoir in order to warn him of what was happening and to see what was to be done, were told by him that he had no orders and that things must be allowed to go their own way.'[1]

Troops and police stood by while looting was going on before their eyes and were seen joking with rioters. Most of the officers of the *Gardes Françaises* had gathered in the cathedral of *Nôtre Dame* for the blessing of their banners. Biron, their commander, had been advised by Maurepas that morning to go ahead with their ceremony, despite the threat to public order. A zealous group of young musketeers shut a dozen rioters in a cellar. When they turned them over to the police they were told that the police had no orders to make arrest.

By about eleven o'clock the rioters had gone to every baker in the city centre and after lunch there was little else for them to accomplish. Turgot arrived in Paris from Versailles in the late morning, by which time there was not a loaf to be had in the whole of Paris. Outside his office a small crowd were protesting at the price of bread and were holding up pieces of bread which they had bought in the market. When these samples were later examined, they were found to have been cooked earlier that day and mixed with some substance to give them a revolting green colour. Turgot summoned Lenoir and Biron to discover why, in view of his advanced instructions, a mob had been allowed to run riot through the capital. Turgot was not satisfied by their answers.

After lunch the troops were stationed at strategic points and Lenoir issued an ordinance supporting the right of bakers to sell at the market price and ordering the police to arrest anyone interfering with the bakers' trade. During the afternoon the police made about forty arrests. The rioters dispersed, having attained their desired object of throwing the bakery trade into fearful inactivity. They had played their role and, if the government were to be kept under further pressure, other agents were needed to maintain the riots.

The *parlement* met during the afternoon to consider the events and the first president read the king's letter requesting *parlement* to stay out of the affair. The magistrates instructed their first president to tell the king how devotedly they supported him at this time.

Turgot returned to Versailles during the evening. His report of what had happened that day persuaded the king to call an extraordinary Council, which went on sitting until the early hours of the next morning. At Turgot's instigation the Council dismissed Lenoir, although, as a protégé of Maurepas, he seemed invulnerable, and other police chiefs. Albert was appointed in his place. Turgot wrote to Lenoir next morning, 'I do not hide from you that I have proposed to the king your dismissal and the nomination as lieutenant of the police someone

---

[1] *Hardy's unpublished journal* Bibliothèque Nationale Paris.

with a character more appropriate to the present needs.'[1] The army was split into four commands: Biron retained command of those in Paris and the others were deployed on the banks of the upper and lower Seine and the Marne to protect grain vessels bound for the capital. Turgot wrote to Lenoir to explain the reasons for his dismissal: 'I am persuaded that you had done what you could to prevent the troubles of the previous day. But these troubles occurred and I do not doubt that the policing facilitated an event, which in my view was easy to prevent, as everything was announced the previous evening and we had agreed on the measures to be taken . . . These measures were not put into effect, as you know; you have been badly served. Without making a crime of it, the situation is so crucial and tranquility is essential at present in order to assure the subsistence of the inhabitants and town of Paris . . . I regard it a strict duty not to leave anything to chance and not to risk a second day like today. I will not conceal from you that I have proposed your dismissal to the king and the appointment of someone as lieutenant of the police with a character more appropriate to the present circumstances.'[2] Lenoir opposed the policy of free trade in grain and it is clear that his sympathies lay with the opponents of Turgot's policy, be they found in the *parlements* or on the streets.

It is clear that there was no mob running around Paris on the 4th, as on the previous day, but rioters did re-appear and a number of scuffles were followed by arrests, sentries were insulted, paving stones torn up and placards were put up declaring, 'If the price of bread does not come down and if the ministry is not changed, we will exterminate the king and all the household of Bourbon.'[3] Two soldiers were placed on guard outside each bakery shop and it was evident that on this occasion they were ready to deal with any trouble. They were kept on this duty for the following five months.

Despite the compliant note of the *parlement* on the previous day, the magistrates were troubled by the news that arrests had been made and convened the following day to consider what they should do. Their worry was that trial procedures were being introduced without their participation. The magistrates passed an arrêt reserving to *parlements'* courts jurisdiction to try all matters arising out of the riots and they added a paragraph designed to undermine the king's stand against the riots: 'the king will be implored very humbly to take more and more measures which will inspire in him his care and his love for his people in order to lower the price of grain and bread to a level more appropriate to the needs of the people and thus to remove from evil men the pretext and the occasion which they abuse in order to excite peoples' minds.'

The magistrates also refused to register a royal declaration reserving criminal proceedings arising from the riots to another court called La Tournelle. The *arrêt*

---

[1] Schelle, op. cit., vol iv, pp. 425–6.
[2] Ibid, p. 427.
[3] Lavisse, *La Régne de Louis XVI* vol 9 pp. 33–4.

enacted by *parlement* had been sent to their printers, so that copies could be posted up to give the impression that the parlement could initiate measures. The effect, and probably the purpose, of the *arrêt* was to continue the unrest, if not the riots, as the bakers would almost certainly refuse to sell their bread below the market price. The Council, at Turgot's insistence, no doubt, ordered that the printers' impression of the arret be destroyed and posters already put up should be covered by the ordinance forbidding anyone demanding bread at a price below the market level. In order to set up the special courts, despite the opposition of the *parlement*, Turgot persuaded the king to exercise his prerogative power to hold a *lit de justice*, or exercise of royal prerogative, whereby a royal enactment became a binding law, despite the refusal of the *parlement* to register it. The magistrates were summoned to Versailles in their black robes to hear the king override their opposition. The reason for bringing those arrested before special courts, was to avoid the tedious delays and partiality of leading proceedings before the courts of *parlements*; the special courts could get to the heart of the matter and punish the offenders swiftly, in order to stamp out the remaining sparks of the riots. The Keeper of the Seals explained the temporary need for these courts:

> Mobs of ruffians are spreading through the countryside, entering towns in order to commit disorders which it is necessary to suppress with the greatest expedition; their itinerary seems linked; their coming is announced; public rumours indicated the day, the hour and the places where they were to commit their violations. It would seem that a plan had been formulated to desolate the countryside, to intercept navigation on rivers and to prevent the transport of grain by road in order to bring about starvation of cities and of Paris in particular . . . and if the king had not take the swiftest and the most just measures in order to arrest the disorder, which is as dangerous in itself as it is cruel in its effects, His Majesty would find himself in the sad necessity of multiplying indispensable examples which are only really effective when they are made without delay.[1]

The king addressed the magistrates in a firm manner and his commands were accepted. 'Some demanded the old regulations', wrote the king to Turgot, 'but the majority backed down a great deal from their impertinence of yesterday and were afraid. I hope that will give us some peace . . . But as from misfortune one sometimes gains some good; from this it will have been that I am not as weak as some believe and that I will be able to effect what I resolve to do. The truth is that I am more embarrassed by one man than by fifty . . . It is really dreadful that our suspicions are confirmed already and that the very embarrassing decision has to

---

[1] Schelle, op. cit., vol iv, p. 425.

be taken but unfortunately it is not these only who have said as much. I hope for my good name that it is only malicious rumours.'[1] The king was referring, it would seem, to someone in the royal family, whose connection with the riots would be damaging to the crown. He could have been referring to his brother, but the most likely person appeared to be the prince de Conti. Shortly afterwards the king wrote to Turgot, reiterating his determination to have the riots exposed: 'The people have opened their eyes and realise that they have been deceived . . . I would very much like to discover the leaders of this odious machination.'[2]

The riots continued on the path south-east of Paris and attracted the support of country people. In two towns the troops prevented disorder breaking out. There was less pillage and the mob confined themselves to demanding bread at 2 sous a pound. By 10 May the riots had petered out. Soulavie, a contemporary historian, who had followed the disorder, reported that the rioters had distributed fake decrees in the name of the Council ordering farmers to sell their grain at half price, and that in the regions of the riots there was no shortage of grain in the markets. The rioters had entered Paris hoping to create shortages. Like many observers, he believed the riots had been orchestrated as a protest against Turgot's policy on the grain trade, though in appearance they might seem to have been a spontaneous rising by the country people.

Turgot sent a memorandum to the priests in the provinces in order to expose the real nature of the riots and to explain the principles of his edict on the grain trade:

> The maintenance of public order is a law as much of the gospel as of the state, and everything which disturbs it, is equally criminal before God and before man . . . The riots were not caused by an actual shortage of corn and, in the regions where the riots broke out, the markets were well provisioned. Nor was it caused by distress . . . The riots were not the result of misery either . . . The disorders in country districts had been incited by men who were strangers to the parishes which they had come to destroy. Sometimes these perverted men, concerned only with stirring up minds, did not want the grain pillaged even for their own account and at other times they took the grain for their own profit, doubtless to resell another day and thus satisfy their greed . . . the mischief has gone as far as burning barns full of corn and entire farms. It seems that the aim of this plot has been to create a real famine in the provinces around Paris and in Paris itself, in order to arouse the people by need and despair to wild excess. The method, employed by these enemies of the people, has been to incite them to pillage everywhere by claiming to be the defenders of

---

[1] Ibid, pp. 428–9.
[2] Ibid, p. 442.

the people. In order to seduce the people, some pretended that the views of the king were hardly favourable to the welfare of his people . . . others . . . have not been afraid of circulating the rumour that the king approved of their conduct and wished that the price of bread was lowered . . . One of their most cunning tricks has been to sow division between the different classes of citizens and to accuse the government of favouring the rich at the expense of the poor . . . Destructive projects attributed to the government, false anxieties maliciously aggravated, slander of the most respectful names have all been employed by these treacherous men to serve their passions and their designs . . . The farms which have been pillaged and the shops which have been devastated constituted a resource available for difficult times and would have provided the food until the next harvest.[1]

He asked the priests to tell their parishioners the truth about these riots in order to encourage them to co-operate with the police and the troops.

Julie Lespinasse wrote to Condorcet shortly after the riots: 'You will have been told of all the troubles of these last days and that they occurred as if they had been spontaneous. Our friend [Turgot] has remained calm in the midst of the storm; his courage and clear head have not left him. He has worked day and night and I die of fear that his health may give way under the strains . . . The king has shown much wisdom, good sense and firmness throughout the affair.'[2]

Eight days after the trials had begun before the special courts no verdicts had been returned and La Vrillière asked the senior judge, Papillon, the reason for the judicial inaction. The court responded immediately by condemning two rioters, one a gauze-maker and the other a wig-maker, to death by hanging. The purpose of the courts was to elicit guilt among ringleaders rather than punish the followers with death, and, not surprisingly, on the day of the hanging a general amnesty was issued to all those who had joined the rioters, provided that they returned to their homes and made full restitution of money or grains stolen. About 100 arrests had been made but no evidence of a plot was discovered. As late as 11 May the king was still keen to expose the ring leaders. But thereafter the matter was dropped, and neither Du Pont nor Condorcet dwelt on the origins of the riots in their biographies of Turgot.

An explanation, which confirms the existence of a plot and throws light on the sudden abandonment of its investigation, is supplied by Weber, the foster brother of Marie-Antoinette, who wrote, 'The mercy of the king wished to hush up the investigation of the sedition.'[3] Weber's opinion was shared by Soulavie, who wrote, 'The king, when he had collected more information and become more

---

[1] Ibid., pp. 436–40.
[2] Ibid., p. 452.
[3] Weber, *Mémoires* vol i, p. 84.

cautious, resolved to conceal the causes of the riots. He burnt with his own hand the notes and the papers which he had received on the matter. In the Council there was sufficient wisdom to preserve silence in regard to these political crimes which would be difficult to prove and dangerous to punish.'[1] Dupuy, speaking almost a decade after these events, was unable to penetrate the mystery. 'Will the lamp of history', he wondered, 'one day bring to bear so sure a light on one of the strangest events of the century in order to reveal its origin, its mind, its secret agents? Perhaps it is desirable on all counts that it should be buried in the obscurity in which it was conceived.'[2]

Professor Rudé has made a detailed study of these riots[3] and concluded that they had been evidence of spontaneous protests against the unfair price of bread. Rudé also was persuaded by the price rise in grain on the eve of the riots. He pays no regard to the wider factors outside the actual riots, such as the opposition of the *parlements*, the financiers, Necker and the court against Turgot; the circumstantial evidence and the opinions of many credible observers – factors which point to a concerted rather than a spontaneous rising. By concentrating only on the riots, Rudé excluded much of the relevant evidence and adduces too little to establish his conclusion that the riots were spontaneous movements. Faure argues along the same line to the same conclusion but he goes to further lengths to cast doubt on several factors, which have often been cited as evidence of a conspiracy. While he may have presented the falsity of some of these factors, he does not cast any greater doubts on the conspiracy theory than Rudé.

The instigators were probably led by the Prince de Conti and included a great many leading figures, including Necker, who wished to see the end of Turgot and his revolutionary ideas. Métra recorded that the flour riots 'did not originate directly from the people, but from a wicked and powerful cabal'.[4] Véri reported six months after the riots that it was believed the Prince de Conti had been the leader of the riots.[5] De Tocqueville thought they had been planned.[6]

Immediately after the riots preparations were in hand for the coronation. The king, who loved popularity, did not want to cloud the event, which promised to be a popular celebration, with the shadows of the riots. It was enough for the king that the riots had been quashed so swiftly. Perhaps it was not only the complicity of the royal prince which had frightened the king, but of a large number of other leading figures. This explanation is consonant with the initial desire of the king and Turgot to get to the bottom of a conspiracy and the abrupt termination of their interest and the almost complete lack of comment by Du Pont, who was acting as Turgot's personal assistant at that time and who would surely have

[1] Soulavie, *Memoires of the reign of Louis XVI* trans. [1802] vol 11, p. 29.
[2] *Acadèmie des Inscripition*, vol 45 pp. 121–45.
[3] *Annales Historiques de la Révolution Française* vol 28, p. [1958].
[4] Métra, *Correspondance*, 3 May 1775.
[5] Véri, vol ii, 20 Dec. 1775.
[6] Tocqueville, *Coup d'Oeil Sur La Règne de Louis XVI*.

known the truth, and the absence of speculation by Condorcet, who must have known or suspected it.

Marie-Thérèse, the Empress of Austria, dismissed the riots in a letter to Marie-Antoinette, her daughter as 'just one of those troublesome events by which this century is marked too much ... In general this spirit of mutiny is beginning to become familiar everywhere; it is the consequence of our enlightened century.'[1] Her main purpose in writing, however, was to order her daughter to sleep in the marital bed, for it was widely rumoured that she had moved into a room of her own. Her marriage had not yet been consummated.

The king of Sweden wrote to Turgot a few weeks after the riots to offer his admiration for the way the freedom of the grain trade had been defended in France: 'It is to posterity above all that someone like yourself ... must invite judgement of their actions.' To which Turgot replied immediately, 'I have no other merit, Sire, except that of invariably serving principles which theory and experience have shown me over many years and whose certitude are known to Your Majesty better than anyone. If the efforts by which one has attempted to put them into practice have not been in vain, this success has been due entirely to the firmness which the king has shown and which he has drawn from the purity of his views and the love of his people.'[2]

[1] Mercy-Argentau *Correspondance entre Marie-Thérèse et le comte de Mercy-Argentau* vol ii letter 2 June 1774.
[2] Schelle, op. cit., vol iv, pp. 471–2.

18

The Coronation

The king decided on a traditional ceremony at Rheims, spread over a week of expensive celebrations. Turgot, who had to find the money amounting to about 7 million livres, had suggested that the coronation should be held in Paris, in order to save expense. The coronation was an important moment for the king and nation as it marked a departure from the disorder of the previous reign. A move to Paris would end the traditional superstition that Rheims possessed miraculous powers.

There was a coronation oath which was openly offensive to Protestants. French kings had been swearing for many coronations to 'exterminate entirely from my States all heretics specially condemned by the Church'. The oath was in conformity with the spirit of religious intolerance in France.

Turgot drafted a new set of oaths which omitted reference to religious heretics. Turgot proposed he should promise to 'govern my kingdom according to justice and to laws; to go to war only for a just and indispensable cause; to employ my authority to maintain the rights of each of my subjects; to defend them against all oppression, and to labour all my life to make them as happy as it is possible for me to do.' Turgot proposed that in addition the king should promise 'that all churches may count on my protection and my justice'.[1]

On the eve of his coronation, which was to take place on 15 June 1775, the king replied to Turgot's proposals:

> I have not had you summoned, Monsieur, in order to give you my response to your letter of yesterday, because I prefer to give you a written statement of my pledge of my thinking on your ideas at the moment. I think the proposals, which you have made on my behalf, are those of a very honest man, who is deeply attached to me. I am most grateful to you and I will always be indebted to you for speaking to me so frankly. I do not wish, however, to follow your advice at this time. I have considered it deeply and I have consulted with some advisers and I think

---

[1] P. Foncin, *Essai sur le Ministère de Turgot*, p. 250.

that there is less inconvenience in changing nothing. But I am no less obliged to you for your advice and you can be sure that it will remain secret and I beg you to keep this letter to yourself.[1]

It was as well that the matter was kept confidential because Turgot's views on toleration were not shared by his fellow ministers; Du Muy was almost a fanatical supporter of the Catholic Church and Maurepas was in favour of toleration, but not at the risk of upsetting the churchmen.

A month after the coronation the clergy held an assembly and among its remonstrances were contained these extracts: 'Complete, [Sire], the work [of] Louis the Great had inspired and Louis the Beloved [Louis XV!] had continued. It is reserved for you to deliver this last blow to Calvinism in your states. Order the scattering of the schismatic assemblies of Protestants . . . Exclude the sectaries without distinction from all branches of public administration. Your Majesty will thus assure among your subjects the unity of Catholic worship . . . [referring to the illicit marriages solemnised by Protestant priests, of which the clerics complained] that against the wish [of Your Majesty] children of tender years are torn away every day from the ministers of our saintly religion in order to be presented to the master of error who makes them suck his poison with the milk.'[2]

After the coronation Turgot, undeterred by the king's responses to his proposals, wrote a paper on religious toleration for him. Unfortunately only a part has been preserved. Véri warned him that the king was opposed to toleration and lacked the strength of character to change his attitude. But Turgot replied that if the argument was put in a clear way, it would be possible to engage his sympathies.

Your Majesty, while rendering justice to my views was afraid of the storm that might have resulted from the action I had proposed. You know how much I regretted your submission to the obligation formulated in times so lacking in light. But all is not lost and Your Majesty cannot be bound by injustice . . .

It is a known fact that there exist on the surfaces of the globe a multitude of religions and the followers of each believe that their religion is the handiwork of God and the one pleasing to Him . . . The Protestants and the Catholics recognise the truth of Christianity and the divinity of the Scriptures . . . But the Jews do not admit all the Scriptures. A large part of Asia follows the religion of Mohammed and rejects that of Jesus Christ. The Moslem countries are as extensive as those of Christianity. The rest of the earth, of even greater extent, recognise neither Mohammed nor Jesus Christ and follow different religions . . .

[1] Schelle, op. cit., vol iv, p. 554.
[2] P. Foncin *Essai* . . . p. 250–1.

If the fate of men throughout eternity could depend on other men, should there not at least be a reasonable certainty that they were endowed with light, either innate or acquired, superior to ordinary men? Without such light, and even with it, but without an express mission of the Deity, what man could dare take upon himself the eternal happiness or misery of other men? What man would not quake to be charged with such a mission? The charge of kings is to secure the welfare of their people on earth. It is sufficiently noble and fine and the burden is sufficient for the strength of any man ... Louis XIV knew very little. He admitted with candour that his education had been neglected. Yet, having made this confession, he dared to judge the religion of his subjects; he believed he had the right to remove from the Protestants the liberty of conscience solemnly assured to them by Henri IV, whose crown was cemented in blood. Louis XIV reduced the Protestants to despair by continual persecution exercised in his name, the details of which make one shudder, when one reads the mmoires of the time and he punished the misdemeanours caused by this despair with death. He believed that he was acting laudably and with piety; what deplorable blindness of a ruler who, though well intentioned, did not know how to distinguish his duties as a man and his rights as a prince ... the interests of the priests of the court had always been to confound these two matters and to abuse the ignorance of the rulers in order to establish their credit and serve their passions. This was not the only mistake of this kind which they caused Louis XIV to commit. The miserable disputes of Jansenism and Molinism, which have caused ruin to so many individuals and supplied the pretext for unrest which was dangerous to the monarchy, has happened only as a direct consequence of this mania, which makes the government intervene in questions in which it has no interest or right to involve itself as a consequence of that unfortunate inclination of Louis XIV to believe the priests at court and the *dévots*.

How can religions command sovereigns to use their power to constrain their subjects in matters of religion? Can religion command or permit crimes? To order a crime is to commit one.[1]

The coronation was an occasion when the Church reminded temporal rulers that, in addition to interceding between heaven and earth, it was a powerful body outside its cloisters and confessionals. The matter of taxation particularly concerned the pious ecclesiastics. In an age of privilege and exemption, they wished to avoid the vulgarity of taxation.

The clergy met every ten years in assembly to vote a sum to the crown in lieu

---

[1] Schelle, op. cit. vol iv, pp. 557–66.

of taxation. The sum voted was called a *don gratuit*, or free gift. This had been the practice for centuries. When the early kings had needed money above their private resources in order to finance wars and adventurous campaigns, they used to have to go to Rome cap in hand. Eventually the crown won permission to approach the clergy direct. The French Church acted quickly to preserve their wealth from the greed of the state by offering a gift. It was a small fraction of what they might have been liable for under the normal taxes but it obviated the humiliating resort to begging. It was accepted and long usage established the practice. The clergy assembled in July 1775 and settled an address to the king on the morality and general condition of his kingdom. The archbishop delivered the address: 'The activity of your paternal foresight has spread confidence and spared you, Sire, for ever the responsibility of punishing or pardoning these worrying disturbances which cannot be justified even by the reasons for them, any more in the eyes of religion than in those of government. By one of these mischances, which sometimes disturbs empires, magistrates have taken alarm to its extremes; but within a short time Your Majesty has calmed them by preferring the gentleness of a beneficent authority to the harshness of power.'[1] It was a barely disguised censure of Turgot, whom they regarded as a fallen priest.

[1] Ibid., p. 659.

19

The Queen Enters Politics

The coronation was a moving event and Marie-Antoinette could not restrain her tears. 'It is quite astonishing', she wrote to her mother, 'and very gladdening to be so well received two months after the riots [it was actually one month] and despite the shortage of grain, which unfortunately persists.'[1]

By the spring of 1775 Marie-Antoinette was exercising political influence and attracting diverse parties at court, who soon realised how to manipulate her. For example, the Choiseulists, followers of of one the grandees of French politics the duc de Choiseul, began to pay court to the queen in the salon Guemene, in order, through her influence to bring about his return to government. Choiseul had arranged her marriage to Louis XVI. She was, therefore, particularly disposed to him. In early May, Mme Brionne, the mistress of Choiseul, presented a paper setting out the rather unhealthy state of the country, which needed the experienced hand of Choiseul. When the queen showed it to the king, he dismissed it, with a wish never to hear mention of the name of Choiseul again. Choiseul was keen to prepare for the moment when Maurepas might step aside or fall into his grave. By 1775, however, it was becoming plain that Maurepas was as tenacious of life as of office.

At about this time a trial opened over an incident which had occurred five years before between Guines, the ambassador in London, and his secretary, Torte de la Sonde. La Sonde had speculated on the money market in London on the probability of a war between Britain and Spain over the Falkland Islands. When it failed to materialise, he had lost heavily. He told his creditors that he had been acting as the agent of Guines. In order to quieten him, Guines had him consigned to the Bastille in Paris. When he was released in 1772, he repeated his allegations and Guines sued him for defamation.

There was, however, another dimension to the trial. For in 1770 Aiguillon, the minister for foreign affairs and the nephew of Maurepas, had attempted to recall Guines from his posting in London. It was alleged that Aiguillon was acting in concert with de la Sonde to discredit Choiseul by attempting to dismiss Guines,

---

[1] Schelle, op. cit., vol iv, p. 554.

who happened to be his protégé. When the trial opened in 1775 the reputation of Aiguillon was as much in issue as the contentions of de la Sonde. Both Aiguillon and Guines wanted to refer to state papers in order to clear themselves. But the minister for foreign affairs in 1775, Vergennes, prevented them doing so on the ground that these papers contained state secrets.

The king read the papers requested by either side and declared that Aiguillon had acted honestly and that Guines should not reveal his own papers. In due course, the documents relied on by Aiguillon were leaked and the Choiseulists asked the queen to persuade the king to allow Guines to use his papers during the trial. This she arranged, showing for the first time her ability to get her way in political matters. But the king subsequently changed his mind – no doubt he had spoken to Maurepas and forbad Guines to produce his papers.

By protecting his nephew, Maurepas had unwittingly irritated the queen and Véri advised him to make his peace with her, for she might have proved to be a difficult enemy. According to Véri what especially irritated the queen was that her attacks on Aiguillon produced no evident resistance from Maurepas. Having failed to provoke Maurepas, she began to use her charms to get round him.

A few days before the coronation she had a meeting with Maurepas at which she specified her terms for reconciliation: the exile of Aiguillon, who had years earlier set Louis XV against her, called her the 'little redhead' and treated her like a coquette. Maurepas calculated that his own political survival was a higher priority than protection of relations and, obligingly, he exiled his nephew.

While the Choiseulists had not been able to drive a wedge between the queen and Maurepas, they had been given proof of her attachment to Choiseul. Bésenval, a leading Choiseulist, who had won the friendship of the queen by teaching her to play backgammon, was able to arrange a meeting between her and Choiseul himself a few days during the coronation festivities. First she had to obtain permission from the king, who had banned even the use of his name. 'You will hardly guess', she later admitted to a friend, 'the way in which I approached him so as to make it seem that I was not asking his permission. I told him that I desired to meet M. Choiseul, but my difficulty was in fixing the hour. I carried it off so well that the poor man arranged the most convenient time for me himself. I think I made good use of my rights that time.'[1]

The interview with Choiseul did not change the king's opinion of him, but it did reveal the queen's readiness to enter the political arena bearing a visible standard. Having failed to unseat Maurepas, as they had planned to do, the Choiseulists turned to consider the position of Turgot and realised that he, rather than the ageing Maurepas, posed the real threat to their hopes of regaining power. For not only were his ideas and reforms opposed to their views but, worse still the king had become infected by them as well.

---

[1] D. Dakin, *Turgot and the Ancien Régime* p. 212.

'The partisans of Choiseul', wrote Véri in June, 'attacked Turgot in the presence of the queen in order to lead her to dislike this minister whom she had treated until that time with esteem and trust. They thought that the operations of the finances and the grain trade gave them reason to attack Turgot. His dry nature along with his awkwardness and impatience with opposition would help them a great deal. His intentions and his integrity will never be attacked, but his noble views will be represented as dangerous systems and his unyielding manner will be held up as hard and domineering. The cries of those who will suffer from the reform of the abuses will be passed off as the wailings of the people.'[1]

The queen was young, headstrong and quicker-witted than her husband, whose passions were for affairs of state. She found Versailles large and lonely. Her marriage gave her no security and no happiness. It is not surprising that her time was spent in games and parties among the folk at Versailles. At length, she entered the game of politics; she could play sometimes better than her wooden husband and his leading minister. She lacked the character to effect any worthwhile political reforms and the intellect for exploring the high ground of political thought; she was willing to be moved around the board like a chess piece, each move circumscribed by her likes and dislikes and dictated to her by her manipulators.

---

[1] Schelle, op. cit., vol iv, pp. 682–3.

20

Reform of Taxation

There was nothing speculative, blind or dogmatic in Turgot's economic thought, as many writers have alleged. He reached his own conclusions with care and not even his most inveterate opponents have been able to question his integrity, motive or intellectual power. Nonetheless without attempting to understand his ideas about taxation, his opponents have dismissed them as irrelevant, misconceived and even deranged.

The first priority of a *contrôleur-général* was to ensure the continuance of national credit and confidence. Therefore the profound reform of taxation was postponed temporarily. He knew that this was a fundamental reform needed to introduce justice into the distribution of wealth. It was certain to provoke shrill protest from the court, the nobles, the financiers and the *parlements*.

The longer the reform of taxation was delayed, the harder it would be to put into effect because Turgot's opponents would have more time to plot against the reform by devious and dishonest means. Only the king, an enlightened political thinker and those whose property consisted entirely in their labour, might support the reform. This last category of potential supporters were a silent majority, for they possessed neither press nor constitutional position.

Turgot believed that the foundation of taxation was based upon the division of property between public and private property. The idea that private property should be exempt from taxation had been in Turgot's mind since he had read *The Two Treatises* of Locke while at the House of the Sorbonne. Locke had declared that one main purpose of society came into existence to protect the private property of the individual; in short, individual earnings. Turgot believed that taxation should be levied only on public property, to which every member of society had equal right.

In his essay *Reflections* Turgot had identified public property as the *produit net* of agricultural land. Before the industrial revolution production was undertaken almost exclusively on agricultural land. The *produit net* was the natural surplus which remained in the landowner's hands after costs, wages, interest and profit had been deducted.

The argument had been advanced after the industrial revolution, when production had been largely transferred to towns and factories. Land attracted, as before, a value according to the demand for its use. Since the demand arose from an entire society, so the value of land – be it agricultural, industrial or residential – remained public property.

Lacking a just foundation, taxation had been levied on private property of every description. The only type of property to escape taxation was that which Turgot had identified as public property: that which was reflected in the value of land. Thus landowners have enjoyed an income derived from a natural element that no man ever made and which nature has bestowed and continues to bestow on mankind in common. The amount of the landowner's income varies according to the value of land which is set, not by him, but by public demand. According to Turgot's thinking what is naturally private property has become public property and what is naturally public has been converted into private property.

In order to transfer taxation from individuals, that is from their labour and consumption, to the value of the *produit net* of agricultural land, a register of land valuation would have to be compiled. Though this register would demand much work to set up, it would be simple to keep it up to date. The compilation of such a register would have been attacked as a move against agricultural landowners; though it was in fact it would be the basis of a community's taxation policy. Turgot was not attacking landowners as a class; his motives were higher than that. The landowners may have constituted themselves into a rich, powerful and self-interested class, but they were one small body in the society. Turgot had shown that the *produit net* was a gift of nature and that it was for the benefit of the whole community. So he was proposing to bring this natural order into the realm of taxation. The private appropriation of land value constituted, in Turgot's thinking, a basic injustice. What had been created by a whole society was being appropriated by landowners.

Many opponents have claimed Turgot as the enemy of the private possession of land. Such claims are misconceived, for he never referred to private possession, either directly or obliquely. What he was against was the ownership of the value of land, or its *produit net*.

Unfortunately Turgot did not write specifically about taxation while a minister. So his ideas on the matter have to be gleaned from other less reliable sources. But he asked Du Pont, his secretary, to write a paper in August 1775 on provincial assemblies, or municipalities which is significant in this regard.

Du Pont's paper came to light in 1787 in a curious way. Du Pont used to visit Honoré Mirabeau, the son of the marquis de Mirabeau, in gaol every Sunday and they discussed political ideas. Mirabeau begged him to give him any papers or articles of interest, because he was dying of boredom. Du Pont gave him his piece on the municipalities. When Mirabeau was released he gave the paper to Calonne, the *contrôleur-général*, as his own work, and later Mirabeau sold it to a bookseller as the work of Turgot.

Clearly Turgot and Du Pont discussed the matter at length and the ideas formulated by Du Pont have been regarded as an accurate summary of Turgot's thought. But Du Pont's enthusiastic speculations were far removed from the manner of Turgot's mind. It is not safe, therefore, to regard the memoir of Du Pont as an accurate reflection of Turgot's thought on this matter.

Condorcet summarised the main principles of Turgot's thinking with more detachment and his account seems more reflective of Turgot's thinking. Turgot planned to introduce assemblies for groups of villages and towns. Owners of property, of unspecified values, would be entitled to be elected to these assemblies, which would elect their representatives to sit in assemblies of cantons or administrative districts. One of the main functions of these assemblies was to supervise the valuation of land, the compilation of a land register and to oversee the assessments of tax as between taxpayers. In addition, these assemblies would become responsible for public works, the relief of poverty and education, within the guidelines prescribed by central government. These local services would be paid out of a fund of local taxation levied on land value, which would increase in step with local services; one only has to think of the effect of the provision of street lighting, sewerage, paving and police on urban land values. Turgot thought that he could introduce these village, urban or cantonal assemblies without reducing the power of the crown, for, as he explained so often to the young king, the concentration of power in the hands of a central government ultimately becomes self-defeating; the point is reached whereby a government is hamstrung by holding too much power. Burdened with so many powers and responsibilities a government is unable to act at all.

Thus the king had everything to gain from sharing his power with his people; the exercise would raise their intelligence like nothing else. A child becomes adult only by exercising his own independence. Therefore he had no intention of setting up provincial assemblies which could become the focal point of hostility to the crown. De Tocqueville stated that Turgot planned to give a national assembly, formed by these provincial assemblies, the power of registering royal enactments, leaving to *parlement* only their legal and judicial functions.

Condorcet's summary of Turgot's ideas was a plan to point France away from a centralised despotism towards a decentralised democracy. Turgot seems to have preferred this plan of municipal assemblies rather than that of recalling the States-General, with its representation from the three Estates of the realm; the nobles, the clergy and the people. The States-General had last met about 160 years before and Turgot did not want to revive its composition and its constitutional role, which were based on medieval rules and traditions.

Nothing survives, if it ever existed on paper, of Turgot's scheme for education which he intended the municipalities should oversee. It is possible, however, to imagine some of his ideas about an educational system – because he was a consistent thinker. He would have almost certainly devised a system for all types of students, from the scholastic to the practical, in which intellectual and practical abilities would be rewarded and developed; he would have encouraged scientific education in the fields of pure science as well as technological application; he would have wished for a system more considerate of the child's intellectual and emotional needs than a system which bred conformity with the existing attitudes and institutions of society; and he would have liked a more liberal system, looking forward to new possibilities.

There can be no doubt that he would have wanted to introduce into the educational curriculum instruction about the nature of society, in order to explain the civil and economic rights of individuals, the powers and the limitations of government and its essential duties, both local and national.

Thucydides had declared at the funeral of Pericles, the Grecian father of democracy, in 429 BC that Pericles had wished to teach to Athenians political wisdom. But, unhappily, the Peloponnesian War thwarted that reform. Political wisdom has rarely been comprehended, let alone taught. It is often supposed that political matters should never be taught as part of a public education syllabus; better indeed, it is supposed, for children to be reared on rumour, gossip and prejudice, honoured by society at large and by their parents. Almost everything involving doubt and ambiguity has what might be called a political element. The addition of two plus two equals four; so much is a matter of certainty and common agreement. There is no political factor involved in this simple arithmetical sum. Similarly, an education based on principles of justice and reason, would dispel many of the doubts attendant on political questions, implant reasonable principles and explain the several essential workings of society. Indeed, one of the great failures of western political thought is that it has left so much unexplained, it has become dominated by vested interest and obscured by impenetrable expertise and complexity. As Turgot often explained to the king, political thought involved matters that anyone could begin to understand if they had been disciplined to reason on these simple matters.

According to Du Pont, Turgot wanted to submit his own contribution to the king in July 1775, so that the municipalities could be created by the beginning of the fiscal year on 1 October, but he was so preoccupied by the *guerre des farines*, particularly during the weeks which followed the riots, that he decided to shelve the reform of taxation and the establishment of the municipalities until the following year.

When Necker produced his plan for provincial assemblies in 1777, Turgot spoke to Véri about his intentions. Turgot explained that there was the usual opposition of the nobles, but his reason for not rushing into the formation of provincial assemblies was due mainly to the youth of the king. He wanted to wait awhile until the king could judge the matter for himself, until he could see the need to cede some of his royal power. Each assembly would encompass 20–40 parishes. They would deal with local administration and assessment of taxes. There would be no privilege or rank and the members would be landowners. National affairs, such as war and taxation, would remain to be determined by the king and his ministers.[1]

---

[1] Schelle, op. cit., vol v, pp. 627–8.

21

The Support of Malesherbes

Remonstrances of the *Cours des Aides*

In the early summer of 1775 the *Cours des Aides*, the court of the *parlement* of Paris with jurisdiction in fiscal matters, presented its Remonstrances on taxation and government expenditure, as the king had requested them to do. Malesherbes, the president of the court, had drafted this forthright document himself. He was not sparing in his criticism of the system and the methods of tax collection and the profligacy of government expenditure.

The *Cours des Aides* was a cell of the *parlement*, sharing its interests and its prejudices, but Malesherbes seemed to have introduced some uncharacteristic zeal for reform into its deliberations. For example, on the eve of the exile of the *Cours* in 1770 he had told his fellow magistrates that: 'It is absurd that all men are not equal in the eyes of the law, when they are all equal in the eyes of nature. It is the business of the law to protect equality there. All privileges are founded on prejudices or injustices. Those who have not been rewarded by chance with privileges hold them as a result of a short-sighted view which fails to take into consideration the unhappiness of others. There is no privilege accorded to one which has not harmed another. It is unjust to favour one part of a nation at the expense of another . . . You may not prescribe against the interests of the people.'[1] Such forthright exposure of the injustice of privilege was rare in France. The *économistes* could hardly contain their enthusiasm that a public figure was speaking their language.

After the recall of the *parlements* the previous autumn, Malesherbes reminded the *Cours* of their chief concern: 'Gentleman, there is one [virtue] which is the foundation of all others and which at present should constitute the chief motive of your actions; and that is the love of the public welfare.'[2]

Malesherbes was not a revolutionary political thinker; rather a brilliant scholar with a deep sense of justice. He was prepared to pursue an idea or an argument fearlessly to its conclusion. Furthermore, he could express himself in the language of poetry and with the precision of a lawyer.

---

[1] J. Allison *Lamoignon de Malesherbes* 1938, p. 71.
[2] Izouard, *Life of Lamoignon Malesherbes*. p.

The ministers of the Council, apart from Turgot, were alarmed by the attack against the forms of taxation, privilege and tax collection, Their alarm was even greater because the attack had not come from an *économiste*, from whom it might have been expected, but from one regarded as a highly respected figure in the nation.

At the end of the month Malesherbes went to hear the reaction of the king. 'I will apply myself', said the king, 'to introducing reforms one after another on all the matters needing them. But this will not be the work of a moment; it will be the task of my whole reign.'[1]

Maurepas and Miromesnil attempted to suppress the publication of the Remonstrances on the pretext that it would stir up resistance among the tax payers and render the collection of the taxes difficult. Both, however, were published and widely read. Turgot was delighted by the plain speaking of the Remonstrances. If he had not guessed the strength of the opposition to fiscal reform within the Council, he now had proof of it. He realised that his position was difficult, for within the Council he was the only voice in favour of fiscal reform. He needed the weight of a Malesherbes, if he was to embark on his plans of reforms.

Malesherbes enters the Council of Ministers

Maurepas feared that the Choiseulists would press their candidate into the position vacated by La Vrillière. Therefore, he backed the cause of Malesherbes, who was not identified with Choiseul. The king had some reservations about the links between Malesherbes and the *encylopédistes*; he had been taught to distrust them by the priests at court. Maurepas was able to dissolve any doubts in the king's mind and, uncharacteristically, the king made up his mind on the spot. He appointed Malesherbes to the Council.

It was well known, however, that Malesherbes did not seek political office. A deputation of Turgot, Véri and Blondel was formed to persuade Malesherbes that only his appointment would block that of a Choiseulist. If this appointment of a Choiseulist were to happen, Choiseul himself would eventually be brought back into government, which would not only bring with it the abject incompetence associated with him but the real threat of war with Britain. For the British heartily distrusted Choiseul.

'All these points of view', recorded Véri, 'were not denied by M. de Malesherbes. However, he persisted in his refusal. He believed that no one thought him competent to transact daily matters. He knows only how to speak and throw out ideas; that if he was needed only to advise and not to act, he might be of some help, but he is unsuitable for an active role; that the goodwill he had received

---

[1] P. Foncin, *Essai sur le Ministère de Turgot*, p. 222.

145

from the *parlements*, that he had earned by appearing to help them, would turn into dislike as soon as they see him placed through good fortune in a position to oppose them.'[1]

After reflection his decision was unchanged. Turgot and Véri showed his letter to Maurepas at Versailles. Maurepas had just emerged from a meeting with the queen. 'You know already my desire to proceed,' she solemnly told Maurepas, 'to proceed in step with you. It is the good of the state, it is good for the king and, consequently, it is good for me too. M. La Vrillière is going to retire and M. de Malesherbes refuses the vacant place. I want it for M. de Sartine and the ministry of the marine for M. d'Ennery. I do not understand what you tell me about the disagreements that will take place between M. de Turgot and M. de Sartine over questions relating to the king's household . . .'[2]

'Our reflections', wrote Véri, 'on this matter were neither long nor many. It was the moment *du combat* which must decide the continuance or the retreat of this administration. If the reply of M. de Malesherbes had been to accept, the whole problem would have disappeared. The king would have ordered the place to be offered to him, its acceptance would have prevented the place being vacant.'[3] They decided to see the king the next morning and Turgot went to see Vermond, the guardian of the queen appointed by her mother. He was astonished to hear what the queen had said to Maurepas, since she had talked to him quite reasonably about the matter that same morning. He presumed that someone had spoken to her and counselled her to be tough with Maurepas who was old, compliant and weak. Vermond assured him that the queen would soon quieten down to accept any appointment in a short time. Later that evening the queen made her demands for the appointment of a Choiseulist to the king. The king replied firmly, 'I know your desires, Madame, quite well. But it is I who must decide.'

After his meeting with Vermond, Turgot sent a courier to Malesherbes to relate the latest developments. Still Malesherbes rejected the position. The next morning Turgot and Maurepas went to the king to play their last card; the king should write to Malesherbes. The king agreed to write and did so as follows: 'M. Turgot has told me of your aversion for the position which I have offered to you. I still think your love of the public welfare must overcome it. You do not know the pleasure which you will bring me by accepting at least for the meantime, if you do not want to commit yourself completely. I believe that this is absolutely necessary for the good of the state. Louis.'[4]

Véri delivered the letter to Malesherbes, who exclaimed, 'With the exception of a mortal illness, nothing more fatal could have happened to me. But one cannot

---

[1] Véri, vol i. pp. 313–14.
[2] Ibid., p. 315.
[3] Ibid., p. 315.
[4] Ibid., p. 316.

refuse a wish so much more powerful than an order.' In his reply to the king, Malesherbes stressed that his limitations 'have been able to give me some aptitude for framing legislation, but I am completely incapable of the detailed work of administration'.[1] The Choiseulists had been rebuffed and Bsenval observed succinctly, 'This gave victory to Maurepas and what in the language of intrigue is called a snub to the queen.'

The appointment of Malesherbes as minister for the king's household was announced weeks later. He became responsible for ecclesiastical matters, the roles of benefices, courtiers' pensions and different allowances and gifts awarded to members of the court and the government of Paris and several *pays d'etat*, or provinces which enjoyed a certain measure of self-government. His appointment was popular generally, except with those who saw it as a move to strengthen Turgot's position.

In so many fields Malesherbes and Turgot were kindred spirits; both came from noble families with long traditions of public service, they were intellects of the first order and students of science and literature, champions of individual freedom, of religious toleration, of a free press and of the rule of law. They had known each other from childhood. Malesherbes saw liberty consisting in civil freedom. Great things were hoped of this enlightened partnership and there was universal joy at its announcement, except among the clergy who did not like them because they had been *encyclopédistes*, *philosophes* and thinkers with little respect for the Church and its dogmas. Besides, they had the air of men who thought too much. The church preferred ministers who merely kept the national status quo; they distrusted reformers. While there was widespread jubilation at Malesherbes's appointment the 'clergy were almost in despair'.[2]

Lord Shelbourne was impressed by Malesherbes. He spoke about him to Julie Lespinasse who wrote, '[Shelbourne] told me "I have seen for the first time in my life what I did not believe could exist – a man whose soul is absolutely free of fear and hope, but who, nevertheless, is full of life and passion. Nothing in the world can disturb his peace of mind, nothing is necessary to him, but he interests himself in all that is good." '[3]

Malesherbes insisted on continuing to wear his magisterial robes and wig, even at Versailles where ministers were expected to acquit themselves more formally in morning dress and with a ceremonial sword. 'All the exteriors of the Court may be reduced to an exterior of confidence and friendliness which deceive no one in general and very many people in particular,' explained Malesherbes. He was not at ease among the courtiers, whose overriding pursuits consisted of diversions and intrigue. Their minds were concerned with nothing profound or interesting.[4]

---

[1] Ibid., p. 317.
[2] Métra, *Correspondance* vol ii, p. 69.
[3] Lespinasse, *Lettres*: letter 22 Oct. 1774.
[4] J. Allison, *Lamoignon de Malesherbes*, p. 89.

'I trembled', Malesherbes admitted, 'at my accession to the ministry. I found myself seated at my desk opposite a single clerk and I was the most absolute master pronouncing arbitrarily the most terrible condemnations.'[1] One area in which he wanted reform was in that of the *lettres de cachet* and in the imprisonments of suspects before trial. But when he looked into the matter, he became aware of the need to hold suspects like deranged delinquents and others considered dangerous to the public peace. He proposed, therefore, that *lettres de cachet* be taken out of the hands of a minister and entrusted to a committee. The Council, however, rejected this reform. As to the imprisonment of suspects he wrote, 'I have examined the cases of more than half those committed to the Bastille and Vincennes over the last fifteen years. They became insane or so disordered in their minds as to render it highly dangerous to restore them to liberty.'[2]

Economies in the ministry of war and in the royal household

Over half the state expenditure was accounted for by the military, and, if economies were sought, it was reasonable to expect them in the military departments. But Du Muy, the minister of war, resented Turgot's calls for economies and brushed them off as the ranting of a mere bookkeeper. Thus as long as he remained in office, Turgot could not expect to make economies in the ministry of war.

When Du Muy died suddenly after an operation at the beginning of October, Turgot hurried to Paris to head off any attempts to fill this important department with a Choiseuliste or some other pliant appointee. On meeting Maurepas he admitted, 'I have an idea which you will find ridiculous, but it seems to bear examination. I do not want to be reproached for remaining silent. I have in mind M. Saint-Germain'. 'Ah well, Monsieur', replied Maurepas, 'if your thoughts are ridiculous so are mine, for I was going to set out for Fontainbleau with the aim of proposing his name to the king'. At Fontainbleau they discussed the idea with Malesherbes. None of them knew much about the sixty-year-old Count Saint-Germain, except that he had been respected as a soldier and he had been employed in the service of the Danish court before retiring some years earlier. Maurepas remembered that the count had sent him a paper upon his retirement in which he had outlined various reforms in the French army. The three of them read it, were struck by his desire for reform and became convinced of their earlier decision to advise the king to appoint him.

Maurepas told the queen and she accepted it without reservation. The count was fetched from his country retreat. He was delighted to be rescued from a tedious retirement and readily accepted. 'If I do nothing good', he said, 'then my country retreat is always ready to receive me.'

---

[1] Soulavie, *Memoirs of the Reign of Louis XVI* vol 2, pp. 322–23.
[2] Ibid., vol ii, p. 322.

When he arrived in Fontainebleau for his investiture he took an uncomfortable room in a modest inn. 'Have you not something a little more comfortable?' he asked. 'We have nothing else', replied the innkeeper, 'because a crowd of people are here waiting for the new minister of war who will be arriving shortly.' Saint-Germain's appointment was greeted with the same public acclaim as that when Turgot had become *contrôleur-général*.

Having already secured the appointment of Malesherbes at the royal household, Turgot was now supported by two ministers who were keen to effect reform in two expensive departments of state. He was primarily concerned with the preparation of six edicts which, were published in January. Having been unable to introduce fundamental reforms of taxation for the fiscal year beginning 1 October 1775, Turgot could hope only for cutting and controlling public expenditure which would secure the basic financial aims written in his original letter to the king.

Malesherbes proved to be a popular choice, but the courtesy shown to him from all sides began to worry him. He told the king that it was a sure sign that he was doing his job badly and that he was not standing against those seeking his favours. 'I can prepare the case for reforms, but it is a gross illusion to imagine that I can effect them,' he confided to Véri. 'My character is not suited for this task. I am too inclined by nature to agree with whoever comes to talk to me. Furthermore, this work has nothing in common with the work which I have been doing up to now. It tires me so that, I, who used to go to my office eagerly every day, have to make a great effort to go there now and even get up from my bed. I said so at the outset and experience has confirmed my initial reactions. I am worth nothing when it comes to day-to-day details. I am good only at discussing the general ideas with the king or his ministers and leaving the execution to others.'[1] Within a short time it became clear that Malesherbes was not suited to making economies. He did not have the resolve or the nature to fight for expenditure cuts against the clamour that this exercise arouses.

Malesherbes was a distinctive figure and it is impossible to criticise him for incapacities, of which he himself was aware. Nor would it be fair to criticise Turgot for having hoped for more than Malesherbes could achieve, for he had only the choice between acquiescing in the appointment of some vain and obstructive courtier or of bringing into government a friend of known wisdom and talent. Perhaps he had hoped that public office would inspire latent capacities. At the royal household Turgot had need of a fellow spirit in the necessary exercise of economy; but instead he had a friend who was out of his depth and who was becoming increasingly frustrated.

Saint-Germain, however, plunged into the work of the ministry of war and began effecting reforms at once. Within a short time the queen wrote to her

[1] Véri, vol i, pp. 373–4.

mother that Saint-Germain's principle reform was to cut wasteful expenditure in order to recruit 40,000 additional soldiers who would bring the French forces up to the strength of the Prussian and Austrian armies. Turgot was saddened that Saint-Germain's praiseworthy efforts to cut out waste was devoted to preparing for a future war, which France was unable to sustain when it was so weak financially. Thus the hopes Turgot had of cutting expenditure in the ministry of war and the royal household were dashed.

Throughout the summer of 1775 Turgot had examined the budgets of the spending departments and consulted many officials so that his knowledge of government became extensive. Turgot wrote, according to Du Pont, two letters in October to Saint-Germain proposing immediate reforms amounting to a saving of 2 million livres and other reforms which over a year would have saved 15 million. Besides these specific financial proposals Turgot outlined a number of other reforms in the army. Among these was the ending of the death penalty for desertion, except for desertion on the field of battle, for the large majority of deserters came from the ranks of the conscripts selected by the *milice*. This reform was accepted weeks later. In November he wrote again to Saint-Germain to describe how the provisioning of cavalry in eastern France had been arranged by means of a monopoly, which destroyed the local markets, and he asked the minister to instruct his commanders on how much the army would gain by forgoing the monopoly and buying their supplies in the open market.

By mid-December Saint-German seems to have come to resent Turgot's desires for reform and while the rift between the two ministers widened, Maurepas, who could have brought the two together with no trouble, allowed them to drift further and further apart. Thus by the end of 1775 Turgot could no longer hope for assistance in his search for economies in expenditure from the two ministers whom he had helped to bring into the Council.

22

Further Injustices of the *Ancien Régime*

Before dealing with some injustices of the ancien régime, Turgot had to assert control over an outbreak of foot-and-mouth which broke out during 1774 in the southwestern provinces of Bayonne and Pau. The methods employed are still those employed in Britain today – an embargo on the movement of cattle, the slaughter of infected herds and burying the carcasses in lime. These measures required strict compliance with orders otherwise the outbreak would never be stamped out during the winter months and would spread in the warm weather.

It is necessary to explain one episode of the outbreak, in order to defend Turgot against the attack which modern writers have made against his reputation. It concerned the conduct of the intendant of Auch and Bayonne, M. Journet, who seemed to have lost control of his subordinates. They were openly critical of the regulations imposed and were unwilling to execute them. Turgot wrote to the intendant and threatened to investigate breaches of his instructions and to put the offenders on trial for inciting disobedience of the law. A few weeks later he wrote again to complain that Journet's staff were not paying compensation promptly for the slaughter of animals. Days later he wrote again to complain that the amount of 2 million livres already paid and 5 million livres reckoned to be owing exceeded the amounts paid in the neighbouring provinces. Turgot believed that the intendant's subordinates were converting large sums for their own use. Journet sanctioned payment of a fee of six sols to the soldiers for every animal slaughtered, without having received higher authorisation to do so. Finally, in December Turgot recalled Journet to Paris. 'I pay full due', wrote Turgot, 'to your honesty and to your love of the public welfare. I am even prepared to think that you have spared neither cares nor efforts to arrest the progress of the outbreak. But in a matter so important and when the welfare of the state is at risk . . . one is forced to conduct oneself by the principles which pertain in war . . . It is then that the welfare of the state becomes supreme law.'[1] Faced with an enquiry Journet committed suicide. In an attempt to conceal the cause of his death officials seized and imprisoned his servants. There is no question of Turgot having had anything to do with this cover-up.

---

[1] Schelle, op. cit., vol v, p. 88.

Faure, Turgot's fiercest modern critic, implicates him in the suicide: 'The text [of Turgot's letter] is moreover of a quality which goes far beyond the needs of the situation . . . The maxims [cited above] brought no comfort to the man who is down: he committed suicide . . . and this affair was attributed to the harshness of Turgot.'[1] He fails to add that those who attributed the suicide to Turgot were not innocent and impartial bystanders, but the enemies of Turgot, who seized, like Faure, every chance to do him down. The more objective reporters dismissed the rumour as ridiculous.

In September the *parlement* of Toulouse ordered the municipal and parish authorities to convene meetings in order to consider the measures being taken by the government. The magistrates were disturbed that, in such a large and important matter , they had been afforded no standing or authority. Turgot issued an *arrêt* confirming the measures which he had been taking and forbade the *parlements* from interfering in any way. He even banned the publication of a book which criticised the policy being pursued, because he thought that it would undermine it. In this case, the champion of a free press was acting in an emergency under the supreme law of the welfare of the state.

During the autumn of 1775 foot-and-mouth disease broke out in Calais and in the north, probably because hides received from the south had not been correctly treated. The outbreak had to be stamped out, in order that it was not to continue until the spring and summer.

The *milice*

Turgot abhorred the *milice* and, in particular, the way of choosing recruits by the drawing of lots. He hated the brutal disregard of individual liberty. He hated as much the disturbances to which the annual recruitment gave rise. Du Muy, the previous minister of war, was not minded to proceed with the reform of the *milice* proposed by Turgot. Instead he regarded the *milice* as a mechanism of raising the annual intake of 12,000–40,000 soldiers. In December 1775, however, the edict for the intake of that year had to be renewed and the king, mindful of Turgot's desire for reform, ordered that a committee of six ministers should consider the question of the renewal of the *milice*. On the committee three members, Maurepas, Bertin and Turgot who had each served as an intendant, favoured the reform and two war ministers, Du Muy and Sartine, opposed reform. In order to resolve the deadlock, Turgot appealed to the king.

According to Véri, the king accepted the reforms proposed by Turgot, but only in principle, and thus was inclined to continue the present arrangements until a more propitious moment for radical reform.

---

[1] E. Faure, *La Disgâce de Turgot*, pp. 113–14.

The transport system

The postal, courier and transport systems outside the main cities were operated by private contractors, who had purchased monopolies, concessions and privileges from the state. This created complexity and inefficiency and these services yielded further examples of injustice which permeated the *ancien régime*. Unsurprisingly, neither the state nor the public benefited. The poor communication throughout provincial France was hampered by expense and inconvenience to the traveller.

The journey from Paris to Dieppe took as much as four days, that from Paris to Bordeaux up to fourteen days and Paris to Lyon up to six days. The journeys were made in uncomfortable carriages on poorly made roads with frequent interruptions for masses at wayside chapels. The fares were extremely high: 80 livres to Bordeaux and 66 livres to Lyon. Tobias Smollet, the English novelist, wrote of the five-day journey from Paris to Lyons. He travelled by carriage, called a *diligence*. 'The inconveniences attending this way of travelling are these. You are crowded into the carriage, to the number of eight persons, so as to sit very uneasy, and sometimes run the risque of being stifled among very indifferent company. You are harried out of bed, at four, three, nay often at two o'clock in the morning.'[1] Services were infrequent and inconvenient; carriages from Paris to Chartres and to Rouen left at three in the morning and to Orlans at five! In short, the transport system in France furnished every reason to stay at home.

Undoubtedly the transport system was ripe for reform. But the difficulty facing Turgot was that many financiers, who were his most determined enemies, were involved either directly as transport contractors or as lenders to the contractors. 'It is well known', reported Métra, 'that the contractors maintain the grandest style of living, entertain large numbers of mankind, throw magnificent parties and have acquired a large number of dependants. A large number . . . protest that this operation may ruin 20,000 people, while in fact, leaving aside the parasites, hardly 50 clerks and concessionaires [who were to be compensated] will suffer from it.'[2] Turgot feared that by attacking the privileges and monopolies of the contractors and the financiers, private investors would not come forward to contract with the government on reasonable terms. Turgot wanted to attract new contractors to build more efficient carriages, to increase the relays of horses and to modernise the staging posts along major roads. He also wanted to recover a greater sum for the state, for estimates showed that extra revenue of 4 million livres per annum could be earned. As he doubted that private enterprise could create an efficient transport system within a short time, he decided to proceed with a state board – a semi-public body.

In June 1775 Turgot demanded the intendants to require transport monopolists

---

[1] T. Smollet, *Travels Through France and Italy*: letter dated Oct 19, 1763.
[2] Métra, *Correspondance* vol i, pp. 149–51.

to prove their title to the privileges claimed by them. Two months later he announced that the state would take over the transport system and pay fulsome compensation to contractors. The *arrêt* announcing the take-over undertook to restore transport to private contractors and to open it to competition, once it had been successfully established under state management. Within a short time new carriages were introduced, new timetables and cheaper tariffs were issued and journeys became more comfortable, more convenient, cheaper and swifter. Carriages on the main routes were exempted from the tedious and regular customs checks. Sections of the Church opposed these new-fangled experiments. 'The entrepreneurs of the former undertakings', lamented abbé Proyart, 'were obliged to secure travellers the facility of attending mass on the days that he is obliged to attend. The modernisation of carriages will bring about the demise of chapels and the travellers in turgotines [as the new carriages came to be called] may learn to do without the mass, as Turgot does without it.'[1]

Journey times were cut substantially. For example, that from Paris to Bordeaux was cut from fourteen to five and a half days. Security was greatly improved by guards accompanying the carriages during dangerous parts of the journeys and it became possible then to use the post as a means of transferring money between government offices and between banks.

The cabinet noir

Shortly after his appointment as *contrôleur-général*, Turgot took over the position of superintendent of the post, which had been unfilled for several years. Not only did the position give him control of the post, and, therefore, freedom to introduce reforms, it also brought within his control the *cabinet noir*, which operated as the official intercept of private mail. The *cabinet noir* enabled the king and his ministers to open private letters at will. This violation of privacy angered Turgot more than any other. For years he had been writing in a code in order to confound the *cabinet noir*. Now he held this miserable *cabinet* in his palm. He wrote to the king: 'every principle puts the secret correspondence of citizens among the inviolable things, from which the courts, like individuals, must avert their gaze'.[2] Yet the king decided to preserve the *cabinet*; he liked to read intimate secrets and private views. Even Maurepas was unable to wean the king from this unlawful diversion.

'The king', wrote Véri, 'promised to order that the baron d'Oigny [the chief of the *cabinet*] bring him only matters of state ... There is no longer any secret between families and friends committed to the post. The amusement which the king obtains gives long roots to this problem. Through it he discovers something bad about everyone ... The result is that one finds the king is known to hold a

---

[1] P. Foncin, *Essai sur le Ministère de Turgot*, pp. 280–1.
[2] Ibid., p. 282.

bad opinion of everyone and to generally mistrust.'[1] The crown actually lost from the existence of this *cabinet* for it discouraged use of the post and it wasted expense only to reveal a mass of useless and conflicting information.

Once a provincial woman wanted to be presented at court and the king refused to receive her, because her titles were not in order. Maurepas was surprised that the king should have known this defect before her papers had been examined by the official genealogist. The king told him that he knew the situation from her husband. Maurepas became more surprised because he knew the husband lived in the provinces. The king added that the husband had written to his wife about it.

If Maurepas was unable to persuade the king to forego this pleasure, Turgot had to accept that there was nothing he could do. His tenure of the superintendency of the post brought him not only frustration, but also resentment from the queen, who had wanted this position for her favourite, Montmorency.

Beggary in France

'Beggary was one of the worst scourges of the *ancien régime*', wrote Marion. 'It became very extensive.'[2] Clearly it was a universal problem. Through the seventeenth and eighteenth centuries beggars had been imprisoned, enlisted for the galleys, restricted to their places of residence. In 1767 Averdy, the *contrôleur-général*, established depots for beggars. Terray was pleased with the effects of detaining them in depots. This detention had cleared the roads of beggary, but the causes of the problem persisted; the beggars had to suffer life below reasonable expectation, they were herded like criminals with other tramps and society had to bear the cost of these depots. Though Turgot attributed the cause of beggary to poverty and unemployment, he was faced with the immediate problem of beggary. He was unwilling, however, to accept a policy which did nothing to eradicate the cause – unjust taxation.

In October 1775 he attended a meeting at Montigny with Malesherbes, Albert, Brienne and Trudaine to consider the problem. Later he told Véri: 'We met principally to concern ourselves with plans to suppress beggary and to relieve poverty. For it was not necessary to limit ourselves to suppressing the one without relieving the other, as L'Averdy, my predecessor had done.'[3]

In his essay, *Foundations*, written almost twenty years before, Turgot had expressed his dislike of leaving the resolution of poverty to charities, for they had the effect of increasing the number of beggars by reducing the incentive to earn a living, while at the same time leaving the causes of poverty unreformed. Brienne had made a special study of begging and hospitals and presented a paper to the meeting. It is thought that Turgot also presented a paper under an assumed name,

[1] Véri, vol i, pp. 248–9.
[2] Marion, *Dictionaire des institutions de la France: see* Mendicants.
[3] Véri, vol i, p. 363–4.

and sought to keep the meeting out of the public eye, because it was essentially an informal and frank meeting between friends. The document began 'I think one is wasting one's time in seeking to frame a direct law against beggary.' He also shared Brienne's opposition of licensing harmless beggars by providing them with certificates, for he felt that certificates would provide too much security and respectability to a way of life, which should be discouraged as much as possible.

Turgot proposed two simple measures which could be introduced immediately. First, that charitable workshops be set up in districts where beggars, along with the poor, could find no work appropriate to their abilities. These workshops could be employed on unskilled work, such as earth-moving and levelling. Second, that the maréchaussées, or mounted police, be put under the control of the intendants rather than of the army, so that they could deal with the beggars in step with local officials and local conditions.

After the conference Turgot wrote to the intendants: 'It is impossible to destroy begging and unjust to outlaw it inasmuch as the beggar cannot be regarded as blameworthy, as misery forces him to beg in order to live, and as steps have not been taken to provide suitable work for the able-bodied poor.'[1] He ordered that the charitable workshops be set up wherever there were beggars or where the poor could find no work, that details of charitable foundations be compiled and, lastly, that the police should arrest only beggars who were dangerous and all those who could be said to be harmless and of no fixed address should no longer be detained in depots.

A month later he wrote to the intendant of Caen giving fuller instructions on the treatment of beggars and vagabonds. Dangerous beggars were to be sent to five large depots reserved for this class. The harmless and disabled detainees were to be sent home and, if they were incapable of earning their living, the intendants were to give them annual pensions of between 30–50 livres. The mounted police were to arrest and detain able-bodied beggars, who were to be subjected to severe military disciplines in order to sharpen their appetites for work. Young men following the life of beggary were given the opportunity to join companies of provincial workers, which were to be formed, in order to give the men a year of training, provided they contracted to stay with the companies for eight years. Their pay was to be a fixed daily rate plus a fifth of the value of their production. Initial work undertaken by these provincial companies was related to road building.

Beggary is a phenomenon which government cannot solve by making the life of beggars and tramps less wretched, for that would be such an encouragement that their numbers would be bound to increase. Turgot attempted to relieve the problem, as this conference showed that government could do little about its appearance. The choice was either to reform the cause of poverty in society or to endlessly pursue cosmetic policies which were not concerned with the root of the problem.

---

[1] C. Bloch, *L'Assistance et l'État à la vielle de la Revolution* [1908], p. 191.

23

The Manipulation of Maurepas

Turgot had accepted the position of *contrôleur-général* on the strength of the king's promise of support for his reforms, on terms that were just. He had foreseen that his reforms would attract hostility at court, in the *parlements* and Church, among farmers-general and financiers and even the royal family. By the beginning of 1776 what he had foreseen was becoming true. The entire pack of enemies were in hue and cry after him.

They detested the notion of justice, which was inseparably linked with Turgot. Their concern was that he disturbed their privileges, monopolies and pensions. Turgot realised that those, who enrich themselves by injustice, think only of their own interests. They do not possess the flexibility or largesse to consider the welfare of society because they are full to the brim with prejudice and pretension. They pretended to think of the welfare of the nation, its monarch, it history and its honour, but they were unable to appreciate that the jewels of society were the liberties of its citizens. To Turgot they were as precious as the freshness of air or purity of water.

The first attempt to unseat him had been the *guerre des farines*, designed to bring about his public dishonouring. Here, his enemies had condemned him as a simpleton with his fond ideal of free trade, who had succeeded only in reducing Paris to virtual starvation. In France to have caused such confusion to the national digestive system was a greater folly than any other and far greater in France than elsewhere. Though the riots had been suppressed without trouble, it would be a mistake to think that this suppression had been achieved without the rigorous action of the king and Turgot. Far from bringing about the disgrace of Turgot, the riots had enhanced a mutual trust.

Nothing so bold and unsubtle was attempted again. During the remainder of 1775 the various elements paraded their opposition. From the ranks of the established order there was, however, one notable and important exception: the young king. The next move of Turgot's enemies was to sever this regal attachment.

After failing to fill the vacancy of the departure of La Vrillière with a Choiseulist, Bésenval, the leading wire-puller among the Choiseulists, persuaded the queen to enlist the aid of Maurepas. In September 1775 Bésenval explained to Maurepas that the queen was not happy that her nominee had been overlooked in favour of Malesherbes, but it would be a simple matter for him to make his peace again with the queen. For her resentment, according to Bésenval, was reserved only for the *contrôleur-général*. She imagined that he was obstructing her plans, plunging the nation into turmoil with his wild schemes and monopolising the ear of the king. Instead of rebuffing this censure of a fellow minister in a firm and decisive manner, Maurepas said nothing on his behalf.

The relationship between Maurepas and Turgot was recorded in detail by Véri, who was the confidant of both men for the greater part of 1775. In July Maurepas asked Turgot to find a place for M. Longchamp in his department. Turgot did not think much of Longchamp's candidacy. He did not want to employ someone, whom he considered unworthy of the office; he felt strongly that public offices should be held by men of known capability and honesty. Véri told Turgot to heal this quarrel with Maurepas and to appoint Longchamp. 'That', replied Turgot, 'would really displease me, owing to the poor opinion which I hold of the man.' 'What does your opinion count for?' retorted Véri. 'The king and Maurepas, who are the masters, have a good opinion of him and have promised him that position. You are only an instrument of their will ... For, after all that M. Maurepas has done for you these past few days [backed Malesherbes' appointment], it would be unworthy of you to offend him.'[1]

'One can see', recorded Véri, 'from this small incident how M.Turgot forgets everything whether it be other people or decency or personal interest, when something goes against his ideas of rectitude.'[2] Turgot regarded the purposes of government as something greater than the vain ambitions of politicians and he considered it quite unjust that government should be filled by incompetent favourites.

During August Véri retired to the country for a holiday. He received letters from Mme Maurepas complaining about Turgot and from Turgot on how he himself was opposed from every side and how much he needed Véri's support. Véri replied urging him to give way on such a small matter. 'M Turgot', he recorded, 'certainly has more insight and a broader vision of internal administration of the kingdom than M.de Maurepas, but the latter has more weight in the nation and more talent for dealing with people. Nothing is more simple than leading him to sensible ideas than by the means of a little conversation ... Unfortunately it is this conversational ability that M. Turgot lacks.'[3] Within a fortnight Mme Maurepas wrote again to report that Maurepas 'was not happy' with M. Turgot. And Turgot replied to Véri's sermon to say that he had given way on the appointment of Longchamp but that his distaste of the matter was justified. 'M. Turgot does not

[1] Véri, vol i, p. 319.
[2] Ibid., pp. 319–20.
[3] Ibid., p. 328.

believe that it is possible to see things differently from himself. This is the root of his faults.'[1]

When Véri returned from his holiday he was still troubled about the relations between Maurepas and Turgot and in early September he recorded the following conclusion:

> M. Turgot has excellent ideas upon which he has reflected profoundly. Those of M. Maurepas do not have such a solid basis; they are more flexible. M.Turgot has the welfare of the nation at heart, like a good gardener. M. Maurepas also wants the good of the nation but not with the same concern ... In the last 24 hours I have had occasion to be touched by the beauty that reigns in M.Turgot's soul in the midst of a few brambles who are now rallying the Court against him ... His spirit is as calm in the face of the general outcry as in the face of eulogies which have come from other directions. I have seen no more anger in him against the opposition than I have seen enthusiasm for the eulogies. I have been curious to re-acquaint myself with his plans over all branches of his administration. It is not possible to bring to bear a greater purity of intention. Stranger to all questions of personal interest, to ambition; or personal glory; he holds before his eyes only a wrong to be reduced or a benefit to be procured. He may deceive himself on the way but certainly he has no other end in view. I dare to assert that if he is mistaken, he is less so than anyone else. If he does not possess the art of handling those who inhabit the Court, he is amply compensated by the talents of treating things with a rare profundity and an integrity of vision view which is just as rare. Those who do not appreciate him, accuse him of being systematic and of holding dangerous opinions. But his integrity is universally admired. A wicked mind of which I have seen only the unsigned writing, wishes to persuade M. Maurepas that he had no enemy to fear save for the treachery of M. Turgot who wishes to replace him and who only led him to call M. Malesherbes to office, so that he could be pushed into second place, as part of his treacherous plans. Oh heaven! M. Malesherbes and M. Turgot, traitors! Aristide, Turenne and Timoleon had not a soul more pure.[2]

At last Véri had seen beyond his earlier idea that Turgot was blind to the views of others and saw only his own. Véri came to realise that Turgot had an inner serenity, an unshakeable integrity and a desire to promote the welfare of society. Henceforth, Véri ceased to be the confidant of Maurepas. Following this complete

---

[1] Ibid., p. 331.
[2] Ibid., pp. 335–6.

change of heart, Véri discussed with Turgot the opposition forming against him. Turgot had offended the financiers because he was raising loans at cheaper rates abroad. The complaints were made, not by the financiers directly, but by their dependants at court who were threatened by the drying up of their source of loans. But the courtiers could not remonstrate too loudly and they had to rely on the poor to make the louder protest, as they had in the *guerre des farines*.

The reconciliation between the queen and Maurepas was sealed in an interview during September. Bésenval warned Maurepas to expect the interview to begin with the queen giving vent to her displeasure, but he should wait for this to give way to tones of reconciliation and friendship. 'She began with this tone', recorded Véri, 'but hardly had she uttered a few sentences when the king entered the room. The queen appeared to continue with the details of her household and then turning to the king said, "I have realised that I was wrong about M. Maurepas and I must say now that I am extremely happy with him." The king was thrilled and ran to embrace the queen and gripped one of M Maurepas's hands. The queen rising from the sofa to acknowledge the embrace of the king, let fall her head dress which M. Maurepas found himself in a position to reach when he was bending down to kiss the hand of the king. All of this produced a blending of emotion and gaiety which created a harmony, not broken to this day.'[1] Véri may almost have been describing a comic scene in an opera.

The queen's purpose of this reconciliation was to bring herself into government. When that had been effected, she refused any longer to be manipulated by Bésenval and the Choiseulistes. After the sudden death of Du Muy in October, she became irritated by Bésenval's demands for the appointment of a Choiseuliste and decided to discard him. She was more intent on using her new understanding with Maurepas as an entry to government under her own colours. Soon she was able to procure Maurepas's assent to the creation of a post of the superintendent of her household. 'Those who see this position of waste, expense and meddlesome prerogatives, forecast ill for the future,' wrote Véri. Turgot had already provided for the expense of a coronation, the marriage of the king's sister, the provision of a household for the new-born nephew of the king at a time of financial crisis. He could have done without the revival of this nest of extravagance. Véri confronted Maurepas for having compromised Turgot, by agreeing to the extravagance of the queen. He replied weakly that he had witnessed the queen telling her husband that the happiness of her life depended on this appointment.

The leverage, which the queen obtained from the bending of Maurepas, brought her and the court into conflict with Turgot over such matters as dowries and pensions. The position of superintendent of the queen's household was given to princesse Lamballe, who pressed for the maximum emoluments in excess of 150,000 livres awarded to the previous incumbent. Not only was Maurepas happy

[1] Ibid., p. 367.

to make the necessary arrangements, which Turgot opposed in the interests of economy, but Malesherbes went along with the payment. The princesse had already pressed the queen to demand from Turgot a dowry for Mlle Guebriant on her marriage; it was finally paid by the queen herself. Turgot opposed the request of a pension for the comtesse de Ploignac, but it was granted and the queen instructed her to write to Turgot to thank him for paying it. 'I had no part in the favour which has been granted to you,' replied Turgot.[1] The queen was incensed by the reply and enjoined the comtesse to reply but found her letter too soft. So a tougher letter was composed which the comtesse dispatched reluctantly to the impertinent *contrôleur-général*.

Having seen the misery caused by the collection of taxes from peasants, it must have sickened Turgot's soul to see the proceeds lavished on someone who was exempt from taxation. He was not dancing to the tune of injustice, in order to ingratiate himself with his masters or fellows.

By the end of the year Turgot and his friends were defamed in various anonymous pamphlets, none of which contained any specific or substantial criticisms. But they illustrated how much Turgot was loathed in many quarters.

At the end of December, the Marquis de Turgot, his younger brother, wrote to warn him:' Surely you are aware of the infernal cabal which has formed against you and the rumours which they are circulating; the priesthood and the financiers and all who are linked to them, pull together as fishermen in troubled waters.'[2] But Turgot had little time to turn his attention to these rumours, for not only was he preoccupied with a string of reforms for the following year but he had also suffered another attack of gout, which had confined him to his room at Versailles well into January 1776.

'What a nation!' exclaimed Métra. 'Even those with the least interest in maintaining injustices echo the accusations of the scoundrels and the unhappy honest men are too few to raise their voices and make themselves heard in a nation, which is light-hearted and unreasonable in its pleasures, its undertakings and its government.'[3]

---

[1] Schelle, op. cit., vol v, p. 415.
[2] Schelle, op. cit., vol iv, p. 281.
[3] Métra, *Correspondance* vol ii, p. 174.

24

The Six Edicts

At the beginning of January 1776 Turgot presented to the Council of Ministers six edicts on which he had been working for several months. Three of these covered substantial matters and the other three dealt with matters of minor importance. Before setting out the detailed provisions of these edicts, Turgot wrote in the preamble to the edicts a lengthy explanation of the evils to be remedied and the nature of the reforms. He attempted to expose clearly the injustices so that it would be impossible for a future minister to allow them to arise again.

The abolition of the *corvées*

There were no corvées in the regions around Paris, on account of their unpopularity. It was another matter in the provinces.[1] In several the road-building *corvées* had been commuted into a tax based on the *taille*. But there was still a lingering attachment to them in other provinces. The king had already committed himself publicly to the reform of the *corvées*, after reading an earlier paper by Turgot. The edict drafted by Turgot was the first legislative enactment on the *corvées*; they had been introduced as administrative expedients with no legal sanction. He wanted to abolish the *corvée*, which he had experienced vividly in the Limousin.

The burden of building and repairing roads had been put upon the shoulders of peasants who happened to be living near the roadside. Those with broader shoulders, like landowners and their tenants, courtiers, noblemen, *parliamentairies*, clerics were privileged and, therefore, exempt from liability to the *corvée*.

Turgot considered how the roads were to be financed. He rejected a system of tolls on travellers because in the main the charges would be passed into the price of goods and, therefore, bear most heavily upon the poor. He rejected national taxation for the same reason. Yet he perceived that roads increased the value of land along their route and at either end. The demand for land near or on a road increased and the high value reflected the intensity of this demand. High land

---

[1] Schelle, op. cit., vol v, p. 150.

values simply indicated that the demand for the use of land was high and that the land was desirable and low values reflected the poor demand due to the undesirability of the land.

Were the increased land values created by roads to be donated to landowners on a plate? Were the landowners deserving of the peasants' bounty? Turgot thought not. He believed that land value, that is the value of the bare land without improvement or building, indicated the source of a public fund. It owed its existence to the gregarious nature of man. Having not been created by any individual, be they duke or peasant, the value of land belonged to everyone equally or to society. Therefore he favoured that the value of land should be taxed and used in part to finance communal projects such as roads, bridges and the like.

'A tax of this nature', admitted Turgot, 'is beset by difficulties, but, when something is recognised as being just and of absolute necessity, one must not balk at the obstacles; it is necessary to overcome them.'[1] He anticipated fierce opposition from the privileged, who would be backed by the *parlements*. They favoured the private appropriation of a communal asset. In order to defeat Turgot's edict abolishing the *corvées*, they would refuse to register it. As far as they were concerned, that would be the end of the attempt to tax land value. The king, however, would have to make use of his prerogative power to ratify the measure, in a ceremony called a *lit de justice*, which would obviate the need of *parlement*'s registration.

The practical difficulty was the assessment of the tax, for there was no tax based on the value of land, owned by privileged and unprivileged. Turgot's suggestion was to base the assessment on the *vingtième* and to value the land of the privileged, which was not liable to the *vingtième*, on the same basis.

The edict was again prefaced by a lengthy summary of the injustice of the road *corvée*. In a paper to the king, Turgot tried to inspire him to undertake so reasonable a measure:

> At present His Majesty reigns by virtue of his power. He can only reign in the future through the level of reason which will have directed his laws, by the justice which will have formed their foundation and by the agreement of his people. As His Majesty wishes to reign only to effect the good, why should he not aspire to reign after his life through the duration of his good? The solemn declaration by His Majesty that he suppress the *corvées* because they were unjust will constitute an insuperable barrier against any minister who might dare to propose their reintroduction.[2]

It was not the suppression of the physical labour of the *corvées* which incited

---

[1] Ibid., p. 150.
[2] Ibid., pp. 153–4.

the interest of Turgot's enemies, but his provision for the tax to finance them. When framing the edict he was opposed continuously by Trudaine and the officials of the department of the *Ponts et Chaussées*, who were responsible for the construction of roads and by members of the Cours des Aides, whose jurisdiction covered fiscal issues. Those early opponents classed themselves as liberals and friends of reform. They opposed Turgot's ideas on practical grounds, and, only by constant argument and discussion throughout the autumn and early winter, did Turgot finally win their support.

Within weeks of the publication of the edict and its acceptance by the king, Maurepas suggested that Miromesnil, Keeper of the Seals, should examine the edicts and prepare a report for the king. When the king had read the report he asked Turgot to reply to the arguments of the Keeper of the Seals.

The king pondered the positions adopted by his two ministers. The contrasting views represented the qualities of each: a man of unpretentious nobility of character with an eye for justice and a politician who put the nobility of France higher than justice. He preferred the arguments of Turgot.

Freedom of the grain trade in Paris

In the earlier edict of September 1774 Turgot had introduced free trade in grain throughout the kingdom, but he had allowed the old regulations to be continued in the capital, where the protests were most vociferous. The earlier edict had restored the freedom of the grain trade in such natural centres as Bordeaux, Rouen and Lyons where trade had been choked previously with taxes and numerous regulations. But the anomaly continued in Paris, in order to prevent the free passage of grain between the north and south of Paris. This clog on freedom harmed both consumer and producer throughout France either directly or indirectly. 'It would not be possible', wrote Turgot to the king, 'to imagine how absurd these regulations [in Paris] are, if one did not have them before one's eyes . . . they constitute an obstacle, which renders the establishment of the grain trade in the town of Paris impossible because they are like a raised sword with which the magistrates can strike, ruin and dishonour at will any merchant who has displeased them or has been denounced by the popular prejudices.'[1]

The preamble of the edict described how in 1415 it was first forbidden to store grain in markets, so that, while it was held pending sale, grain was exposed to all weathers, and grain brought into Paris had to be sold by the close of the third market following its arrival or at a price fixed below the market price. In 1565 all merchants found guilty of moving grain outside Paris were made liable to flogging. In 1661 merchants were forbidden to purchase grain in the markets and bakers were restricted to purchases of less than two hogsheads of grain. In 1672 a

---

[1] Ibid., pp. 154–5.

merchant selling a cargo of grain had to sell every portion thereof at a uniform price and the person bringing grain into Paris had to sell in the recognised markets personally; he could not appoint agents. Such were some of the regulations operating in 1775.

Their combined effects , according to Turgot, had been to create famine in Paris during the years 1660–3, 1692–4, 1698–9, 1709 and 1740–1 when the price in other provinces was considerably less than it was in Paris. How could a society delude itself into imagining that these controls actually assured Paris a supply of food, when a moment's reflection would have dispelled so perverse a notion? It can only be attributed to the traditional distrust of freedom in France, which had been equated so often with anarchy and disorder; this distrust ran so deep that *dirigisme*, or central control, had become the habitual refuge. Yet, as Turgot had observed, it was only by ignoring these regulations when necessity demanded that Paris had been able to survive famines.

Turgot believed that the first edict would improve agriculture and the second would aid commerce and industry.

The suppression of the jurandes

The *jurandes* had been established in the Middle Ages as craft guilds, which had been formed as corporations under the control of masters. Craftsmen were allowed to associate together in corporations. Gradually these bodies won official recognition, as the state was able to raise cash by selling privileges for the manufacture or sale of goods and services. A clockmaker, a cheesemaker, a bookseller and the like had to purchase the right to engage in their professions or trades. The internal constitutions were arranged to enrich the pockets of the masters and lesser officials: the prince de Conti drew an estimated 50,000 livres per annum from the corporations. As Turgot observed in his introduction to this edict:

> It is without doubt the lure of these means of finance which has prolonged the immense damage suffered by employment and the blow to natural rights on account of these corporations. The illusion has been carried by certain persons as far that the right to work was a royal right which the crown could sell and which the subjects must buy. We hasten to refute such a maxim. God, by giving man needs and making these needs dependent on the resource of industry, has made the right to work the property of all men and this property is the foremost, the most inviolable and the most inalienable of all.
>
> We regard as one of the first duties of our justice and as one of the most worthy acts of our beneficence to free our subjects of all the abuses of this inalienable right of humanity. Consequently we wish to abrogate these

arbitrary institutions which do not allow the poor to live by their work; which repress a sex, whose physical weakness brings with it more needs and less resources and which seem, by condemning it to inevitable misery, to encourage its seduction and debauchery [women were excluded from the crafts by the corporations, even from the craft of embroidery]; which stifled competition and industry and rendered useless the talents of those who are excluded from entry into one of the corporations for one reason or another; which deprived the state and the arts of all intelligence which foreigners could bring to it; which retard the development of these arts by the multitude of difficulties which inventors encounter from different corporations who challenge the right to put into operation the discoveries which they have made; which surcharge industry by an enormous burden, as onerous to the individual as they are valueless to the state, by the immense fees which the craftsmen are obliged to pay in order to acquire the right to work, by the exactions of all kinds which they suffer, by the continual seizures made for the pretended transgressions, by the expense and waste of all kinds, by interminable trials, which break out between all the corporations over the respective claims to exclusive privileges; finally which, by these privileges afforded to the members of the companies to combine among themselves, allow the rich to submit the poorest to their wills and become an instrument of monopoly and encourage moves to increase the price of essential commodities above their natural level.[1]

'I regard, Sire', Turgot had written to the king, 'the suppression of the *jurandes* and the total freedom of all types of work that this edict allows to industry and the poor and labouring sections of your subjects, as one of the great benefits for your subjects. It is, second to the freedom of the grain trade, one of the most important steps that the government can take towards the improvement, rather the regeneration, of your Kingdom. It will be for industry what freeing the grain trade will be for agriculture.'[2]

The remaining edicts were of lesser importance. They concerned the provisioning of Paris, which did not enjoy the freedom of trade conferred on the rest of France.

Turgot's opponents hailed these edicts the handicraft of a deranged mind. Though the edicts themselves were reasonable, it was feared that they were only Turgot's opening moves against injustice. Turgot had to be attacked before he struck down more privileges enjoyed by his enemies.

---

[1] Ibid., pp. 242–3.
[2] Ibid., p. 159.

25

Registration of the Edicts

When the general contents of these edicts became known in late January 1776 the opposition at court, in the Church and in the *parlements* became intense. Before the measures were published Turgot was denounced as a madman, who wanted to overthrow the ancient order in France, only to experiment with these dangerous theories. There was no reasonable argument against the abolition of the *corvée*. The system was unjust, inefficient and damaging to liberty and agriculture. Arguments could be raised against the abolition of the *jurandes* but none could deny that it was the individual's right to work at a trade of his or her choice and that the closed shop was, like every monopoly, repugnant to the liberty of the individual and to the liberties of society. Against the edict of free trade in Paris the traditional, medieval and protectionist arguments could be raised. But arguments for protection are opposed to one fundamental truth: all forms of protection in peace, except perhaps the trade in dangerous drugs and armaments, are at the expense of individual liberty.

Turgot was well aware that his reforms were necessary to abolish real abuses, in which revolution would find its cause. He brought forward the six edicts in order to bring the struggle between the forces of reform and enlightenment and those of reaction and injustice into the open. Having chosen the ground on six edicts of incontestable merit, he hoped to assert the authority of the king and his Council over the opposition of the nobles, the Church and the *parlements*.

The opposition could engineer a noisy public protest, pretend to represent the public welfare and engage in devious conspiracies, but their weakness was patent and would be exposed; they had no solid arguments against the edicts. The king knew that. In fact, the *parlement* dared not print its remonstrances against the edicts. They were published in Holland, where the writ of censorship in France did not run, and the magistrates used every means to prevent them being imported into France.[1]

The six edicts were a prelude for greater reforms, which, as well as reforming inveterate abuses, would have also given the world a leading example of a

---

[1] D. Dakin, *Turgot and the Ancien Regime*, p. 266.

well-governed nation. In short, they were only the first steps and they demanded only the resources of ordinary common sense to comprehend.

The reforms promoted by Turgot during the first three months of 1776 were wide ranging. 'Three months ago', observed Véri at the end of February, 'he would have been renowned only as a visionary, because up to then only lists of his plans, many of which were wild, were merely circulated ... His courage is wholly deployed on behalf of those who have no access to the Court and for whom he destroys the objections of the rich, the courtiers, the financiers, the *parlements*, a party protected by the queen and even of his own colleagues. We have seen ministers care little about the provinces and their people provided that the Court and Paris were content with them. The provinces are well aware that M. Turgot is their support. But their voice does not reach the king, who imagines that everyone without exception hates the *contrôleur-général*'.[1]

Turgot never sought to represent classes or groups of society against other classes. The business of government, he believed, consisted in upholding the interest of the individual, usually against oppressive enactments of government. Though he may have enjoyed provincial support, he never relied on it. He counted on the king's support.

The six edicts and other reforms were enacted in the first three months of 1776. The opposition concentrated their efforts to sever the vital cord of support extended by the king. The threads of this accord were beginning to fray.

There are several examples of rulers who have attempted to revolutionise society or to accelerate its development. They have set their hands on expensive and spectacular projects, embarked on glorious adventures, assembled empires and done many spectacular things. The six edicts of Turgot were the preliminary steps towards something the world had never seen: a free, just and prosperous society.

The six edicts were discussed in the Council during January and Turgot encountered immediate opposition from his fellow ministers; some were open opponents, others were indifferent. As a result of their protests, he had to exempt the clergy from the road-building tax, which considerably weakened his reform of the *corvée*. Thus the new road tax fell to be assessed on the basis of the *vingtième*, the tax for which there were to be no exemptions, from which not only were the clergy exempt but also a number of nobles as well. He acquiesced in this concession because he had plans to reform the *vingtième* and to destroy its privileges.

Before the texts of the edicts were received by the *parlement*, Turgot had a meeting with the president of the *parlement* of Paris to discuss the registration of the edicts. The meeting broke up with the president pledging the opposition of the *parlements* and Turgot threatening a *lit de justice*, or use of the king's

---

[1] Véri, vol i, p. 413.

prerogative, to avoid the need of registration. Meanwhile, the magistrates had united to attack a pamphlet written by Condorcet with his customary fire on the reform of the *corvée*. The Prince de Conti pulled himself from his deathbed to rally the *parlement* against the pamphlet. It was said the 'marks of death were evident on his face'. As he left the *parlement*, the prince asked to be sent a copy of the edicts and declared that if he was ill during the debates he would return in a litter.

In the debate which followed, Espremesnil, a magisterial hack, attacked those who had been preaching liberal doctrines in commerce, agriculture and employment and accused them of stirring up more dangers for the state than the Jesuits. 'M. de Turgot', noted Stormont, 'was more than once reflected upon by name, and ranked among those innovators who, in a wild enthusiasm for their own chimerical opinion, would down every barrier, and to whom no property was sacred.'[1] It is interesting to note that while Turgot's name was cast into outer darkness, that of Necker was garlanded with effusive eulogies. So vehement were the attacks on the *philosophes* and *économistes*, that Turgot had Condorcet's pamphlet withdrawn from circulation.

At the end of February the *parlement* had worked itself into a fury over a reasonable book written by Boncerf, a subordinate of Turgot, on the subject of feudal dues. The principal idea of this inoffensive work was that, as the dues had fallen in value to a level that did not recompense the trouble of collection and greatly encumbered conveyancing, they should be commuted in money and the king should take the initiative by abolishing them on his domains. What irritated the magistrates most was that the book was written as an extension of Turgot's thinking on individual freedom. They denounced the book and ordered that its author be apprehended and the book banned as a punishment for making use of his mind. The king wrote immediately to the President of the *parlement* ordering that the matter be taken no further. Speaking against this modest work of Boncerf, Seguier likened the liberal thinkers to

> a secret party or agent, which, proceeded by thunder and earthquakes, at length throws up a sudden eruption with an ardent stream of ashes, lava and ruin, or bursting out with concentric rage from the bowels of the earth. Every nation has its manners, its laws, its customs and its usages. Political institutions constitute public order. To disturb this order is to assail the very constitution on which government is founded. The laws of every nation invariably partake of the spirit, character and opinion of its inhabitants. Every legislator, who would render a people wiser, or better, should consult their peculiar character and ideas. By what fatality does it happen that the writers of today make it their peculiar business to attack, tear down and subvert everything? The edifice of ordinances, the

---

[1] State Papers.

work of so many ages and the fruit of so many prudent kings and the result of the studies and the vigilance of so many enlightened ministers and magistrates, is treated by the new preceptors of mankind with insulting contempt, to which their imagination inspired by a false and illusive system, would alone be susceptible.[1]

The *parlement*'s remonstrances were presented to the king on 4 March and his reply was written to the magistrates three days later:

I have examined the remonstrances of my *parlement* with great attention: They contain nothing that has not been foreseen and deeply pondered before I had decided to publicise my edicts. My *parlement* ought to have seen that all these laws are intended to assure abundance in my good city of Paris, to deliver commerce from a damaging straitjacket and to provide relief for those of my subjects who live only by their work and who are most exposed to poverty. My intention is not to confound conditions, nor to deprive the nobility of my kingdom of the distinctions acquired by their services and which they have always enjoyed under my predecessors and which will be maintained by me always.

It is not all a question of a humiliating tax, but of a simple contribution to which everyone will do themselves honour by paying, since I have myself given the example by contributing according to my domains. I wish to believe that my *parlement* has only been prompted by its zeal and I will never imagine that it wishes to stray from the submission which it owes to me. But now that I have taken to explaining in person my motivation for persisting with my resolution, I expect that my *parlement* will not delay in proceeding to register the edicts pure and simple.[2]

After reading this letter, Turgot thought the *parlements* would register the edicts without further ado. Despite this firm royal reply, the *parlement* announced that it was 'penetrated with grief in that its faithfulness and its attachment to the king and to the dignity of his service obliges it to represent the arguments so that he will be minded to examine them after the point of view of humanity, beneficence and justice which reign in his heart.'[3]

The king responded by invoking his prerogative in the elaborate and solemn ceremony of a *lit de justice*, to be convened at Versailles on 12 March. This ceremony enabled the king to register the edicts himself, without the approval of the *parlements*. The Keeper of the Seals opened the proceedings before the magistrates, dressed in black facing the throne, by speaking on the purpose and

---

[1] Soulavie, op. cit., vol iii, pp. 1367–68.
[2] Schelle, op. cit., vol v, p. 272.
[3] Ibid., p. 273.

nature of the edicts. Then the magistrates knelt down on their knees, until bidden to rise by the Keeper of the Seals.

The first president of the *parlement*, M. Aligre, opened the arguments of the magistrates. 'You will read, Sire, in all eyes, which are the certain interpreters of hearts, gratitude and joy. This kind of satisfaction so flattering to a king you have tasted from the first moments of your reign and your great soul has appreciated to the full. Why is it necessary that today a gloomy sadness offers itself everywhere to the august looks of Your Majesty? If he deigns to regard the people he will see them anxious. If he turns to the capital he will see it in alarm. If he regards the nobility he will see it plunged into affliction.'[1]

After the first president's brief summary of the feelings of the *parlement*, the Keeper of the Seals crouched before the throne to hear the king's pleasure and then stepped forward to command the registrar to read the edict on the *corvée*. The doors were opened and the registrar walked up to the Keeper of the Seals, who gave him a copy of the edict. He read it. The magistrates were kneeling, until bidden to rise and then Seguier spoke against the edict. This procedure was repeated for each of the six edicts.

After the procedure was adopted for the final edict, the assembly filed out of the chamber in order. On the morrow, in keeping with tradition, the magistrates protested at the illegality of the proceedings. But the edicts had been registered and had become law.

The passage of the edicts was greeted with widespread joy, particularly by those still liable to the *corvée* and those oppressed by the corporations. News spread to England where five or six editions of the edicts were published in translation; '. . . in several cities, in Bristol principally, toasts were drunk, there was dancing and there had been celebrations in honour of our young king and his minister'[2] No doubt these shows in Britain were promoted by expatriate French artisans, who had emigrated in order to escape religious persecution or the restrictions of the corporations.

---

[1] Ibid., p. 277.
[2] Beauchomont, *Memoires Secrétes* vol ix, pp. 181–3.

26

Frenzied Opposition

In late January 1776 Véri had reported that the Council had decided to recall De Guines, the ambassador in London, who had been involved in a law suit with his secretary. The ambassador had caused further trouble by giving an assurance to the British government that if Britain did not side with Portugal in its war against Spain, France would not support Spain. The news found its way to Madrid and the Spanish government checked its veracity with Vergennes, the French foreign minister. The French king picked up the story from the *cabinet noir*, which intercepted the Spanish diplomatic bag as it passed through Paris.

Both foreign minister and king did not want to raise the matter for fear of exciting the queen's support of Guines. But fortified by the knowledge that each other knew, they informed the Council. Malesherbes told the queen that Guines should be recalled and she readily agreed. The king, however, let the matter rest. Maurepas did not want to offend the Choiseulistes by taking the initiative and Vergennes seemed to hesitate as well. Both Turgot and Malesherbes agreed that it was necessary to recall an untrustworthy ambassador, particularly as war was being waged in the American colonies. Turgot, who was scheduled to have the first meeting with the king, undertook to discuss the situation with him. After their meeting the king promised to discuss the matter with the queen, but another week went by without any action. Turgot reminded the king of the urgency of the matter in a letter on another subject.

Finally on 22 January, the decision was taken to recall the ambassador. Later, other follies in the ambassador's conduct came to light: he had informed the Spanish ambassador that the military preparations being made in Britain were for an invasion of Mexico and, in contradiction of orders, he told the British government that France would not intervene in the American struggles. But meanwhile, the Choiseulistes pressed that Guines be given an opportunity to defend himself. They demanded that no successor be appointed until he had be given that chance. Choiseul, who had distanced himself at first, discussed the matter with Aranda, the Spanish ambassador in Paris, and thought that Guines, his former protégé, was innocent. Choiseul demanded that diplomatic papers should be produced to establish the ambassador's innocence. Vergennes advised the king that to do so would bring matters under the gaze of the whole of Europe. After Guines had been recalled to Paris on 3 March, there was no more talk of a defence and the queen seemed to accept the situation, but was active behind the scenes to protect the former ambassador.

In the first week of February 1776 the king was heard to remark, 'It is only Turgot and myself who loved the people.'[1] That was the last recorded kind sentiment expressed by Louis on a minister, who had given himself to illumine his reign with justice, freedom and prosperity.

'The enemies of M. Turgot', wrote Mairobert on 10 April, 'are looking all the time to cover his operations, his confidants and friends with ridicule and odium.'[2] They composed songs, cartoons, satires and plays to deliver their attacks. A satire called *The Dream of M. Maurepas* was a witty, yet unjust, attack on Turgot. It is a dream of a hideous machine taking over the governance of France. Maurepas

> discovered a dark laboratory where embryonic and elementary conceptions of organic and patriotic municipalities were being formed. Science and solemnity reigned everywhere. Here were being concocted unthinkable advantages for the poor and the wretched. Here also were prepared the general annihilation of every social bond and the total subversion of every inequality of fortune and rank. The measures of government were no longer to be influenced by the weight of property and consideration; France was to be thrown into a mould, dissimilar and quite opposite to her former condition. She appeared like a smooth tablet of wax, which twenty novices had scribbled over with their economic plans designed for the good of the nation . . . [then Maurepas awakes] There was another man in France, awkward and ungracious, confused and dull of apprehension, with more harshness than character, with more obstinacy than fortitude, with more impatience than sensibility; a mountebank in government and morals; designed to bring the former into disrepute and as unacquainted with human nature, which he never understood, as with public affairs, which he always misapprehended – that man was Turgot. He was one of those half-witted, seeming thinkers who adopt everything that is visionary and exaggerated. He was held to be profound, but he was superficial to a degree; his enthusiasm, however, as adapted to time and circumstance, was able to seduce. Night and day he muttered to himself those cabalistic terms, 'philosophy, liberty, equality and *produit net*. It was a sort of madness which he made fashionable with watchwords for printers of the day.[3]

[1] P. Foncin, *Essai sur le Ministére de Turgot*, p. 422.
[2] Beauchomont, *Chroniques Secrétes*, vol ix, p. 90.
[3] Soulavie, op. cit., [trans. 1802] vol 2, pp. 108–11.

Small snuff boxes were quite popular in Paris, and on account of their flatness became known as 'platitudes'. The duchesse de Bourbon visited a tobacco shop and when asked what she wanted, she replied 'Some turgotines'. The shopkeeper thought he had misheard and ignored her request. 'Yes', insisted the duchesse, 'some snuff boxes like these'. 'Madame', explained the shopkeeper, 'these are platitudes'. 'Yes, yes', countered the duchesse irritably, 'they are the same thing.'[1]

The *parlements*, incensed by the six edicts, seized upon two incidents in which the peasantry had turned on their noble masters; the marquis de Vibraye locked up a peasant who refused to pay a feudal due, and was besieged by a mob of forty labourers, who demanded the release of their comrade, and the duc de Montemar was attacked by a group of peasants who pretended to be free owners of their holdings. The *parlements* attributed these outrages to Turgot's schemes and particularly to the book written by Boncerf.

The clergy and the Jesuits took every opportunity to denounce the *philosophes* from the pulpit in the most violent language, which would have outdone the most ferocious presbyterian preacher.

While the six edicts were being enacted, Stormont noted that the Church and the magistracy, rarely in agreement over anything, were now united 'by their common interest and common hatreds of the comptroller [as he described Turgot]. The abbé Fauchet, who was both chaplain to the king and a loyal friend of Turgot, was censured by the archbishop of Paris for speaking favourably of Turgot.

Voltaire wrote to Turgot at the beginning of May, 'M. Trudaine witnesses the transports of joy which you have caused in the country all around us. We are seeing the birth of a golden age, but it is really ridiculous that there are so many folk from the age of iron in Paris.'[2]

While the chorus of opposition to Turgot was reaching a crescendo on the public platforms, several leading parts can be highlighted. The baron Rigoley d'Oigny, the head of the *cabinet noir*, had a special relationship with the king: he provided continual diversion and amusement by showing him passages of private letters intercepted by himself. After his elevation to the Council Turgot made a point of sending no *lettres intersantes* through the post.[3] Yet, according to D'Oigny, Turgot had been sending letters critical of the royal family and been receiving similar letters in reply; the letters, however, were forgeries. D'Oigny also produced forged letters critical of Turgot.

Not only did D'Oigny have a duty to amuse and alert the king but he also had a violent dislike for Turgot, who was widely known as an enemy of the *cabinet*. The king, knowing the character of the *contrôleur*, should have discounted the claims of the baron. But it must be remembered that he was ready to believe

---

[1] *L 'Espion Anglais* [1809] vol i, p. 556.
[2] Voltaire, Letter *3 May 1776*.
[3] Schelle, op. cit., vol v, p. 446.

anything coming to him from this grubby source. According to Du Pont, the king showed these forged letters to Maurepas, who did not question their authenticity. This much was corroborated by the comte d'Angivillers, to whom the king divulged his allegations against Turgot.

A second figure at the centre of the conspiracy against Turgot was the marquis de Pezay. The marquis pretended to be an aristocrat, but, according to Sénac de Meilhan, he was plain M. de Pezay. He also gave himself the airs of a poet. He was an accredited lover of Mme de Montbarey, who influenced the grand manipulator, Mme Maurepas. Once Maurepas said that Pezay ruled France. For he controlled, through two women, the chief minister and, thus effectively, ruled France himself. Early in the reign the marquis started writing letters in confidence to the king and among his gratuitous pieces of advice was the dismissal of Terray; it was the same advice that the whole nation seemed to be pouring into the king's ear. According to Véri, his political advice consisted of dressing up general opinions and adding a little spice of his own. Pezay had revealed his identity to the king through Sartine. After some months of gratuitous correspondence, he sought some recognition for his labours with the pen. He asked the king to acknowledge his assent to receiving his letters by pausing in front of a certain window in a vestibule through which the king passed on his way to vespers each evening. The king did as he was requested and the letters continued.

Though Pezay valued his literary labours above price, he needed remuneration. He offered his services to Necker whom Sénac de Meilhan described as 'a rich man tormented by ambition'. Necker opened the vaults to the poetic marquis and it was then, according to Sénac de Meilhan, that 'the marquis de Pezay becomes really interesting'. The marquis also acquired the Prince de Montbarey as his private client. The marquis began communicating the financial ideas of Necker to Maurepas. These, as might be suspected, were as vague, as vain and as interventionist as his earlier writings on the grain trade. One wonders whether interventionists, protectionists and socialists actually believe in their measures or espouse them merely because they concentrate power in their own hands. With Necker, the latter consideration was ever present in his arbitrary calculations. Maurepas gave Pezay and Necker a copy of his budget of 1776. Within weeks [he] was laying before the king Necker's criticisms of a budget projecting a deficit of 24 million livres. 'The arrogant Necker', wrote Sénac de Meilhan, 'went on several occasions to the house of the marquis and waited in his carriage several times for his arrival from Versailles. When one calls to mind that this man had stated so often in his writings of the nobility of his sentiments and of his mistrust of intrigue . . .'[1]

In due course the marquis served his clients well; Necker realised his ambition of becoming the *de facto contrôleur-général*, for as a Protestant he could not hope

[1] Sénac de Meilhan, *De Government . . .* [1792], p. 170.

for a formal appointment. The prince de Montbarey became the minister of war and Pezay himself became an inspector of the coasts at a salary of 60,000 livres per annum. But it went to Pezay's head and he began boasting of his achievements in his last years. 'Such is the story', concluded Sénac de Meilhan, 'of a petit maître, poet, intriguer, who brought into office by his dark manoeuvres a man [Necker] who made the destiny of France.'[1]

---

[1] Ibid., p. 171.

27

The Spring of 1776

In February Turgot 's brother-in-law, the duc de Saint-Aignan, died at the age of ninety-two and his death caused a vacancy in the *Acadèmie des Inscriptions et Belles-Lettres*, to which Turgot's father had also belonged. It was an erudite body, filled with *philosophes*, numbering about forty members. They decided to show their support of Turgot at a time when he was under public attack and, accordingly, elected him a member. Turgot at first refused to become one, thinking it would only afford the enemies of the *philosophes* further reason to oppose him. But he changed his mind and joined the *Acadèmie* in March 1776.

Finances in 1776

In his budget for 1775 Turgot had allowed for a deficit for 37 million livres; in fact, he had limited it to a deficit of only 24 million livres after repaying 66 million livres debt of various kinds, using capital rather than current receipts, and meeting 10 million livres unforeseen expenses, relating to the foot-and-mouth outbreak, the marriage of Mme Clotide and the coronation. He had effected an overall improvement of almost 13 million livres which would accrue in full during the following year, of which 3 million livres can be attributed to increased revenue from a smaller tax burden, 8.5 million livres through reduction of expenditure and an additional 1.5 million livres from the post. The largest savings in expenditure were the reductions in brokerage, commissions and expenses deducted from the receipts and savings in interest, which amounted to 5.7 million and 2.4 million livres respectively. One result of this first year in office was that credit had improved sufficiently to allow the Treasury to borrow directly from the French public and to negotiate a substantial loan in Amsterdam.

The budget for 1776 projected a deficit of 24 million livres on levels of expenditure and receipts comparable to the previous year. This included an increase in military expenditure of 3 million livres and an increase of a like amount in the king's household.

Negotiations were still in progress with the Dutch bankers in regard to the loan of 60 million livres. This loan would enable Turgot to break the monopoly of the French financiers and to repay the more expensive loans.

It had proved impossible to cut military expense, and to curb the wasteful expense of the court. But it would be possible to cut the expense of borrowing by negotiating cheaper rates on loans. Such a saving could be secured without the support of fellow ministers. He estimated in the summer of 1775 that the annual interest on the loans, called the anticipations, advanced by French financiers against the revenue of the following year was 6–7 per cent, which represented a large premium over the international rate of 4 per cent. Terray had destroyed the international credit of France and had made the government dependent on a few French financiers, who demanded high rates and who were able to embarrass the government by withholding funds if their demands were not met.

Having shown his determination to honour obligations dishonoured by Terray, Turgot decided to free the government from its dependence on domestic financiers by borrowing at the lower rates being offered abroad. In July 1775 he had begun negotiations with Dutch bankers and it soon became apparent that 'the operations of the previous reign had greatly impaired the credit of France'.[1] The bankers demanded terms which Turgot felt could not be refused; they were prepared to lend 60 million livres, half at 4 per cent and half in the form of life annuities at 8 per cent. He disliked annuities. The bankers also demanded the guarantee of the Spanish crown, in addition to the French crown. Turgot advised the king to accept these terms and thereby force domestic rates down to the international level.

In March 1776 Turgot's plans for a Discount Bank, *la Caisse d'Escompte*, were announced in an *arrêt*. Turgot thought the Bank should seek its share capital from the public and then the Bank would lend the government 10 million livres over a period of thirteen years at 4 per cent. It would also be empowered to discount private bills up to a limit of 5 million livres, endorsed by at least three reputable names. Though modelled on the Bank of England, the Discount Bank was given no similar monopolies or privileges. Turgot's purpose in establishing a bank was to create a free and active financial market in Paris, which he believed would assist the development of commerce and industry. The government also would benefit from lower rates of interest. The initial capital of 10 million livres was to be lent to the government in order to provide the bank with a secure base. Turgot's hope was that over the thirteen year period it would find its place in the financial market without needing to depend on the government. This was the only attempt to establish a state bank since the dramatic failure of John Law's bank a half-century before. According to Métra the venture incurred opposition from the financiers, who saw it as a move to break their power.

Turgot submitted a paper on internal duties imposed on trade. It explains at

---

[1] Schelle, op. cit., vol v, p. 311.

length why it is so that taxes 'if they impoverish the people, cannot enrich the sovereign'.[1]

The North American Colonies

At the end of March 1776 the king asked Turgot to submit a paper giving a second opinion, after reading the report of the minister of foreign affairs, on the situation brewing in the American colonies, regarding their struggle for independence from Britain. Turgot wanted to preserve the peace, for he knew France could not afford a war. Turgot's paper of nearly 40 pages considered several factors relevant to the interests of France. He suggested that Britain might become reconciled with the colonies, by repealing Townsend's Stamp Act imposed in 1763, which had attempted to impose taxation on the colonies, without allowing representation at Westminster. Then a new British leader could seek compensation in a spectacular war in Europe. This possibility posed a threat to France. Another possibility was that if Britain was successful in America, she might begin conquering Europe. Turgot believed, however, that victory in America would weaken Britain greatly by the debt and the effort needed to maintain a standing army in the colonies and by the loss of trade, which invariably followed war. It was also inconceivable that a defeated Britain would turn against Spain and France, for Turgot doubted that Britain would want to make fresh enemies. The last possibility was that the colonists would triumph and, the longer the war continued, the more certain this result would become – America would become independent.[2]

The whole situation was bound up with the protectionist ideas that colonies could be exploited economically and that they should be tied by trading monopolies to the mother country. He argued that these advantages were chimerical, when weighed against the real cost of protecting the monopolies. With both Spain and Britain attached to protectionist beliefs which complimented their imperialist ambitions, Turgot advised the king that France should introduce a new order by allowing her colonies political and economic independence and so secure the 'complete freedom of trade and navigation'.[3]

He advised the king to stay out of the war at all costs, because the finances were in deficit, the national debt was already overbearing, credit was beginning to revive and the army and navy were in a poor condition. Rather than go to war, France should prepare for any eventuality by putting the navy on alert, with ships held in French ports, by stationing the land forces and munitions near the ports, by deploying spies in Britain and by shipping arms to the colonies through Spanish ports. If France went to war in America, it might also promote a reconciliation between Britain and her colonies, giving rise to a range of

---

[1] Ibid., p. 359.
[2] As Turgot had predicted in 1751.
[3] Ibid., p. 399.

portentous possibilities. However, were France to declare war against Britain, it could be mounted most successfully in Canada, India or Gibraltar. Turgot favoured an attack in India, which he saw was the weakest link in British rule. The power of the British in India 'was as precarious, as it was terrifying. It is a colossus whose feet are made of clay. It is founded on violence, brigandage and tyranny alone. There is no doubt that the cruelties and vexations exercised by the English nation have brought the minds of the population and their rulers to despair. They may be waiting only for a European war, which would give them hope of assistance, in order to revolt. With sufficient forces and good leadership, we could effect the same revolution over there against the English which we ourselves suffered at their hands. And this revolution would not, in turn, suffer a similar counter-attack by the English, if, wiser than we were when we had the upper hand and than the English have been ever since, we did not undertake to succeed their domination; if instead of opposing the natives of this country, we limited ourselves to protecting their liberty.'[1]

Two years later France entered the war in America. It was glorious adventure but the debt it incurred grew to insupportable heights under Necker and the effects of war in America proved to be as fateful as Turgot had feared.

The slave trade

It was rumoured in April 1776 that the French government was on the point of liberating Negroes in their colonies. The directors of trade in Guyana were shaken by these rumours and consulted Sartine, the minister of the colonies. He replied in early April to announce that the king had agreed to pay a subsidy of 15 livres for every slave imported into the colonies. They were not satisfied by the level of the subsidy and appealed to the *contrôleur-général* for a subsidy of 24 livres to run for the next three years. For reasons yet to be described, Turgot was not able to reply, but, knowing his feelings on the subject, one can only imagine that he would have pressed for their emancipation on humanitarian, political and economic grounds. In the same year of 1776, some thirty-one years before slavery was abolished in Britain, David Hartley moved a motion in the House of Commons that, 'The slave trade was contrary to the laws of God and the rights of man.' The emancipation movement began in France thereafter and in 1788 Condorcet became the president of the *Société des Amis des Noirs* which helped to secure the abolition of slavery in France in 1815.

---

[1] Ibid., p. 413.

28

Dismissal

It seemed as though the queen was ignoring De Guines immediately after his return from the ambassadorship in London. In fact, she was working for him behind the scenes, by persuading the king to prevent examination into his conduct in London. She was scheming during April 1776 in another direction, which began when Malesherbes let it be known that he wanted to leave the government. He had always understood that his tenure of office would be brief. The enactment of the six edicts brought him into conflict with the *parlements*. He supported the edicts, not from conviction, but rather out of loyalty to Turgot. Although Malesherbes' desire to leave the administration created an opportunity to replace him with an opponent of Turgot, no charge of betrayal can be laid against him. For Malesherbes had predicted, with characteristic candour, his unsuitability for office.

Throughout April 1776 both the court and Turgot put forward their candidates for the vacancy. The queen and Maurepas backed Amelot, who happened to be Maurepas' nephew. Turgot had agreed to appoint him an intendant of commerce. Turgot felt grave reluctance in appointing him to this modest rank of government, because he believed him to be unsuited for public office. Turgot supported Véri to succeed Malesherbes. Véri , however, had left for a holiday in the country and did not return even when Turgot pleaded with him to return and to mediate between himself and Maurepas.

At this time the king agreed to let Malesherbes go. He began to yield as well to the unrelenting pressure from the queen against Turgot. It proved to be effective because Maurepas made no attempt to support Turgot against the increasingly malicious rumours. Up to this time the king had made only the occasional remark against Turgot and had not faltered in his support for him. In mid-April the king remarked to the queen about the chilly reception which had greeted her at the opera. She retorted that, if the king himself went out with 'his' Turgot and Saint-Germain, he, too, could expect to be booed.

At this critical time two scandals were grossly exaggerated, in order to damage Turgot. It was simpler to damage his reputation by rumour than attack his reforms. The first involved Turgot's brother. In 1763, at the conclusion of the

Seven Years War, France had lost many of her possessions in Canada. Choiseul, then the French foreign minister, decided to build up the colony in Guyana. Emigrants were dispatched from France, but no satisfactory arrangements had been made for their arrival. They soon perished in the equatorial heat and in the floods, which were followed by plague. A year later Turgot's middle brother was appointed governor of the colony. He ordered the arrest of the previous governor, Chanvalon, and sent him home. Against the advice of Turgot's brother the French government dispatched further consignments of emigrants without adequate preparation. They too perished. Turgot's brother became ill and returned to Paris. He tried to clear his name against the charge that he had been negligent. He was dismissed and returned to botanical gardening. Chanvalon was imprisoned and ordered to finance masses for the dead and for the funding of a hospital in the colony. In 1775 Chanvalon lodged an appeal against his imprisonment. Sartine, the minister of the colonies, and Turgot himself heard the new evidence and disallowed the appeal. Sartine re-opened the matter in 1776 by presenting papers referring to Turgot's brother in the whole affair to the king. Sartine asked for a hearing in secret, but he said nothing to Turgot about the move. The king, however, told Turgot about the action of Sartine. Turgot suggested that the matter had only been re-opened by his fellow minister in order to embarrass him. The affair shows how the conspiracy to break the king's trust had reached the Council of Ministers.

There was another incident which was employed to lower Turgot in the king's eyes. A Mme Lebeau had directed a theatre in Lyons under licence of the duc de Villeroi. A subordinate of Turgot, called Delacroix, did not like her or the prosperity of her theatre. He accepted a bribe and then revoked her licence to run her theatre. Mme Lebeau made inquiries of the role of Delacroix and discovered that he had accepted various bribes of 18,000 livres per annum. Armed with proof, she went to see the queen at Versailles. The king confronted Turgot with the claim that a member of his staff was guilty of bribery and Turgot agreed to investigate. Delacroix supplied a reasonable explanation. After the next meeting of the Council, Turgot attempted to defend Delacroix and the king took some papers from his pocket and replied, 'I do not like rogues, nor those who support them.'[1] His meetings with Turgot were becoming brief and terse.

By the end of April 1776 Turgot knew that his relationship with the king was either at an end or in danger of being put to an end. He was not worried about his personal position, as he had explained to Véri a month earlier:

> Basically I want only what I believe to be the good of the king. He has a greater need of me than I of him. If he dismisses me, or if I go because he has made my task impossible, what do I lose? You know my tastes are

---

[1] P. Foncin, *Essai sur le Ministre de Turgot*, p. 526.

not difficult to satisfy . . . This is my remedy; always to tell him the truth and to tell it with the greatest clarity. If he were to dismiss me tomorrow, I would say to him today: 'This is what I think you should do, I cannot serve you tomorrow since you no longer want me anymore, but it is still my duty today to put one truth before your eyes.' If one lacks the art of handling people, constant truth is the best resource. If that does not work, I will leave with it.[1]

On 30 April Turgot wrote to the king, appealing to him to face the realities of his position and to the dangers into which Maurepas was leading him. The letter later appeared to Malesherbes, who collected Turgot's papers after his death, to be so confidential that he even forbade Turgot's brother from reading it. Malesherbes burnt it in order to preserve confidence between monarch and minister. Fortunately Turgot had shown it to Véri, who copied parts of it:

Sire, I do not wish to disguise the deep wound to my heart caused by Your Majesty's cruel silence to me last Sunday, after I had drawn his attention at great length in my earlier letters to my position, to his own, to the dangers threatening his position, to the glory of his reign and to the impossibility of serving him if he gives me no support. Your Majesty has not deigned to give me even a reply.

I do not think, Sire, that with a cheerful heart you would consider sacrificing the glory of your reign and the welfare of your people; it is implied therefore that Your Majesty may not have believed a word of what I wrote and said. It is implied that he may have believed me a rascal or an imbecile who has not seen that which he believes he has seen himself. It is thus implied that he puts no value on my services or on the attachment which I have vowed to him . . . A minister who loves his master, needs his love in return . . . The honest man will serve you as a matter of duty, but when, Sire, an honest and sensitive man receives only indifference in return for his sacrifices, he withdraws into himself and wilts . . .

Sire, I have believed that Your Majesty deserved to be served loyally on account of the love of justice and the goodness engraved on his heart. I gave myself wholly to this sentiment. I have seen my reward in your happiness and that of your people. I have braved the hate of those who profit by several abuses . . . It is a question of your reign, your authority, your glory, your happiness and that of France. I repeat the same thing continually. How can I tell you more clearly? Your Majesty has told me that you need reflection and that you lack experience. You lack

---

[1] Véri, vol i, pp. 414–15.

experience, Sire? I realise that twenty-two years and in your position you have not had the experience of living among equals which enables individuals to judge others. But will you tell me that you have more experience in eight days or in a month and that it is necessary to wait for this tardy experience arrives? You have no personal experience, but you have the recent experience of your predecessor, to enable you to appreciate the dangers of your position? I have depicted all the ills which caused the weakness of the late king. I have explained at length all the intrigues which gradually undermined his authority . . .

At the age of forty Louis XV held authority intact and there was no disorder in peoples' minds. You, Sire, are twenty-two years old and the *parlements* are already more lively, more audacious and more linked to cabals at the court than they were in 1770 after twenty years' effort and success during the previous reign. Peoples' minds are more activated on all matters and your government is more divided and is actually weaker than that of your predecessor. Imagine, Sire, that according to the way of nature you have fifty years to reign and imagine also the progress that disorder, having reached its present temper, can make in twenty . . .

It grieves me greatly to tell you that M. Maurepas is truly guilty, if he proposes M.Amelot, and his weakness will be as damaging to you as an ordinary crime . . . But, Sire, do you know at what point M. Maurepas is weak in character? At what point is he dominated by those who see him often? Everyone knows that Mme Maurepas, who has less intelligence but much more character, continually inspires all his wishes. The opinion of the public also make an unbelievable impression on him. Someone with his intelligence and ability must have his own opinion. I have seen him change his ideas ten times on the *lit de justice*, according to whether he was seeing the Keeper of the Seals, M. Albert or myself. It is this unfortunate uncertainty of which *parlement* is duly appraised, which has so long fortified and prolonged the resistance of this body. If abbé Véri had not helped steady him, I would not have been surprised if he had completely given in and advised Your Majesty to surrender to *parlement*. This weakness has affected my relationship with M. Maurepas . . . The dominant role which I assumed in the riots of 1775 naturally, because it was I who was being attacked . . . hurt him greatly . . . From that moment it was rumoured that I wanted to act on behalf of all departments and become the prime minister. Thousands of people told M. Maurepas that I wanted to supplant him and I do not know in truth if these criticisms against me were believed by him; which shows he hardly knew me . . .

Never forget, Sire, that it was weakness that brought the head of Charles 1 [of England] to the block; that weakness made Charles IX cruel . . . Weakness created all the miseries of the last reign . . .

It is thought, Sire, that you are weak and there have been occasions when I feared your character had this fault. However I have seen you at critical times show real courage. I cannot repeat to Your Majesty too often what I foresee and what the whole world sees as the inevitable consequences of weakness and misery, if plans once begun are abandoned and if the administration, which has put them forward, yields before the resistance mounted before it.

And what will happen, Sire, to these internal disorders if there is added the embarrassment of war (in America), which a thousand imprudent steps can bring or circumstances can force? What hand if it cannot hold the rudder in the calm, will be able to withstand the effects of storms? How would a war be maintained in this fluctuation of ideas and habit of indiscretion which always accompanies weakness?

This is the problem in which you find yourself; a weak and disunited government, all minds in ferment, the *parlements* in league with all the cabals and emboldened by the goverment's weakness, revenue below the level of expenditure, the greatest resistance to economies, no solidarity or fixity of policies, no secrecy in the resolution of your councils. Is it in these circumstances that one proposes to Your Majesty a man without talent whose only merit is that of submissiveness? Not of those ministers who have strength in government, but to the Keeper of the Seals, who, by his insinuations, increases still more the tendency to weakness. It is in these circumstances that Your Majesty cannot fail to be seized of the dangers which I have indicated with so much evidence.

Finally, if I earn the misfortune that this letter brings about my disgrace, I beg that he informs me personally. At all events I rely on His Majesty's confidence.[1]

On the same day, 30 April, that Turgot wrote to the king, he also wrote to Véri, who was on holiday in the country. He told him that it was rumoured that the decision to replace Malesherbes by Amelot had been taken. 'For myself', wrote Turgot, 'I have only one resort: it is to achieve the impossible by making Malesherbes stay in office until Whitsun, so that the secret which has come out spreads to the point that the denunciations of the public will reach your friends [the Maurepas] . . . I tell you that this concerns the honour of your friends, the peace and glory of the king and the welfare of more than 20 million people during his entire reign and perhaps for centuries, for we know what roots evil is weaving in this unhappy land and what it costs to uproot them.'[2]

Véri admitted later that he would not have been absent, had he realised the

---

[1] Schelle, op. cit., vol v, pp. 448–56.
[2] Véri, vol i, p. 430.

seriousness of Turgot's position. On 10 May Turgot wrote again to Véri to say that the withdrawal of Malesherbes was to be announced shortly, simultaneously with the appointment of Amelot and that the king had interviewed a candidate, Clugny, for the position of *contrôleur-général*. 'I need', wrote Turgot, 'only a few days to put before the king a plan for the reform of the royal household. Undoubtedly it will not be accepted and I will demand my freedom. I will depart with the regret of seeing a beautiful dream dissolve and to see a young king, who deserved a better lot, and an entire kingdom lost by him [Maurepas], who should have saved them. But I will depart without shame or remorse and I am taking with me the wherewithal to keep myself occupied in my free time and will make my leisure really useful.'[1]

The following day it was announced that Guines, the recalled ambassador, had been made a duc. 'The queen's plan', wrote Mercy-Argentau to Maria-Thérèsa, 'was to require the king to hound Turgot, to send him to the Bastille on the same day that Guines was made a duc.'[2] However, Marie-Antoinette had a more succinct and sufficient reason to approve of Turgot's departure. She wrote to her mother on 13 June to explain: 'that they [Turgot and Malesherbes] were upsetting almost everyone.'

The day after Bertin called on Malesherbes to acknowledge that his resignation had been accepted. Then he visited Turgot to announce not only his dismissal, but also his disgrace. Véri recorded that 'M. Turgot took his disgrace with the greatest calmness. Indifference to favour as a courtier is characteristic to him. He was not indifferent to public office, which has been his meat and drink since his youth. But when one holds office by this lien, and not for the ordinary motives for dignities and enrichment, one soon acquires some indifference.'[3]

On the day of Turgot's dismissal Maurepas wrote to excuse his absence on the grounds of unavoidable duties, to beg Turgot to believe in the sympathies from himself and his wife. Turgot thanked him for his concern and concluded his reply by stating 'when one has no shame, no remorse, when one has known no other interests than that of the king and the state, when one has not misrepresented or suppressed any truth, one cannot be unhappy.'[4] That conclusion would not have troubled Maurepas' dim conscience. A draft of a letter to Maurepas by Turgot survives. It show the futility of attempting to reason with an unreasonable fool; it is almost like expecting to find backbone in a jelly. Maurepas had few political principles and allowed himself to be blown in every wind, in order not to be blown over.

Some weeks later Voltaire wrote to Turgot, 'You have governed for about twenty months. These twenty months will be an eternal epoch.' To another friend,

[1] Ibid., pp. 430–1.
[2] Mercy-Argentau, *Correspondance Secréte* vol ii, 16 May 1776.
[3] Véri, vol i, p. 314.
[4] Schelle, op. cit., vol v, p. 442.

Voltaire wrote, 'This is a disaster . . . I see only death before me . . . this blow strikes me in the head and the heart I will never console myself for having seen born and perished the age which M. Turgot prepared for us.'[1] Mme Kaunitz, the daughter-in-law of the Austrian Prime Minister, expressed what Turgot's friends felt. She wrote to Véri, 'I am pierced with grief, for I see that the good is impossible. I know that M. Turgot has been overthrown and I weep for France . . . Versailles will rejoice and the provinces will be desolated.'[2]

Turgot, having obtained royal permission through the intervention of his friend the comte d'Angivillers, wrote his last letter to the king a week after being dismissed:

> My whole desire, Sire, is that you may always be able to believe that I have been wrong and that I have indicated chimerical dangers. I wish that time does not justify them and that your reign will be as peaceful and happy for you and your people as your principles of justice and beneficence promise it will be.
>
> There remains, Sire, one kindness to ask of you and I even dare to call less a kindness than an act of justice. The most precious thing which remains with me to keep is your esteem. I will always have claims on it. People will certainly work to make you lose it. They will attempt to blacken in your mind both my administration and myself either by inventing falsities or by disguising true facts. They can cause to reach Your Majesty daily a host of reports cleverly conceived and they will know how to give libel the appearance of greater truth. Perhaps Your Majesty will disdain them at first but, by dint of repeating them, in the end they will sow doubts in your mind and the libels will have fulfilled their purpose without me being able to ward off the blows which I would have ignored.[3]

Turgot did not place much importance in what the king thought of him. He was dealing with a young and inexperienced king, who was surrounded by the wickedness of scoundrels and flatterers. In his letter to the king he wanted to make the king believe in himself, for without inner confidence there could be no basis for government. He was reminding the king of those times when he had shown presence of mind and courage, as in the *guerre des farines* and in the *lit de justice*, so that in the future when he needed it, he might be able to draw strength. Turgot also wanted to encourage the king to preserve the reforms which they had introduced together.

---

[1] E. Lavisse, *La Règne de Louis XVI* vol ix, p. 51.
[2] Véri, vol i, p. 461.
[3] Schelle, op. cit., vol v, pp. 457–58.

29

Retirement

The Choiseulistes, notably Mme Deffand, rejoiced in the triumph of De Guines and the disgrace of Turgot. His friends were devastated. They knew their hopes of a society of justice and humanity had been dashed. Turgot left office with poise and dignity. He did not attempt to justify himself; posterity must decide whether he left in disgrace or whether his fall was due instead to the rottenness of the *ancien régime*. He spent some months in the country enjoying being with friends and having time to discuss science and literature.

Immediately after his return to Paris, he challenged false rumours about his administration, which were beginning to circulate in Britain. The reason why Turgot was particularly concerned with events in Britain was that it was a land enjoying a free press. Turgot regarded that freedom as an essential ingredient of democracy. It was important to him that the British did not become blinded by the *ancien régime* in France, where the freedom of speech was not recognised. In particular, Dr Richard Price, one of the leading members of Lord Shelbourne's circle, accused him of 'want of address', or being politically awkward.

'I might have merited that imputation', conceded Turgot in a letter to him, 'if you had in view no other want of address than incapacity to unravel the source of those intrigues which were employed against me by people, who are much cleverer in these matters than I am, or ever shall be, or, indeed, ever desire to be. But I think you imputed to me a want of address which made my opinions grossly jar with the general opinion of my countrymen. In this respect I think you did justice neither to me nor to my countrymen . . .'[1] Dr Price removed this criticism from future editions of the pamphlet, entitled *Observations on Civil Liberties*.

To another anonymous English correspondent he attempted to answer certain rumours.

> He [Dr Price] is misinformed when he thinks that my dismissal was caused by my lack of regard for the public. He has supposed that the *parlement* was representing political opinion when it opposed my edicts.

---

[1] Schelle, op. cit., vol v p. 533.

But there is very little truth in this as it should be remembered that this body dared not print its remonstrances . . . The edicts for the suppression of the *corvées* and the *jurandes* were received joyfully in the provinces and by the masses in the towns. The reason that these edicts have been revoked is not in response to public demand; on the contrary they were accepted by the public; the sole reason is that M. Maurepas believed that it was his interest to convince the king that there were insurmountable obstacles to their operation and that they were impractical. The outbursts against me were never uttered in the provinces, or in Paris. They were limited to three classes of people; the courtiers who feared reform of expenditure, the financiers who feared simplifications in the collection of tax and the magistrates angered at having to deal with a minister who employed the ways of reason and authority. These cabals were roused secretly by several ministers, particularly by M. Maurepas, who feared that the king would come to enjoy a direct and independent confidence with me. He therefore employed every trick to excite opposition from all sides against me, with the aim of convincing the king that I was an unpopular figure . . . who did not know how to keep in touch with public opinion. I myself am not much disturbed by the reputation given me by the scandals and the intrigues of the court, and, if your friend Dr Price had not reproached me for this fault, I would not have bothered to give this explanation. But I do not want the public to hold such a poor opinion of our nation as is displayed in the assertion that my simple and evident principles, with which Dr Price agrees, have caused the uproar of our people.[1]

The daily news which came from Paris troubled Turgot. Du Pont had written to Maurepas to demand payment of the money he had lost by returning early from Poland in 1774. On 31 May Turgot wrote to him, '. . . what folly to address yourself to M. de Maurepas. How do you not see that this man is animated by the desire for vengeance and busies himself solely to throw on me and my friends all types of smears of rashness. If there is chance to to render your demand unfavourable . . . he would seize it without regard to justice or to consideration of whatever kind. His aim is to represent me to the king as a fool, surrounded by fools . . . In these circumstances perhaps he will go as far as reversing the edicts.'[2] Indeed soon afterwards Du Pont was asked to leave the capital and two *économistes*, the abbés Roubard and Baudeau were formally exiled, and their journal, *Nouvelles Ephémérides*, was suppressed. The Dutch offer of a loan to the French government was withdrawn, the shares of the Discount Bank were

---

[1] D. Dakin, *Turgot and the Ancien Regime*, pp. 266–7; *The Hardwicke Papers* CCCCXCI f. p. 377.
[2] Schelle, op. cit., vol v p. 491.

subscribed only to the extent of 20 per cent and shareholders were demanding their money back, a national lottery (which Turgot detested) was established; the edicts on the grain trade, on the *corvée* and on the *jurandes* were revoked, the parasitical claims of the farmers-general were encouraged and the state grain company was restored.

Saddened by the course of events in France, he turned to the great opportunities for civilisation which were being unfurled in North America. He followed the course of the war between the colonies and Britain with a keen interest. He saw it as a necessary struggle demanding final resolution by arms. Turgot befriended Benjamin Franklin during his visits to Paris in search of a settlement to the struggle. A portrait of Franklin displays Turgot's fitting and elegant epigram, *Eripuit caelo fulmen, sceptrumesque tyrannis*[1] which refers to Franklin's invention of the lightning conductor, as well as his more celebrated political role. Franklin commented on Turgot's epigram, 'I will only say that too much is attributed to me, above all concerning the tyrant; the revolution has been the work of a great number of strong and able men; it is enough to accord to me a small part in it.'[2]

Turgot had endeavoured to explain his ideas about taxation to Franklin, in order to persuade him not to copy the defective fiscal policies of Europe. In particular, he advised American leaders to reject indirect taxes on goods in favour of a territorial tax on the *produit net*. But Franklin was too schooled in the traditional political thinking of the Old World to seize the great opportunity of creating something revolutionary.

Marion, a French historian, depicted the entry into the war in America as fatal to the *ancien régime*. For though France had enjoyed peace for fifteen years its treasury was exhausted before the first shot would be fired. Necker displayed his skills as a banker, and his blindness and irresponsibility as a minister, by financing the war with crippling loans at ever higher rates of interest.

In March 1778 Turgot wrote to Dr Price about his views on the situation in the American colonies. At the outset he stated his belief that the independence of the American colonies was inevitable. His interest was on the question of whether the independent colonies would be happy and free. He wondered why it was that in Britain, where the public enjoyed a great measure of the freedom of speech, many thinkers actually clung to the idea of a mother country enforcing a trading monopoly against a colony. He could only surmise that it was 'party spirit and the desire for public support which has retarded your progress, by inducing your leading writers to treat as vain metaphysics all those theories which aim at laying down the rights and true interests of nations and of individuals on fixed principles'.[3]

He pointed out what he regarded as failings in the constitutions of individual American states. First, that public representatives pledged their belief in the

---

[1] 'He wrestled lightning from heaven and the sceptre from tyrants'.
[2] *Correspondence between Franklin and Laboulaye* 2. p. 117.
[3] He may have been referring to Edmund Burke's *Letter to the Sheriffs of Bristol*.

Christian Church and in Christ. Second, the adoption of a constitutional balance of powers between the council, governor and the peoples' representatives. For the council and the governor were duplications of the British system, which apportioned power between the crown and the people. Since the idea in the colonies was that men should rank equally, such systems would result in needless inequality. Third, the exclusion of the clergy from public office denied the clerics the same interest in the defence of freedom and property as any citizen had and tended to constitute the Church as a body, which might demand privileges. Fourth, the business of the governing bodies was not defined with sufficient precision, as it might be in the constitution of a free society. Fifth, there was no effective separation between legislative and judicial powers, with the consequence that justice became political. Sixth, there was insufficient provision for local assemblies to administer the detailed cares of government which generally cut the ambitious and avaricious politicians down to size. Seventh, no principles of taxation were established, so that every state 'might tax itself according to its fancy by imposing taxes on persons, on consumption and on imports; that is to say that every state may arrogate to itself an interest contrary to the states as a whole.'[1] Finally, he made the general criticism that the constitutions of the American states did not give the hope that a uniform state would arise – there were too many contradictions and diversities:

> This edifice has been hitherto supported on the erroneous foundation of the most ancient and vulgar politique, on the prejudice that nations and states can have in a corporate sense interests other than the interests of individuals – of being free and defending their property against thieves and invaders; on the pretended interest of making greater trade than others, of not buying the goods of other countries; of compelling foreigners to consume their produce and manufactured goods; on the pretended interest of having a larger territory by acquiring such and such a village, island or state; on the interest of inspiring fear in other nations and by outdoing each other by glory with arms, sciences and arts.[2]

Among the practical problems to be solved in North America, Turgot mentioned the constitution of the Catholic Church and the existence of nobles in Canada, the naïve and rigid Puritanism in New England, the religious ban on military activity in Pennsylvania, the existence of great inequalities of wealth in the southern colonies and the existence of a large slave population. Slavery not only offended a free constitution but also threatened to create two nations when they were freed. Another problem was the wild continent in the west, which

---

[1] Schelle, op. cit., vol v, p. 536.
[2] Ibid., pp. 536–7.

would have to be patrolled by a standing army. He argued that the colonies would have to overcome their fear of standing armies by appreciating their utility. Turgot concluded:

> It is impossible not to ardently wish that these people may attain their full potential prosperity. They are the hope of the world. They may become a model to it. They may prove to the world, in fact, that men can be free, peaceful and can manage without the claims of all kinds that tyrants and charlatans in various guises have tried to impose on them under the pretext of the public good. They must set an example of political freedom, religious freedom and of commercial freedom. The asylum they offer to the oppressed of all nations should console the earth and this opportunity this brings them to escape from the effects of a bad government will force the European governments to be just and open; the rest of the world will gradually open their eyes to the empty illusions with which they have been cheated hitherto by their politicians. For this, however, America must preserve herself from these illusions and take care to avoid being . . . an image of Europe – a mass of divided powers contending for territory and trade and continually cementing the slavery of people with their own blood . . .
>
> Britain's present misfortunes and future happiness will be, perhaps, the effect of a necessary amputation. They are the only means, perhaps, of saving you from the gangrene of luxury and corruption. If you could use your present troubles as an opportunity to amend your constitution, by restoring annual elections and by distributing voting rights, so as to render it more equal and better proportioned to the interests of those being represented, you will gain as much as America by this revolution . . . I beg you not to answer me in detail by the post, for your reply will certainly be opened by our bureaucracy and I shall be found too much a friend of liberty for a minister, even for a disgraced minister.[1]

In 1778, shortly before his death, Voltaire returned to Paris, from which he had been exiled for a period of thirty years, to see the opening of his play *Irène*. The play was a great success, which Turgot enjoyed, but the strain hastened Voltaire's death some months later. Condorcet described the meeting of Turgot and Voltaire thus, 'He [Voltaire], in the midst of public acclamations and weighed down with crowns of laurel, advanced equally towards M. Turgot with tottering steps, seized his unwilling hands . . . and cried in a halting voice, "Let me kiss the hand that has signed the salvation of the people." '[2]

---

[1] Ibid., pp. 539–40.
[2] Condorcet, *La Vie de Turgot*, ch. 7.

Retirement gave Turgot an opportunity to pursue his love of literature and of science. During his life he had completed several translations from works in several languages and he presented them to the *Acadèmie des Inscriptions et Belles-Lettres*, of which he became the president in 1778. Unfortunately his works perished in the revolution.

He studied and worked at geometry with Bossut, chemistry with Lavoisier and physics and astronomy with Rochon. He helped Rochon with his work on thermometers, a method of copying documents without printing them, the construction of rope cables and the distillation of liquids. He may claim the discovery of the distillation of liquids *in vacuo* as his own. He installed a still in his study and a receiving vessel connected by a tube was put outside in order to create a vacuum. During the winter months he observed that distillation had occurred on account of the difference in temperatures.

Turgot became increasingly prone to attacks of gout. After each attack had passed he immediately returned to work or concerned himself with his friends and their plans and works. During the beginning of 1781, however, the attacks became more prolonged and regular. He died in Paris on 18 March 1781 in the presence of the duchesse d'Enville, Mme Blondel and Du Pont.

30

Revolution

While at the Sorbonne, Turgot had declared in his First Discourse, 'Unhappy are those nations in which false principles of government have actuated their legislators . . . Almost all have neglected to keep open the door for improvements of which all the works of mankind have need . . . The abuse that remains – Revolution – is one sadder than the abuses themselves.'[1]

He speculated, uncharacteristically, upon the creation of a just society. In a letter, dated 12 December 1769, to the duchesse d'Enville[2] he had written, 'Political ideas are too complicated, interests too disunited and too difficult to disentangle for a well-constituted republic to arise for some time. Since the world began government has been essentially of two kinds: "brigandocracy" and "rascalocracy" and that will continue until the reign of enlightenment.'[3] The progress towards the tragedy of revolution can be briefly charted. Necker, being foreign and Protestant, could not assume the title of *contrôleur-général*, but between 1776–81 he acted as such. War was declared in America and financed by borrowings which, by 1789, had risen three times the total bequeathed by Terray in 1774. He presented his national accounts in a way which disguised the real position. He was popular for financing a war without resort to taxation. His pretentious boasting was believed until he began making demands to control military expenditure and have a voice in foreign affairs. His fellow ministers refused such demands and Necker resigned. The most distinguished of his successors, Calonne, established order in the finances of France, in order to facilitate borrowing anew. But by 1786 the nation's credit had been consumed and no new borrowings could be arranged. Then Calonne introduced his plan to impose a general land tax, along the lines of Du Pont's paper on Municipalities, to which there would be no exemptions for the privileged. It failed and he was undermined by privileged folk and by Necker's friends. His successor appealed to the nobles and then to the *parlements* for resources. Both bodies refused to co-operate and urged that the demands be put instead to the States-General, who

---

[1] Daire, *Oeuvres de Turgot*, vol ii, p. 593.
[2] *Lettres de Turgot à la Duchesse d'Enville* [edn. 1976] Professor J. Ruwett.
[3] Enlightenment here meaning wisdom, rather than age of enlightenment.

represented the nation. The *parlements* were exiled in August 1789. Absolute rule by the king proved deeply unpopular and a month later the *parlements* were recalled amid scenes of public rejoicing. Immediately they demanded the convocation of the States-General, which had met last in 1614. For want of other remedies, Necker was recalled. His former demands for greater control were met and thus his fellow ministers were reduced to political dwarfs.

The States-General was composed of three equal parts: the nobility, the Church and the people, who were represented by the unprivileged and professional middle class. This last body , known as the Third Estate, had grown in power since 1614 and demanded a larger share of power. Necker and Louis XVI were both committed to winning popularity and agreed to a doubling of the Third Estate, which was hailed as passing greater control to the people, away from the privileged. The States-General met on 5 May 1789. Louis had not decided to back either the privileged nobles or the Third Estate. Six weeks passed without resolution and the Third Estate met alone and claimed to have become the National Assembly of the people. On 23 June a royal session of the States-General allowed Louis to outline plans to develop a constitutional monarchy. In reality he was perceived as allying the monarchy to the nobles. Necker, perceived as a champion of the people, was dismissed and foreign troops were massed around Paris. Mobs formed each day and on 14 July they gathered around the Bastille, a fortress with guns trained on the poor quarter of Faubourg St Antoine. It was stormed, its governor killed, its seven prisoners were released and the Bastille was destroyed. Louis entered in his diary the simple entry, 'Nothing'. He was referring to his failure to kill any game. 'Then came the Revolution, brutal, terrible, with the splendour of its pools of blood', wrote a French historian.[1] The unrest in Paris spread throughout France, which had been experiencing grain riots since the spring of 1789. In rural parts the peasants rose to throw off the feudal shackles, which existed for the enrichment of the privileged.

Turgot was spared the chilling spectacle of the French revolution, which broke out ten years after his death. It is difficult to imagine how a soul so imbued with justice would have endured it.

Among the friends of Turgot, who witnessed the revolution, it was Morellet who recorded the most vivid pictures:

> I spent a large part of the evening of 13 and 14 [July 1789] at my windows in the rue Saint-Honor near the place de Vendôme, watching men of the lowest sort, armed with rifles, meat-hooks and pikes, opening the doors of houses and demanding food, drink, money and arms. I saw canons dragged into the streets, the streets torn up, barricades and church bells were sounding the alarm . . . I knew then that the people were going to become tyrants to all those who had something to lose, to all authority,

---

[1] F. Funck-Bretano, *Ancien Régime*, p. 365.

magistrates, troops, the Assembly, the king . . . I confess that I was seized with fear at the sight of this great power which began to feel its strength and put itself in a position to use it.[1]

He also described the daily scene in 1794 as thousands, including such friends of Turgot as Brienne, Lavoisier, Trudaine and Boisgelin, were guillotined:

> I could not go along the Champs-Élysées in the afternoon without hearing the cries of wild people applauding the fall of heads. If I went out following the road of my faubourg to the city I used to see these same people running in crowds to the Place de la Révolution to feast themselves on this spectacle, and sometimes I met, unavoidably with the fatal charettes. It was thus that I had the misfortune to see, without especially looking at them, the comte de Brienne and his family going to execution with Mme Elizabeth [Canisy]; that frightful image has pursued me for a long while.[2]

In July 1794 Morellet was denounced to the local revolutionary committee. He was summoned to answer questions about his whereabouts on certain key dates and whether he was happy about certain revolutionary events. In the course of the questioning, he mentioned the name of Turgot and the leader of the committee observed that Turgot had been the best *contrôleur-général* of all. After two minutes of discussion Morellet was restored to liberty.

The fortunes of Turgot's friends were various, some were less fortunate than Morellet. Du Pont retired after Turgot's dismissal but was recalled in 1786 by Vergennes. After holding various offices he became president of the Constituent Assembly, created by the National Assembly, in October 1790. The role of this Assembly was to draw up a new constitution. In August 1792 he voted for the continuance of the monarchy, which had attempted to flee from Paris in June 1791. Consequently he had to go into hiding in a conservatory, where he wrote a book, entitled *Philosophie de l'Universe*. He was arrested and imprisoned in La Force. But he was saved from execution by the fall of Robespierre, the revolutionary leader, in July 1794. He resumed his political activity and became a member of the Committee of 500. He opposed the Jacobin party and after the Republican triumph in 1797 he escaped transportation through the offices of a friend. In 1799 he went to America where Jefferson renewed his friendship, gave him work and assisted his son to set up a powder manufactory in Delaware, which flourished to become one of the world's largest chemical companies. After three years he returned to France and served under Napoleon.

---

[1] Morellet, *Mémoires* vol ii pp. 1–2.
[2] Ibid., vol ii pp. 1–2.

Véri observed on the outbreak of violence that 'The scaffold and popular justice are a thousand times more terrifying than the *lettres de cachet*.' At the end of 1793 he was imprisoned for having been a priest and a nobleman. He was condemned to death for fanaticism along with two others, one of whom was an eighty-five year old woman. In prison she became mad. They were due to be executed, but he too was fortunately spared by the fall of Robespierre. He returned home after nine months in gaol and retrieved the manuscript of his journal from a wall, where it had been partly nibbled by rats. He hid it again for fear of a fresh wave of violence and only two years before his death did he feel safe to put it in some sort of order.

Condorcet continued to serve as the secretary of the Acadèmie des Sciences, a position which he had held since 1773. In 1782 he had become a member of the Acadèmie française and his reputation in mathematics, physics, chemistry and literature brought him invitations to join academies in Turin, St Petersburg, Bologna and Philadelphia. During the 1780s he wrote biographies of Voltaire and of Turgot. The latter work is a masterly eulogy, in which his richness of expression merged with his understanding of Turgot's philosophy and his admiration of Turgot's character. However, Condorcet did not see the great merit of his economic thought. Lord Shelbourne, the British Prime Minister, who made peace with America in 1783, was very impressed with the work. He did not meet Turgot but he was in close touch with Morellet and Mme Lespinasse. He arranged to have an English translation published because it would help educate young politicians in the principles of government. In 1790 Condorcet entered, the Legislative Assembly which succeeded the Constituent Assembly, as representative of the municipality of Paris. After the flight of the king in 1791, he was one of the first to declare for a republic and he drafted plans for the National Convention. In 1792 he drew up a plan for a system of state education. But he voted against the trial of the king by the Convention, because it was not a judicial body, and protested at the arrests of the Girondistes. He invited the censure of the Convention. Duly they declared him *hors de la loi*, or outlaw. He hid in the attic of Mme Vernet in Paris, who accepted him despite the risks of discovery by declaring, 'The Convention has the right, Monsieur, to place you outside the law, but it cannot outlaw you from humanity. You will remain here.' While in hiding he wrote a book describing the historical progress of the human mind, taking as the central theme the idea of the perfectibility of man, as had been outlined some forty years earlier by Turgot. Surrounded by chaos and disorder, he sought in the gradual evolution of man something higher and more permanent than the evidence around him. He wrote other books in Mme Vernet's attic, including one teaching children how to count without tears, and political memoirs.

But soon he discovered that the house was under surveillance and so he effected an ingenious escape. He sought refuge in the country with a friend, who showed him the door. He wandered among the quarries in Clamart, near Paris, in search of M Suard. They met and discussed things. Condorcet appeared in a distressed state and said that he would return next evening. On the night of 7 April 1794 he went to a café and ordered an omelette containing a dozen eggs. He aroused suspicions and, in answer to questioning, he pretended to be a carpenter. But his questioners saw that his hands were smooth. He was arrested. He was marched in bare feet until he fainted and then was taken on the back of a horse to Bourg-la-Reine, where he was flung into a damp cellar. At first light he was found to be dead; probably he had poisoned himself.

Malesherbes retired to his provincial estate after his resignation in 1774. There he busied himself by writing a sixteen-volume work on herbs, which was not to be published. He walked in the Alps, Pyrnes and Brittany gathering material. The king invited him to serve briefly as a minister in 1787. The trial of the king followed the discovery of royal correspondence with Austria, against whom France had declared war in the Netherlands during April 1792. When Louis XVI was arraigned for treason against the Republic, Malesherbes offered to defend him. Louis accepted the offer. Malesherbes returned to Paris in December 1792. He contrived to have every ground of appeal raised. However, the king was guillotined in the Place de la Révolution in Paris on 21 January 1793. Malesherbes retired to his home near Bondy once again. A few weeks later four thugs, armed with swords and belonging to the local revolutionary committee seized his daughter and her husband. Malesherbes went on his knees to beg that they take him instead. Shortly afterwards his grandchildren and Malesherbes were arrested. As he left, he stumbled over the threshold of his home and commented that a Roman would have considered that a bad omen. The family was split up in Portlibre prison. He was charged with offences of plotting with the British Prime Minister, writing to his children, who were deemed to be the enemies of the state, and wishing a poor summer for the winegrowers. He refused to defend himself against charges with so little semblance of truth. He was condemned to death. On 1 May 1793 he had to watch the execution of his daughter and his son-in-law before exposing his own neck.

At the end of the eighteenth century there arose, as happens so often after ruinous upheavals, a national hero who became the Emperor in France in 1804. He built up the idea of a centralised bureaucratic control. Without legal knowledge, he imposed a Civil Code amounting to more than 2200 clauses and then other codes for criminal and commercial administration. Education and religion were controlled by the state. Censorship denied freedom of speech – and art did not flourish under state control.

Napoleon was fêted as a god, who was destined to lead France to victory over Europe, allowing revolutionary fervour to spread and suppress the liberties of mankind. Fortunately, his navy was defeated at Trafalgar in 1805 and his army was defeated in retreat from Moscow in the winter of 1812/13. He was exiled to Elba but after eleven months he returned to power but was defeated finally at Waterloo in 1815. The period of Napoleon may have seemed, in hindsight, a romantic interlude, his military campaign was extraordinary and his memory is shrouded in the mists of legend. Tocqueville said of Napoleon: 'He was as great a man as can be without morality.'

The tragedy of the revolution was not that the intelligensia and the aristocracy of France were murdered, but that most of the injustices of the *ancien régime* were allowed to continue. France chose mindless violence after the rejection of just reform, which though incomplete, would have extirpated the causes of both economic and civil injustice. Much more would have been accomplished by reform than by butchery. France would have become a model for mankind, instead of one of its brutal abattoirs. The number of executions is unknown and estimates vary downwards from 2,500,000, or about 10 per cent of the population. Turgot stood for revolution in political thinking and, much as he hated injustice, he hated violence even more, because it could never reform the original cause.

Condorcet opened his biography of Turgot with these powerful and eloquent paragraphs:

> Among the multitude of ministers, who, during a short period, govern the fate of nations, there are a few who merit the attention of posterity. If they merely held principles and prejudices in common with the age in which they lived, of what moment is the name of one who has done what a thousand others in his place would have done as well?
>
> General history serves to record the events in which they had a share. There we find that such a minister, raised from the crowd of the ambitious, was more eager to obtain his office than to deserve it; that he was more anxious to prolong his administration than to make it useful. There we see the ill that such men do from ambition, the ill that they permit from ignorance or irresolution; sometimes the good that they have attempted without success, and more rarely the good that they have been able to effect. The history of their ideas, and even of their virtues, may be read in the opinions and prejudices of their contemporaries.
>
> But if there appear among these a man, who has received from nature a superior strength of reason, accompanied with peculiar virtues and principles of action, and whose genius has so far outrun the acquisitions of his age as not to be understood by it: the life of such a minister may be interesting to all ages and all nations. His example may long be useful. His authority may give to important truths that sanction, which reason itself sometimes stands in need of.[1]

The Enlightenment bequeathed to mankind some of the greatest music and, in Paris, the bright light of political thought. Unfortunately, both Turgot's thinking

---

[1] Condorcet, *La Vie de Turgot*, p. 1.

and his example have been ignored and man staggers forward bearing the heavy burdens of injustice, imagining them inevitable, and possessing little aspiration to achieve democracy, justice and prosperity. Perhaps the grand and glorious example of Turgot may help to inspire the noble endeavour to overthrow injustice in society, in order that Man can emerge from poverty. For Turgot believed it both unnecessary and unnatural.

Index

critical of Quesnays ideas, 25–6, first attack of gout, 27, appointed intendant, 27, proposed *taille tarifée*, 39–40, modifies milice, 43–4, lightens *corvées*, 46–9, *Reflections*, 50, writes on magistrates, 62–3, international tade, 66–8, famine 70–5, appointed Minister, 87, sadness at leaving Paris, 76, appointed to King's Council, 87, celebrations of, 94, minister of the Marine, 88, on colonies, 89, international commerce, 66–8, 89, letter to king, 91–3, on finances, appointed *contrôleur*, 94, restores free trade, 108–9, acts on grain contract, 111, recall of *parlements*, 115, gout attack, 116–17, grain riots, 122–31, coronation, 135, taxation, 139–43, memo on America, writes to king, 187, 186, dismissed, 186.

Turgot, Michel Etienne, [father], character of 1–2, death of, 10.

Turgot, Magdelène-Françoise, [mother] ubringing of T, 2.

Turgot, marquis de, [brother], 2, warns T, 161, 181.

Turgot, sister, 2, marries, 2.

Vaines, 95.
Vauban, 26.

Venality, 31–2.
Vergennes, Charles, 86, 137, 172–3.
Véri, abbé, 5, 86, on T & Milice, 90, describes *contrôleur*, 94, on Terray, 103, 107, 109, on courage of T, 118, 133, on queen, 138, taxation, 142, on Malesherbes, 145, 152, beggary, 155, on T, 158, changes mind on T, 159, 182–3, copies resignation letter, 183, 185–6, on T after dismissal, imprisoned but freed, 197.

Vermond, abbé, 90, 94.
Vingtième, 37–8, 41, 98, 99.
Voltaire, François, 2–3, T studies Voltaire's poetry, 3, meets, 27–8, greets T's appontment, 28–9, *The Man with Fory Crowns*, 53–4, trade, 58, 87, translation of Virgil, 81, views on trade , 58, on appointment of T, 87, restoration of free trade, 109–10, on iron age, 174, T's dismissal, 186–7, last meeting, 192., T speculates, 194.

Weber, opinion on grain riots, 129.

Yang & Ko, 50.
Young, Arthur, 33–4, on Brive, 36, on roads, 48–9, on grain, 66.